Teaching Statistics

Resources for Undergraduate Instructors

ISBN: 0-88385-162-8

Library of Congress Catalog Card Number 00-103315

Printed in the United States of America

Current Printing

10 9 8 7 6 5 4 3 2 1

Teaching Statistics

Resources for Undergraduate Instructors

Edited by

Thomas L. Moore
Grinnell College

Published jointly by
The Mathematical Association of America
and
The American Statistical Association

The MAA Notes Series, started in 1982, addresses a broad range of topics and themes of interest to all who are involved with undergraduate mathematics. The volumes in this series are readable, informative, and useful, and help the mathematical community keep up with developments of importance to mathematics.

MAA Notes

11. Keys to Improved Instruction by Teaching Assistants and Part-Time Instructors, *Committee on Teaching Assistants and Part-Time Instructors, Bettye Anne Case,* Editor.
13. Reshaping College Mathematics, *Committee on the Undergraduate Program in Mathematics, Lynn A. Steen,* Editor.
14. Mathematical Writing, by *Donald E. Knuth, Tracy Larrabee, and Paul M. Roberts.*
16. Using Writing to Teach Mathematics, *Andrew Sterrett,* Editor.
17. Priming the Calculus Pump: Innovations and Resources, *Committee on Calculus Reform and the First Two Years,* a subcomittee of the Committee on the Undergraduate Program in Mathematics, *Thomas W. Tucker,* Editor.
18. Models for Undergraduate Research in Mathematics, *Lester Senechal,* Editor.
19. Visualization in Teaching and Learning Mathematics, *Committee on Computers in Mathematics Education, Steve Cunningham and Walter S. Zimmermann,* Editors.
20. The Laboratory Approach to Teaching Calculus, *L. Carl Leinbach et al.,* Editors.
21. Perspectives on Contemporary Statistics, *David C. Hoaglin and David S. Moore,* Editors.
22. Heeding the Call for Change: Suggestions for Curricular Action, *Lynn A. Steen,* Editor.
24. Symbolic Computation in Undergraduate Mathematics Education, *Zaven A. Karian,* Editor.
25. The Concept of Function: Aspects of Epistemology and Pedagogy, *Guershon Harel and Ed Dubinsky,* Editors.
26. Statistics for the Twenty-First Century, *Florence and Sheldon Gordon,* Editors.
27. Resources for Calculus Collection, Volume 1: Learning by Discovery: A Lab Manual for Calculus, *Anita E. Solow,* Editor.
28. Resources for Calculus Collection, Volume 2: Calculus Problems for a New Century, *Robert Fraga,* Editor.
29. Resources for Calculus Collection, Volume 3: Applications of Calculus, *Philip Straffin,* Editor.
30. Resources for Calculus Collection, Volume 4: Problems for Student Investigation, *Michael B. Jackson and John R. Ramsay,* Editors.
31. Resources for Calculus Collection, Volume 5: Readings for Calculus, *Underwood Dudley,* Editor.
32. Essays in Humanistic Mathematics, *Alvin White,* Editor.
33. Research Issues in Undergraduate Mathematics Learning: Preliminary Analyses and Results, *James J. Kaput and Ed Dubinsky,* Editors.
34. In Eves' Circles, *Joby Milo Anthony,* Editor.
35. You're the Professor, What Next? Ideas and Resources for Preparing College Teachers, *The Committee on Preparation for College Teaching, Bettye Anne Case,* Editor.
36. Preparing for a New Calculus: Conference Proceedings, *Anita E. Solow,* Editor.
37. A Practical Guide to Cooperative Learning in Collegiate Mathematics, *Nancy L. Hagelgans, Barbara E. Reynolds, SDS, Keith Schwingendorf, Draga Vidakovic, Ed Dubinsky, Mazen Shahin, G. Joseph Wimbish, Jr.*
38. Models That Work: Case Studies in Effective Undergraduate Mathematics Programs, *Alan C. Tucker,* Editor.
39. Calculus: The Dynamics of Change, *CUPM Subcommittee on Calculus Reform and the First Two Years, A. Wayne Roberts,* Editor.
40. Vita Mathematica: Historical Research and Integration with Teaching, *Ronald Calinger,* Editor.

MAA Service Center
P. O. Box 91112
Washington, DC 20090-1112
800-331-1622   fax: 301-206-9789

Introduction

The opening article in this volume is a piece by George Cobb titled, "Teaching Statistics: More Data, Less Lecturing." That title summarizes succinctly the basic tenets of what might be called the statistics educational reform of the past 10 to 15 years, tenets around which the statistics profession has formed a surprisingly strong and supportive consensus. This volume aims to be an "instructor's manual" for that statistics educational reform for teachers of statistics at the undergraduate and secondary school levels.

The most recent CBMS survey of mathematics and statistics departments shows that for every student taking a statistics course in a statistics department there are more than three students taking a statistics course in a mathematics department [3, p. 4]. Yet many of these mathematics departments do not have a statistician on their faculty. Consequently, mathematicians are forced to become teachers of statistics, often with little formal education in the discipline. Under these conditions, it is almost natural, and had been observed, that more theory would be lectured on than data models presented. Aware of this fact, the ASA-MAA Joint Committee on Undergraduate Statistics conceived of the STATS project in 1993 to provide faculty development opportunities to those mathematicians teaching statistics. STATS workshops focused on modern methods for teaching elementary statistics using activities, projects, software, and authentic methods of assessment. The MAA administered the STATS program with two grants from the National Science Foundation, ending in the fall of 1999.

These STATS workshops have helped tremendously those who attended them. The original purpose of this volume was to provide a "companion text" for those workshops, helpful both for those who attended and for those who did not. Since the conception of this volume, AP Statistics has burst upon the scene with an amazing popularity and with goals and syllabus very similar to those of the standard college-level introductory course, so that AP statistics teachers should also find this volume to be useful. Indeed, even experienced teachers of statistics should find the volume of much benefit.

The MAA Notes series has produced two other volumes of interest to the teacher of statistics. *Perspectives on Contemporary Statistics* [2] contains nine original essays by eminent statisticians on modern statistical topics, topics selected to impact teaching practice. *Statistics for the Twenty-First Century* [1] contains 25 original articles by leading statistics educators. These articles deal with a wide variety of issues and practices in the teaching of statistics. We highly recommend both of these volumes to teachers of statistics be they mathematicians or statisticians.

Since publication of these two volumes in 1992, we have seen the development of several projects for teaching statistics that help us implement the "more data, less lecturing" reform in statistics education. This new volume describes some of the best of these projects and also includes original (or updated) articles on current thinking about the various ingredients to good statistics education.

The volume is organized into six main sections:

- *Hortatory Imperatives:* Where we learn why "more data, less lecturing" is a good idea.
- *Teaching with Data:* Where we get useful advice on incorporating real data into the classroom experience and into assignments.
- *Established Projects in Active Learning:* Where we learn about three published books that use active learning to teach statistics.
- *Textbooks:* Where we get advice from two experts on how one should go about choosing a statistics textbook.
- *Technology:* Where we learn about the ever-widening array of technological resources for teaching statistics.
- *Assessment:* Where we learn about how assessment can go beyond the assigning of student grades to the enhancing of student learning.

Within the volume you will find a mixture of original articles, articles that have been previously published, and "samplers-with-commentary." The sampler-with-commentary model is our way of describing an existing project, such as the Activity-Based Statistics project, so that you can better decide if the project is something you want to find out more about. Each sampler-with-commentary provides you with: (1) the published preface or a brief description of the project, (2) a "companion piece" about the project, (3) a complete table of contents for the project, and, in most cases, (4) a representative sample (or two) from the project. Articles written by the developers of projects are clearly indicated as such. Companion pieces are original articles written by teachers who have used a specific project but who were not involved in its development.

Finally we need to say a few words about the genesis of this volume and about its completeness. The idea evolved over the past couple of annual meetings of the Statistics in the Liberal Arts Workshop (SLAW). SLAW comprises a group of statisticians from liberal arts colleges who meet annually. It is not our goal with this volume to describe all possible published resources and ideas on statistics education. We choose instead to describe those resources and ideas that we feel would be most useful for anyone teaching statistics, given our original guiding principle of what would be most useful for our mathematical colleagues called upon to assume that responsibility. Having said that, we caution the reader to keep in mind the lag between the writing of the volume and its publication and to keep in mind that new products or projects are constantly being developed.

What this all implies is that we hope you will use this volume, find good advice within its covers, but that you will "keep your knees bent" and always be alert to other good resources that further what we consider to be the over-arching goals of good statistics education: "more data, less lecturing." And because we also feel the need to keep our knees bent, we will maintain a web site for this volume that allows us to provide information on good ideas that come along later. The web address is: `http://www.math.grinnell.edu/~mooret/maa-notes/`.

Acknowledgements

I wish to thank SLAW for conceiving this volume and for providing continuing and substantial advice and support during its production. These SLAW participants are Don Bentley, George Cobb, Katherine Halvorsen, Pete Hayslett, Gudmund Iversen, Robin Lock, David Moore, Rosemary Roberts, Allan Rossman, and Jeff Witmer. I thank the Exxon Education Foundation for its long support of SLAW. I thank the authors of articles and the developers of projects that we have included in the volume; many of these people also gave us good suggestions for the volume beyond the portion of it for which they were directly responsible. I thank the MAA Notes Editorial Committee, especially Tina Straley, Mary Parker, Roger Nelsen, and Sheldon Gordon, for their advice and encouragement. I thank Karen Thomson, Vicki Wade, Judy Hunter, and Emily Moore at Grinnell College who helped with many aspects of production, and I thank the publications staff of the MAA, who gave valuable advice on the manuscript and who efficiently processed the completed manuscript; thanks particularly to Beverly Ruedi and Elaine Pedreira. Finally, I wish to thank the Department of Mathematics, Statistics, and Computer Science at Mt. Holyoke College for its support of this project during my sabbatical there in 1997/98.

Thomas L. Moore
Department of Mathematics and Computer Science
Grinnell College
Grinnell, Iowa 50112
`mooret@grinnell.edu`

References

[1] Gordon, Florence and Sheldon Gordon (eds.), *Statistics for the Twenty-First Century,* MAA Notes Number 26, 1992, The Mathematical Association of America.

[2] Hoaglin, David C. and David S. Moore (eds.), *Perspectives on Contemporary Statistics,* MAA Notes Number 21, 1992, The Mathematical Association of America.

[3] Loftsgaarden, Don O., Donald C. Rung, and Ann E. Watkins, "Statistical Abstract of Undergraduate Programs in the Mathematical Sciences in the United States," MAA Reports Number 2, 1995, The Mathematical Association of America.

Contents

Section 1
Hortatory Imperatives

George Cobb's article, "Teaching Statistics: More Data, Less Lecturing," sets the tone for the entire volume. If your pragmatic side has the better of you, this short piece may suffice to launch you on to the rest of the volume where you can learn practical implementation strategies for statistics education reform. If, on the other hand, you want or need more motivational reading, you should investigate the articles listed in our "Bibliography of Resources for Teaching Statistics."

Editor's note. In the spring of 1991 George Cobb, in order to highlight important issues to the mathematics community, coordinated an email Focus Group on Statistics Education as part of MAA's Curriculum Action Project. This article gives a brief version of a report from that Focus Group. The lengthier, full report is George Cobb's "Teaching Statistics" article, a full citation for which appears in the attached "Bibliography for Resources for Teaching Statistics."

> Statistics has moved somewhat away from mathematics back toward its roots in scientific inference . . . The most important driving force in this shift of emphasis is the computer revolution.
> —David Moore, Purdue University

Teaching Statistics: More Data, Less Lecturing[†]

George Cobb
Mount Holyoke College

How Statistics Changed in the Last Two Decades

Change has occurred simultaneously on three levels, corresponding to technique, practice, and theory. On the technical level, cheap, powerful computing has made possible a number of important innovations: graphical methods for data display, iterative methods for data description, diagnostic tools for assessment of fit between data and model, and new methods of inference based on resampling techniques. On the level of practice, pattern-searching, model-free description, and systematic assessment of fit have all become more prominent, at the expense of formal inference, most especially hypothesis testing. Statisticians now put more effort into the complex process of choosing suitable models, less effort into doing those things—simpler by comparison—which take the choice of model as given.

On the level of theory, two kinds of changes have invigorated discussions about statistical reasoning. First, foundational discussions of long standing (Should unknown parameters be regarded as fixed or as values of random variables? Should inferences be conditional or unconditional?) now take place much more often in the context of real applications. Second, statistical practice has partly outgrown its mathematical theories, which are consequently less relevant. Important new elements of data analysis (model-choosing, model-checking, and model-free description) don't fit the older, theoretical frames, while the influential area of statistical process control offers new ways, not yet mathematically developed, to frame the enterprise of learning from data.

What does all this mean for the teaching of statistics? We offer two recommendations:

A. *More Data and Concepts*: Almost any course in statistics can be improved by more emphasis on data and concepts, at the expense of less theory and fewer recipes. To the

[†] This article originally appeared in *UME Trends*, **3**(4), October 1991, a publication of the Mathematical Association of America.

maximum extent feasible, calculations and graphics should be automated.

B. *Emphasize Statistical Thinking*: Any introductory course should take as its main goal helping students to learn the basic elements of statistical thinking. Many advanced courses would be improved by a more explicit emphasis on those same basic elements, namely:

1. *The need for data*: "To recognize in one's own citizenship, the need to base personal decisions on evidence (data), and the dangers inherent in acting on assumptions not supported by evidence." (Walt Pirie, Virginia Polytechnic Institute and State University)

2. *The importance of data production*: "It is very difficult and time-consuming to formulate problems and to get data of good quality that really deal with the right questions.... Most people don't seem to realize this until they go through this experience themselves." (Jim Landwehr, AT&T Bell Labs)

3. *The omnipresence of variability*: "Variability is ubiquitous. It is the essence of statistics as a discipline... it is not best understood by lecture—it must be experienced." (Dick Gunst, Southern Methodist University)

4. *The quantification and explanation of variability*: "(a) Randomness and distributions; (b) patterns and deviations (fit and residual); (c) mathematical models for patterns; (d) model-data dialogue (diagnostics)." (David Moore)

5. *Effective learning requires feedback*. "Students learn what they practice doing; they learn better if they have experience applying ideas in new situations." (Joan Garfield, University of Minnesota)

How Students Learn: What Research Tells Us

Shorn of all subtlety and led out of the protective fold of the education research literature, there comes a sheepish little fact: *lectures don't work nearly as well as many of us would like to think.* This rather discouraging assertion follows from two clusters of research results—the first shows what makes learning hard and lecturing often ineffective, the second shows what does seem to work when lecturing doesn't.

1. *Basic concepts are hard and misconceptions persistent*. Ideas of probability and statistics are very difficult for students to learn and conflict with many of their own beliefs and intuitions about chance and data. Students correct erroneous beliefs reluctantly—only when their old ideas don't work. Learning is enhanced when students are forced to confront their misconceptions, a process for which lectures are not generally effective.

2. *Learning is constructive*. To absorb the full impact of these three words, you have to push their implied metaphor to its limits; concepts are constructions, learning is building. Common sense principles of carpentry, applied to the process of teaching and learning, lead to the same conclusions as those derived from research on how students learn: to teach students to build, spend less time lecturing and spend more time on site, where you can focus your comments on the work students are actually doing.

Taken together, the two sets of results lead to a third and final recommendation.

3. *Foster active learning*. As a rule, teachers of statistics should rely much less on lecturing, much more on the following alternatives:

i. *Projects, either group or individual*. "Real learning takes place when students buy into the course. This is best accomplished by having students design simple experiments and collect their own data." (Jack Schuenemeyer, University of Delaware)

ii. *Lab exercises*. "Statistics should be taught as a laboratory science, along the lines of physics and chemistry rather than traditional mathematics.... Students must get their hands dirty with data." (Dick Scheaffer, University of Florida)

iii. *Group problem solving and discussion*. "I do not lecture at all. Instead, students are required to read the textbook guided by a handbook containing study questions and sample problems. Each day we first discuss the study questions, often arguing about issues....Students then work in small groups on activities, usually analyzing a set of data and discussing questions about these data sets." (Joan Garfield)

iv. *Written and oral presentations*. "Students come to us with primarily an intuitive understanding of the world. It is part of our job to ferret out those intuitive processes and correct the incorrect ones. As far as I know, this can only happen by having students discuss and write about their understandings and interpretations of problems..." (Dick Scheaffer)

v. *Demonstrations based on class-generated data*. Even within the traditional lecture setting, it is possible to get students more actively involved. Our full report will include examples of class exercises and demonstrations devised by Howard Taylor of the University of Delaware.

Each of these recommendations will be expanded in our full report, which will include important sections on "Examples" and "Making It Happen." We intend our three recommendations to apply quite broadly, e.g., whether or not a course has a calculus prerequisite, and regardless of the extent to which students are expected to learn scientific statistical methods. Although we spent most of our time thinking about introductory courses, several of us know from experience that the spirit of what we urge can infuse courses devoted to experimental design and analysis of variance, sample survey design, regression, time series, or multivariate analysis, to name just five.

Although the work of the Focus Group ends with the completion of our report, many members of the Focus Group will continue to work on these same issues, especially on efforts at dissemination and implementation, as members of a joint ASA/MAA Committee on Statistics Curriculum.

Bibliography on Resources for Teaching Statistics

Cobb, George and David S. Moore, "Mathematics, Statistics, and Teaching," *The American Mathematical Monthly*, **104** (1997), 801–823.

> Two eminent statisticians and teachers discuss how statistics differs from mathematics and what implications these differences have for the teaching of statistics.

Cobb, George, "Teaching Statistics," in *Heeding the Call for Change*, MAA Notes No. 22, edited by Lynn Arthur Steen, 1992, The Mathematical Association of America, 3–46.

> This is in a sense the "full, unabridged version" of the piece by Cobb included in this volume. It provides fuller explanation and more motivation for the recommendations of the Focus Group.

Garfield, Joan B., "Teaching Statistics Using Small-Group Cooperative Learning," *Journal of Statistics Education*, `http://www.amstat.org/publications/jse/v1n1/garfield.html` (on-line), **1**(1), 1993.

> Garfield provides both theoretical underpinnings and practical suggestions for implementing cooperative learning strategies in one's statistics courses. She also gives references to many other good articles on cooperative or activity-based learning.

Garfield, Joan B., "How Students Learn Statistics," *International Statistical Review*, **63**, (1995), 25–34.

> Garfield is one of the leading experts in the theory of statistical education. She is also an accomplished teacher of statistics. The result of those two expertises is this excellent set of teaching guidelines and their relationship to educational research.

Gordon, Florence and Sheldon Gordon (editors), *Statistics for the Twenty-First Century,* MAA Notes No. 26, The Mathematical Association of America, 1992.

> This volume includes 25 widely-ranging articles on the teaching of statistics written by experienced statistics teachers. In particular you'll find lively "hortatory" pieces in Part I and other (extensive) bibliographies in Part IV.

Hoaglin, D.C. and D.S. Moore (editors), *Perspectives on Contemporary Statistics,* MAA Notes No. 21, The Mathematical Association of America, 1992.

Eminent statisticians provide overview articles for beginning teachers on topics central to the teaching of statistics. Topics include: data analysis, computers and modern statistics, samples and surveys, statistical design of experiments, probability, inference, diagnostics, and resistant and robust procedures. This is good background reading for most statistics teachers.

Journal of Statistics Education. This electronic journal began publication in 1993. *JSE* produces many excellent articles on the teaching of statistics. The web address is: `http://www.amstat.org/publications/ jse/index.html`

Moore, David S. and discussants, "New pedagogy and new content: the case of statistics," *International Statistical Review*, **65**, (1997), 123–165.

David Moore is at his best in this article about "...synergies between content, pedagogy, and technology." The discussants include well-known statisticians, teachers, and experts in research on teaching and learning. The result is a "must read" from the hortatory menu.

Moore, David S. and discussants, "Should Mathematicians Teach Statistics?" *The College Mathematics Journal*, **19** (1988), 3–34.

If the title doesn't get your attention, surely the first sentence will: "No!". This classic in the statistics education literature is intentionally provocative and the numerous and varied discussants enliven things even more. If you are one of the many mathematicians who do teach statistics, this article should interest you.

Proceedings of the Section on Statistical Education of the American Statistical Association. Each year at the annual meeting of the American Statistical Association (August) the Section on Statistical Education sponsors several sessions. Many great ideas for teaching statistics come from these sessions and many of these papers are published in the annual Proceedings. Ordering information is available from the web at: `http://www.amstat.org /publications/proceed.html`.

Rumsey, Deborah J., "A Cooperative Teaching Approach to Introductory Statistics," *Journal of Statistics Education*, `http://www.amstat.org/publications/jse/v6n1/rumsey.html` (on-line), **6**(1), 1998.

Introducing the "more data, less lecturing" paradigm into statistics courses can be a time-consuming and otherwise daunting experience for instructors. Rumsey describes experiences at Kansas State University to make this transition to data-centered, activity-based instruction manageable, successful, and satisfying by using a team-oriented approach to course organization.

Section 2
Teaching with Data

Getting "more data" into our statistics courses, in the form of classroom examples, student projects, and case studies is not a complex matter, but it requires some careful thought and preparation. Fortunately, a number of teachers of statistics have had extensive experience and have been able to create practical guidelines that will help to ease the task.

Karla Ballman describes the process of bringing data into the classroom in her very practical article, "Real Data in Classroom Examples." She prescribes a two-step path to a more lively classroom: (1) Find interesting data, and (2) Ask your students interesting questions about the data. Karla introduces us to some of her favorites among the resources currently available for finding real data and the stories behind them. Data from these resources also make for excellent homework or exam questions, so that nary a fake data set need ever again find its way into your teaching. Robin Lock's article—"WWW Resources for Teaching Statistics"—which appears in Section 5, points the way to further on-line data repositories to which you can apply Karla's principles for producing effective classroom examples.

Another way to use real data to teach statistics is through student projects. Student projects are defined as assignments that ask students to formulate a research question of their own invention, to devise a plan of producing data and analyzing data to answer the question, and, finally, to report the results. Joan Garfield, in her "Beyond Testing and Grading" article (Section 6), gives us the rationale for assigning student projects from her perspective as an expert in the learning of statistics. The articles in this section provide both moral and practical support to her rationale.

In his "Small Student Projects in Introductory Statistics," Robert Wardrop provides plenty of motivation for using student projects in one's teaching. His theoretical reasons correlate strongly with Joan Garfield's and his examples of student projects from his own classes add engaging particulars to Garfield's sound generalities.

Katherine Halvorsen and Thomas Moore have been assigning projects to their students at Smith and Grinnell Colleges for many years and their article, "Motivating, Monitoring, and Evaluating Student Projects," provides their very practical suggestions for structuring the entire project assignment—from day one to the final, written report.

An annotated bibliography of the student project literature follows these two projects papers.

This section ends with Norean Radke Sharpe's "Curriculum in Context: Teaching with Case Studies in Statistics Courses." Teaching with case studies is an old phenomenon in some disciplines, but relatively new in statistics. Sharpe has been a leader in the development of the case studies approach in statistics and her paper demonstrates her wisdom on both why we should consider this approach and how we might implement it. Sharpe's paper ends with the bonus of an annotated bibliography on recent case studies books in statistics.

Real Data in Classroom Examples

Karla Ballman
Macalester College

Statistical concepts are best learned in the context of real data sets. Fortunately, using the computer to automate calculations and graphics makes it possible to work with real data without becoming a slave to the mechanics.
—George Cobb [1992, p. 7]

We believe that data should be at the heart of all statistics education and that students should be introduced to statistics through data-centered courses.
—Thomas Moore and Rosemary Roberts [1989, p. 81]

This sentiment is echoed throughout recent literature on statistics education; the repeated message is "use real data." There are several compelling reasons for statistics instructors to heed this advice:

- Real data convey the importance and relevance of statistics. Introductory courses are often service courses and many students are not convinced statistics is something other than an academic hurdle.
- Real data have real information. Since statistics is used in numerous fields, authentic data allows instructors to venture into other subject areas without the fear of presenting misleading information.
- Real data, if used well, can emphasize the problem-solving nature of statistics. In particular, they dispel the misconception that doing statistics is doing calculations and taking exams.

Real data should be used in all aspects of a course: the classroom, homework, case studies, projects, and exams. Many resources exist for data-based homework problems, and to a lesser extent projects. However, how-to descriptions for creating classroom examples using real data are relatively scarce. What follows are some guidelines I use to develop classroom examples. Since the guidelines are very general, I illustrate them with an extended example.

I. What Is a Classroom Example?

It is important to distinguish computational drill from conceptual exercises. Although drill can be based on real data, the goal is to teach mechanical facility, rather than the broader skills of synthesis, evaluation, and communication. Because most textbook examples emphasize drill, my emphasis here is on how to construct a classroom example that requires problem-solving skills beyond mere calculation.

Specifically, data-based examples can be used to show:

- how to translate discipline-specific problems into questions appropriate for statistical techniques;

- how to provide an answer, no matter how imperfect, in those situations that demand one;
- how to check or control data quality;
- how to enhance a statistical analysis with effective use of relevant discipline-specific material;
- how to distinguish between the types of information statistics can and cannot provide;
- how to select statistical procedures appropriate for the problem; and
- how to determine when it is appropriate to generalize the results of a statistical analysis.

Most examples cannot incorporate all these components of a statistical analysis. Rather, a classroom example should downplay the computational component and highlight at least one of these other aspects of statistical problem solving.

Finally, there are a variety of delivery styles for a classroom example besides the traditional lecture:

- A data analysis exercise, where students first analyze a data set with a partner, answer short questions about the data, and the class then convenes to discuss the answers.
- An in-class critique, where students read a short article from the newspaper involving the use of statistics, answer questions about the article in small groups, and then the various groups are responsible (perhaps through a spokesperson) for answering different questions.
- A worksheet, where small groups of students complete a set of questions pertaining to a discipline-specific problem and accompanying output from relevant statistical procedures. Comments and explanations are interspersed among questions that require students to complete various steps of a statistical analysis. After completing the worksheet, each group writes a summary of what they learned from the example.
- An out-of-class critique, where groups critique a published statistical study. During a subsequent class, one group is selected to present their findings to the entire class and lead a class discussion.

A rough rule for all styles is that the more student involvement, the better. To effectively provide students with the experience of statistical problem-solving requires that they become actively engaged with the issues.

II. Guidelines For Producing a Classroom Example

When I construct a classroom example, I generally follow the steps presented here. As you develop a data-based example, you should remember that the first time you use it,

it will not be perfect. It is impossible to create an ideal example from scratch. No matter how carefully I develop an example, improvements become apparent only when I actually use it in class. Furthermore, the success of an example is somewhat dependent upon the personality of the class. I have used the same example, on the same day, in different sections of the same course and experienced drastically different results.

1. Identify the general goal

The general goal will spring from current classroom goals and should help you identify a small set of appropriate data sets. Each individual data set will then suggest its own collection of subgoals. An example of a general goal is: *Explore the effect of an outlier on a confidence interval.*

This goal has two characteristics: (1) it is broad enough to capture a number of data sets, and (2) it downplays the computational aspect of estimation. Often, I have a more specific idea of what I would like to illustrate with an example than the general goal indicates. However, as I locate data sets that satisfy the general goal, they often have characteristics that suggest subgoals I had not considered. Consequently, my finished example has a different (and better) focus than I had initially conceived. Finally, the general procedure needs to downplay computational aspects so that the in-class example does not become a drill exercise.

2. Find a pool of relevant data sets

Once you identify a general goal, you must select data sets that can teach to the goal. While this takes time, there are excellent resources available which are extremely helpful. The annotated bibliography of data set resources at the end of this article describes the ones I have found particularly helpful. My search for the above general goal produced three data sets:

Baseball Free Agency
Source: A Casebook for a First Course in Statistics and Data Analysis, Chatterjee, Hancock, and Simonoff (1995), pages 101–111.

These data describe the difference in a major league baseball player's batting average the year before and the year after a player changes teams as the result of free agency. (All data affected by the 1981 strike are ignored.) A question of interest to baseball management is the average size of the difference. The outlier in this data corresponds to Ivan DeJesus who went from a 0.222 batting average in 1985 for St. Louis to 0.000 for the New York Yankees in 1986.

Speed of Light
Sources: (1) Introduction to the Practice of Statistics, Moore and McCabe (1993), pages 3, 14–15 and
(2) DASL web site:
`http://lib.stat.cmu.edu/DASL/Stories/`
`EstimatingtheSpeedofLight.html.`

The data contain speed of light measurements made by Simon Newcomb between July and September, 1882. There are a total of 66 observations including two outliers. The data were used to estimate the speed of light.

Weights of Rowers
Sources: (1) A Handbook of Small Data Sets, Hand, Daly, Lunn, McConway, and Ostrowski (1994), data set No.414 on page 337, and
(2) DASL web site:
`http://lib.stat.cmu.edu/DASL/Stories/`
`Rowersvs.Coxswain.html.`

The data are the weights for the crews in the 1992 Cambridge versus Oxford 8-sweep boat race. There are two outliers in the data that correspond to the two coxswains.

3. Use subgoals to choose a data set

While each of our three data sets satisfies the general goal—to explore the effect of an outlier on a confidence interval—the different research questions and the nature of the outliers suggest a different set of subgoals for each data set.

For example, the outlier in the baseball data can be used to motivate nonparametric tests as a means for reducing the effect of outliers; it can also be used to discuss the difference between statistical and practical significance. The speed of light data set motivates the idea of ignoring outliers when the focus of the research question is the center of the distribution. In general, these data can be used to illustrate the use of judgment in the handling of outliers. The outliers in the rowers' weight data differ in that they comprise an identifiable subpopulation of the athletes on the boats: coxswains.

So in this step, choose a data set from the pool based on the subgoals that you decide to illustrate. For my example, I might choose the third data set, weights of rowers, because its subgoals are more interesting to me or because they teach a valuable lesson that the students have not yet learned. This data set allows me to discuss outliers that arise from an identifiable cause other than chance error in measurement, or a typo.

Subgoals are by nature more fluid than goals. Goals are closely tied to the course syllabus, whereas subgoals reflect lessons that are important, but whose precise placement in the course is less critical. Allowing data sets to

suggest subgoals eases the job of creating a good classroom example and leads, I feel, to richer classroom examples.

4. State all subgoals for the chosen data set

Having settled on a particular data set, identify all subgoals of the data set that you will put into the lesson.

The subgoals I identified for my data set are:

- to define the target population associated with the research question of interest.
- to use confidence intervals to draw conclusions about a population or process.
- to identify and investigate outliers.
- to learn that different research questions require different methods for handling outliers.

A deficiency of the data I selected is the lack of accompanying background information. I chose this data anyway because of my own knowledge of crew. Instructors without this knowledge or with little experience with creating examples would probably select a different data set from the candidate pool, one that provides more background information. This is yet another reason for locating several data sets that satisfy the general goal.

5. Develop the discussion questions

An example has two parts: the background information, and the questions designed to generate discussion. Ultimately, the example is a means for teaching students the process of statistical problem-solving by making them active participants in the process of addressing the relevant issues. Because students have little experience in doing this, questions posed by the instructor should lead students through this process.

At this stage of the example development, I ask myself what statistical or substantive issues I would have to consider if I were solving the problem. These issues turn into questions to pose to the students. Good questions generate significant student discussion. They strike a balance between being too transparent and too challenging. Questions that are too transparent cause students to lose interest which decreases discussion. Questions that are too challenging cause frustration which also decreases discussion. Creating good questions is not a trivial task, but it becomes easier with experience. Ultimately, you want to generate questions that highlight the statistical issues of importance, and that promote significant student discussion.

You should not worry about generating an ideal set of questions. The questions are meant to be a starting point for discussion. However, there are times when even a good question fails to generate discussion. Hence, you always need to be prepared to help class discussion by posing related questions or by asking individual students for their opinions. Sometimes, a question may just prove to be bad. In such a case, I might choose to explain the intent of the question and the type of discussion I had hoped it would have inspired. Other times, I abandon the question entirely and move forward. For future uses of the example, I make sure that I replace or modify this question.

In general, open-ended questions are best. These do not have a "right" answer but some answers are better than others. Students gain the experience of formulating an answer and then defending it on the basis of its statistical merits. Avoid numerical questions. Remember, the classroom example is not a drill exercise but rather one designed to instill higher-order statistical thinking. Finally, be open to formulating and addressing new questions during class. Often, good discussions generate additional questions. In some cases, students pose questions I had not considered. Student questions provide a wonderful opportunity for the class and instructor to jointly explore various solutions. In the process, students have the opportunity to observe how the instructor reasons about statistical problems in real-time, which has tremendous educational merit.

The example I present in the next section uses questions designed to lead students through an analysis of data that contains outliers. Depending upon the experience and ability of the class, examples can be more or less structured than the one I present.

6. Choose a delivery style and implement the example

Section I describes four possible delivery styles for an example. If you primarily lecture, a classroom example provides a good opportunity to try a different delivery style. In the case of the rowers data, we could choose either a data analysis exercise or we could use an in-class worksheet (with output provided) to implement the example.

III. An Extended Example

Below is a classroom example I use based upon the rowers data set. This is followed by a discussion of my objectives, some comments on classroom delivery, and some comments on alternative approaches.

1. The Example

Weights of Race Boat Crew Members[1]

Like running, rowing was a means of survival long before it was a sport. The Greeks rowed, the Phoenicians rowed, and the Vikings rowed, as a means of transportation and as the primary method of maneuvering during war on seas. Rowing as a sport in modern times was initiated with "gentlemen" competitions beginning in 1829 in the Oxford-Cambridge races on the River Thames. Competitive rowing in the US began on the Charles River with the Yale-Harvard races in 1952.

The sport of rowing is divided into two distinct categories: sweep rowing, where each rower handles one oar, and sculling where each individual has two oars. Boat crews range from 1 to 8. Larger boats may have an additional member called the coxswain who does not row but has other responsibilities such as steering.

Compared to athletes in other endurance events, successful rowers are lean but heavier and taller. The average weight of the mens' 1992 US Olympic team was 196 pounds. [2] The very best oarsmen, winners of international medals, tend to be slightly heavier with an average weight slightly over 200 pounds. We have weight data from the men in the 1992 Cambridge-Oxford 8-man sweep race. The mean weight of the team members was 181.4 pounds.

Major questions of interest are: (1) How does the weight of British oarsmen compare to members of the 1992 US Olympic team and to the weight of elite international oarsmen? and (2) How does weight of a crew affect boat performance?

Discussion Questions.

I. The 95% confidence interval for the average weight based on these data is 167.4 to 195.4 pounds. For what population(s) is this interval reasonable?

II. Suppose we assume these individuals are representative of race boat crews associated with British institutions of post-secondary education. Discuss how the average weight of men in this category compares to the average weight of oarsmen on the 1992 US Olympic team. Be sure to identify plausible explanations for any differences you may observe.

---

[1] Much of the background material for this example is found at two web sites: (1) Rowing Physiology and Performance by Stephen Seiler at http://www.krs.hia.no/~stephens/rowing.htm, and (2) FAQ: Physics of Rowing by Dr. A. Dudhia at *http://www-atm.atm.ox.ac.uk/physics.html*.

[2] I have added two pounds to the actual value to make the pedagogy cleaner.

III. What additional information, if any, is needed to ascertain the validity of the estimates and conclusions above. Explain fully.

IV. Based on the displays of the data given below, would you change your answers to (I) and (II) above. If so, explain why and how your answers would change.

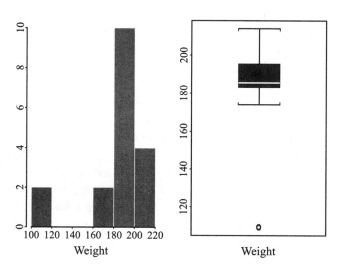

FIGURE 1
Boxplot and frequency histogram of weights, in pounds, of crew members.

V. Using the output below, explain how you could compare the average weight of a British oarsman based on this sample, to the average weight of an oarsman on the 1992 US Olympic team and to the average weight of elite international oarsmen. Make the comparisons, draw some conclusions, and make relevant observations.

Sample:	All Members
Sample size:	18
Sample mean:	181.4167
Sample stddev:	28.16143
Standard error of the mean:	6.637713
95 % CI for mu:	[167.4123 , 195.421]

Sample:	Without Coxswains
Sample size:	16
Sample mean:	190.4375
Sample stddev:	10.84416
andard error of the mean:	2.711040
95 % CI for mu:	[184.6591 , 196.2159]

VI. Many people analyze the affect of weight on the speed of a boat. In these studies, the average weight of a crew member is used. Suppose you are a statistician hired by a researcher who is interested in the questions:

(a) How significant an advantage is more weight with regard to boat speed?

(b) What is the relationship between power and weight?

(c) What impact does the total weight of the boat have on its speed?

Discuss the most appropriate estimates of weight for each of the research questions above.

VII. Summarize the major lessons of this example.

2. Objectives of the questions

We now discuss what I expect to accomplish with each question. When facilitating student discussions of the questions, I try to ensure that we consider each of the main points mentioned below.

Question I. Some students do not understand that inferential techniques, such as confidence intervals, allow for generalization from the sample to a larger population. These students answer this question by defining the population too narrowly as being the sampled participants in the 1992 Oxford-Cambridge 8-man sweep race. They forget that inferential techniques have no meaning in a census. Other students, reluctant to stray too far from the sample itself, allow only that larger populations be individuals in this particular race in a five-year interval around 1992. Discussion allows students to challenge others' ideas about what reasonable populations might be. Doing so allows them to justify their own position and also to observe that different individuals have different perspectives, thus reinforcing the lesson that there is no right answer, but some answers are better than others, and some are plain wrong.

Note: Although the data contain the weights of the coxswains, I make no indication one way or the other that this is the case. Occasionally a perceptive student questions whether the data contain these individuals. Rather than answer the question directly, I ask how the presence of coxswains would affect responses to the questions and how they might determine whether the data include coxswains.

Question II. This question demonstrates the types of conclusions that can be drawn from confidence intervals. The discussion of plausible reasons for the apparent differences in the average weight is usually animated (and often amusing). I encourage students to support their statements with relevant information and statistical concepts. My objective is to illustrate how statisticians use knowledge about an issue in conjunction with statistical knowledge to postulate explanations for differences that appear to result from something other than random chance. I take care to teach students that it is not possible to identify a definitive reason for the difference based on this sample. However, it is possible to develop conjectures which can be investigated with a new study. Again, it is possible that a perceptive or knowledgeable student suggests that the difference may be the result of having coxswains in the sample. This provides a natural lead-in for the next question.

Question III.   The emphasis of this question is that conclusions based on inferential procedures are valid only if the underlying assumptions are satisfied by the data. Specifically, inferential procedures describe only sampling error, which revisits the question of how representative the sample is of the target population, and inferential procedures are dependent upon the sampling distribution of the statistic which gives rise to the technical assumptions. One cannot overemphasize the need to check underlying assumptions. A final lesson is the importance of looking at a graphical display of the data. Statisticians never blindly accept the results of a computation; they always look at their data in many different ways.

Question IV.   First, students recognize the presence of outliers. Second, the conclusions to (I) and (II) are invalid in the light of this new information and need to be modified. For (I), the sample is not representative of the identified population due to the presence of the coxswains. For (II), outliers violate the technical condition that the data are from a normal population; at best, the data are from two different normal populations. Finally, to indicate how their answers would change, students must grapple with the issue of how to best handle the outliers. Clearly, the outliers are not the result of typos or measurement error and so cannot be discarded. Furthermore, the outliers are indicative of two distinct populations of crew members: individuals who row, oarsmen, and those who do not row, coxswains. It is instructive to discuss the issues surrounding the presence of these two groups. It again illustrates there is no one correct approach but that there might be several reasonable approaches.

Question V.   This presents students with a specific situation for which the data can be used. In this case, it appears more reasonable to use the interval for the data without the coxswains. One should now ask students whether all assumptions have now been satisfied to ensure the validity of their conclusions.

Question VI.   Through discussions of this question, students encounter undefined and ambiguous terms which in turn make the questions ill-defined. This is to encourage them to clarify what is wanted by asking an expert in the field (a role played by me). Next, students discover that different research questions require different approaches to the outliers. A common mistake in addressing the third question is that students use the 95% confidence interval based upon all the sample data, including the coxswains. Although the point estimate for the average weight of a member of the entire crew of nine is valid and can be used to estimate the total weight (multiply average weight by nine), the corresponding confidence interval is not valid because the presence of outliers violates the underlying normality assumption. Moreover, the answer to the question may not even warrant the use of a confidence interval based on all nine crew members. In particular, the coxswain's weight only serves to slow the boat since he is not rowing. This suggests a better approach to this question is to determine the average effect of a coxswain's weight on the speed of the boat, which requires a different type of analysis.

Question VII.   This question encourages students to actively reflect on the example, which helps them understand the lesson at a deeper level than if the instructor merely tells them what they should have learned. If all ends well, the students should have generated a set of lessons that includes the subgoals stated for the example.

At times throughout the example, I ask additional leading questions related to an explicitly stated question so that the ensuing discussion takes the direction for which it was designed. Also, I am flexible and if something does not appear to be working, I abandon it. On the other hand, if the class seems to be on a promising line I had not considered, I allow the class to proceed along that line.

3. Comments on the delivery of the example

When I use this example, I introduce the background information and the issues of interest. Next, I divide the class into groups of four individuals each. Each group is given a set of the discussion questions and must record their answers. As the groups work, I circulate among them to answer questions, to provide additional information at appropriate times (e.g., give them handouts with the displays and additional confidence intervals), and to assist a discussion when a group appears to be stalled. After most groups have addressed all the questions, the class reconvenes as a large group to share answers and partake in a larger discussion. The purpose of the small groups is to get as much student participation as possible; smaller groups generally promote greater participation. The larger group discussion at the end exposes students to more ideas than those of their own group and presents them the opportunity to defend their positions if they are challenged. Finally, during the large group discussion, I ensure that the points I deem important have been raised and considered by all.

In this delivery style, as well as most others, students often appear anxious to get the instructor's opinion about whether they are on the right track. I try to encourage them to talk among themselves by: (1) refusing to offer my opinion, and (2) asking members in the group for their opinions. My main purpose for circulating among the groups is to discover what the groups do and do not understand.

4. Alternative ways to develop an example

There are alternatives for developing a data-based classroom example than the full development outlined above. First, many drill exercises found in textbooks can be modified so that they move beyond the mechanical aspects of the solution to a statistical problem. Simple extensions include: (1) the identification of appropriate formal technique(s) to be used on the data, (2) a check on the validity of using a specific technique (i.e., have the assumptions been met and what are the implications of violating an underlying assumption?), (3) a determination of whether additional information is needed about the study, and (4) the selection of the most effective and informative presentation of the results. Generally, I like to make my extensions authentic which sometimes requires additional information beyond that provided by the text. The web is a great resource for this as you have seen from the rowers example. Overall, the goal is to use in-class examples as a means for going beyond the drill practice that students can get from the text.

IV. Other Uses of Real Data

The focus of this article is using real data for classroom examples, but real data should be used for all aspects of a course. Other places to use real data include assignments, case studies, projects, and exams. The objective remains the same for all coursework: to move beyond computation and teach statistical problem solving. Using real data throughout the course is a way to reinforce the lessons taught by data-based classroom examples. The resources cited below can be used to develop case studies, projects, and exams and other articles in this volume discuss how to implement projects or case studies.

Sources for ready-made classroom examples as discussed in this article are rare, but there are numerous resources of data sets and ideas that can provide the basis for such examples. Typically, the instructor needs only to find a data set and develop some discussion questions which are relevant to her goals. The ultimate challenge is to get as much student participation and involvement as possible.

Annotated Bibliograpy of Data Set Sources

1. Data and Story Library (DASL), `http://lib.stat.cmu.edu/DASL/`
   A nice feature of DASL is that it crosslists the data sets and stories by statistical methodology.

2. Journal of Statistics Education, `http://www.amstat.org/publications/jse/`
   The Journal of Statistics Education is an electronic journal. Although helpful articles can be found throughout the journal, the Datasets and Stories section of the journal is particularly useful. Generally, the data sets are accompanied with suggestions of how to use them in class. Some articles in the journal are also useful in that they provide good models or templates for developing your own examples.

3. Hand, D. J., F. Daly, A. D. Lunn, K. J. McConway, and E. Ostrowski, *A Handbook of Small Data Sets*, 1994, Chapman & Hall, London.
   This book contains 500 real data sets that are on an accompanying diskette. Identifying a relevant set in this book requires more work than some other sources. The book has an index of the data sets based upon the structure of the variables but I do not find it particularly useful. Typically, I scan the data sets themselves to find those that satisfy my goal. Although this initially requires time and effort, you benefit in that you can make note of interesting data for later examples. In fact, reading through the data sets often generates ideas for future examples.

4. Chatterjee, Samprit, Mark S. Handcock, and Jeffrey S. Simonoff, *A Casebook for a First Course In Statistics and Data Analysis*, Annotated Edition for Instruction, 1995, John Wiley and Sons, New York.

An excellent resource on many levels. First, it contains a significant number of data sets (on diskette). The authors provide extensive background information for each set. In addition, the case studies have a list of keywords that allows you to quickly determine if the data are relevant to your goal. Secondly, the case studies provide a good model for a data-based class example. The authors emphasize problem-solving aspects, and downplay the computational aspects of statistical analysis. Finally, many data sets are subjected to a variety of different analyses, which demonstrates that it is possible to analyze the same data in a variety of ways depending upon what the research question of interest is.

5. Witmer, Jeffrey A., *Data Analysis: An Introduction,* 1992, Prentice-Hall, Englewood Cliffs.

   This text is a short course supplement that includes some basic techniques of data analysis and many interesting data sets. Identifying data that satisfy the general goal is straightforward. In addition, this is an excellent source for examples of different aspects of data analysis. The examples also provide a good model for creating your own examples.

6. Chance News, `http://www.dartmouth.edu/ ~chance/chance_news/news.html`

   Chance News contains abstracts for articles with a probabilistic or statistical element that have appeared in major newspapers or science magazines. *Chance News* is an excellent source for current examples on statistical issues such as the quality of study design. Furthermore, some discussion questions, relating to the articles, are included with the abstracts. The web site contains current and past issues. An especially nice feature is that it is possible to search across all issues of *Chance News* for articles on a particular topic.

7. Textbooks.

   Many textbooks contain a large number of data sets that are usually used for drill exercises. Often, there is enough background information provided so that you can develop a classroom example. If not, it is sometimes possible to locate the original source of the data which provides more details about the data and corresponding statistical analysis. A nice feature of data in texts is that they are arranged by statistical method. Some texts I use to obtain data sets include:

Introduction to the Practice of Statistics, 3rd Edition, by David S. Moore and George P. McCabe (1993, Freeman.)

Introduction to Statistical Reasoning, Gary Smith (1998, McGraw-Hill.)

Exploring Statistics: A Modern Introduction to Data Analysis and Inference, 2nd Edition, Larry J. Kitchens (1998, Duxbury.)

References

[1] Chance News, `http://www.dartmouth.edu/ ~chance/chance_news/news.html`.

[2] Chatterjee, Samprit, Mark S. Handcock, and Jeffrey S. Simonoff, *A Casebook for a First Course In Statistics and Data Analysis,* Annotated Edition for Instruction, 1995, John Wiley and Sons, New York.

[3] Cobb, George, "Teaching Statistics," *Heeding the Call for Change: Suggestions for Curricular Action,* Lynn A. Steen (editor), 1992, MAA.

[4] Data and Story Library (DASL), `http://lib.stat. cmu.edu/DASL/`.

[5] Dudhia, A., "FAQ: Physics of Rowing", `http://www-atm.atm.ox.ac.uk/physics.html`.

[6] Hand, D. J., F. Daly, A. D. Lunn, K. J. McConway, and E. Ostrowski, *A Handbook of Small Data Sets,* 1994, Chapman & Hall, London.

[7] Journal of Statistics Education (JSE), `http://www. amstat.org/publications/jse/`.

[8] Kitchens, Larry J., *Exploring Statistics: A Modern Introduction to Data Analysis and Inference,* 2nd Edition, 1998, Duxbury, Pacific Grove, CA.

[9] Moore, David S. and George P. McCabe, *Introduction to the Practice of Statistics,* 3rd Edition, 1998, Freeman, New York.

[10] Moore, Thomas L., and Rosemary A. Roberts, "Statistics at Liberal Arts Colleges," *The American Statistician,* **43** 1989, 80–85.

[11] Seiler, Stephen, "Rowing Physiology and Performance," `http://www.krs.hia.no/stephens/rowing.htm`.

[12] Smith, Gary, *Introduction to Statistical Reasoning,* 1998, McGraw-Hill, New York.

[13] Witmer, Jeffrey A., *Data Analysis: An Introduction,,* 1992, Prentice Hall, Englewood Cliffs, NJ.

Small Student Projects in an Introductory Statistics Course

Robert L. Wardrop
University of Wisconsin-Madison

Introduction

The key to effective public speaking, I have been told, is to begin with a funny story. Thus, I will begin this article with a story.

> There was a one-room school house in a remote rural area. Periodically a regional supervisor would visit the school to evaluate the performance of its teacher. On one visit the supervisor viewed a unit on the addition of fractions. The teacher wrote on the board, $2/3+4/5 = 6/8$. After school that day the supervisor spent a great deal of time ensuring that the teacher understood the correct way to add fractions.
>
> On the next visit to the school the supervisor was dismayed to find the teacher again was using the incorrect method of adding fractions. Confronted later in the day, the teacher replied, "I tried your method, but mine is easier to teach."

The method's benefit to the teacher is, of course, overwhelmed by its disservice to the students. I will share briefly some ideas I have on what makes a statistics course good or bad. In particular, I will argue that on certain occasions a teacher should opt for a more difficult way to teach statistics.

My ideas can be summarized quite well by the paradigm: be willing, not willful. Below is an example of a willful statistics exercise.

> Sally has a random sample of size $n = 10$ from a normal population with unknown mean and standard deviation. Use Sally's data to construct a 95 percent confidence interval for the mean of the population.

This exercise is willful because its author tells the student exactly what to assume in order to complete it. This exercise is easy for the instructor because there is a known unique correct answer.

A willing exercise would provide a description of the scientific problem that motivates Sally's work. It would carefully describe how Sally obtained her data. Finally, a willing exercise would ask the student to explain what can be learned from Sally's data. The willful exercise amounts to teaching the student to turn a crank or push a button. The willing exercise forces the student to think; to draw upon ideas presented in the class along with other knowledge the student might have and combine these in a creative way. The willing exercise is difficult for the instructor because he or she does not possess the unique correct answer. I learned long ago that if I assign willing exercises, I must check my ego at the door—frequently one of my students finds a clever and creative answer that I missed.

Certainly, some willful exercises have a place in the best of courses. My complaint is with courses whose only goal is to prepare students to satisfactorily complete willful exercises. There is a great temptation to omit any willing exercises from a course. *Willing exercises take time.* As long as there are powerful people who judge a statistics course by "How many topics are covered," teachers will face pressure to omit willing exercises, leaving more time to cover more topics.

I consider the subject of statistics to be a collection of concepts, principles, and methods that help scientists learn about the world. (I define a scientist as any person who wants to understand better his or her natural, political, or social worlds.) Mathematics is a critical component of statistics, and, I believe, all other things being equal, the person who is the better mathematician will be the better statistician. If my view has any validity, should not our introductory statistics courses make some effort to help students become better scientists? For example, the first day of class I announce that the fundamental goal of my course is:

> To enable students to discover that statistics can be an important tool in daily life.

I want my students to learn that statistics is useful because it can help *them* learn about things that *they* find interesting.

My fundamental goal has an impact on various aspects of my course: the choice of text, the material presented, the methods of presenting the material, and the methods of evaluating the student's learning. In this paper I will limit attention to one aspect of my course: my use of small student projects. See [2], [3], [4], and [5] for related work. As will become immediately obvious in Section 3, student projects can give rise only to willing exercises.

Limitations

Beginning in the next section, I will present several examples of student projects from my classes. As will become obvious, my students deserve all the credit for the creativity and cleverness their work demonstrates. My main contribution is that I assign this work to them. I believe that an ideal introductory class would require each student to do several projects. Limits on my time, however, require that I assign only two projects in my course.

Based on my teaching experiences, I fervently believe that a student learns more by analyzing data that he or she has collected, than by analyzing data collected by another. This discovery did not surprise me. What did surprise me is that most of my students prefer studying other students' projects to "professional" research that I present. I do not know why this is true; I conjecture that there is less variation in interests within students than there is between the students and me. This is the first of two reasons I use numerous student projects as examples in lecture—my students find them to be interesting. The second reason is that I learned in the early days of assigning projects that few students are creative without models of good projects, but almost every student is creative when provided models of good projects. (This partly explains why this paper contains numerous projects; if you choose to assign projects you might want to make the project topics below available to your students.)

Figure 1, taken from [1, p. 9], displays four possible study designs and notes their allowable inference(s), if any. Units can be selected at random or not at random, and can be allocated to groups by randomization or not. If units are selected at random, then inferences to populations are valid. If units are allocated to groups by randomization, then causal inferences are valid. All introductory Statistics texts present inferences to populations, but relatively few discuss causal inferences. This is unfortunate. Arguably a key component of statistical literacy is the ability to dis-

Allocation of Units to Groups

Selection of Units	By Randomization	Not by Randomization
At Random	A random sample is selected from one population; units are then randomly assigned to different treatment groups	Random samples are selected from existing distinct populations.
Not at Random	A group of study units is found; units are then randomly assigned to treatment groups.	Collections of available units from distinct groups are examined.

FIGURE 1
Statistical inferences permitted by study designs (from *The Statistical Sleuth* by Ramsey and Schafer [1, p. 9]). For the designs in the first row, inferences to populations can be drawn; for the designs in the first column, causal inferences can be drawn.

tinguish between causal and noncausal links between variables. It is difficult to distinguish a difference if one is never taught that such differences exist.

I want my students to be able to perform valid inference, but I do not want them to expend the time and effort necessary to obtain random samples. Hence, my students "work in" the lower left entry in Figure 1; they can draw causal inferences, but not population inferences. I refer to such inference as *randomization-based inference*. For details on randomization-based inference see [3], [4], and [5].

Eleven Projects with a Dichotomous Response

For many of my students, their daily life includes working to obtain enough money to continue school, and these students are very interested in ways to earn more money. The first four projects below were executed on-the-job. (Note: My students have given me permission to use their work, and I will identify each project with the first name(s) of its author(s).)

1. **Lori** worked as a waitress and wondered whether suggesting a specific appetizer upon greeting her customers would lead to an increase in the sales of appetizers. Her data, though not statistically significant, ran counter to her belief—mentioning a specific appetizer decreased the sales of all appetizers!

2. **Nell** worked at a coffee cart which offered two sizes, small and large. Of course, some customers specified the size when they ordered, but Nell was interested in those who simply ordered coffee. She found that the question, "Would you like a large?" was statistically significantly superior to the question, "Would you like a small or a large?" at eliciting the purchase of a large cup of coffee.

3. **Andre**'s work problem was similar to Nell's. He sold ice cream which could be served in a plain or a waffle cone. His store made a much larger profit on the waffle cones. For customers who did not specify the cone type in their order, Andre found that the question, "Would you like a plain cone or a homemade waffle cone?" elicited significantly more sales of waffle cones than did the same question with the adjective "homemade" deleted.

4. **Mary's** job duties included the purchase of used compact discs from customers. Mary wondered which of the following statements to the customer would be more effective.
   I will give you $X.
   How does $X sound?

(The value of X was appropriate for the number and quality of the compact discs offered for sale.) Mary found that the first statement performed better (at getting an acceptance of the first offer) than the second, but that the difference barely missed achieving statistical significance.

The following project was motivated by the experiences of its author and many of his friends.

5. **Tuan** was interested in the problems an international student faces at the University of Wisconsin–Madison. He showed 25 graduate students part of an essay he said was written by "Jack McConnell, a student from Iowa." He showed 25 other college graduates the *same essay*, but said it was written by "Hsiao-Ping Zhang, an international student from China." When asked, "Do you detect any grammatical errors in this passage?" 64 percent who had read the Chinese student's essay said yes, compared to only 20 percent who had read the Iowa student's essay! This huge difference is highly statistically significant.

6. **Ruth** visited a minimum-security federal prison camp to obtain her subjects, first-time nonviolent offenders. The first version of her question read,
   The prison is beginning a program in which inmates have the opportunity to volunteer for community service with developmentally disabled adults. Inmates who volunteer will receive a sentence reduction. Would you participate?

The second version was the same, except that there was no mention of sentence reduction. Ruth was surprised when her data revealed that the second version received a much higher proportion of yes responses than the first version, but the difference did not quite achieve statistical significance.

In the above studies, the experimental units are people. More often, my students choose units that are trials. The remaining examples are of this latter type. Frequently, my students choose to use statistics to investigate longstanding hobbies or pastimes.

7. **Erin** began her project with the following statement.
   Ice-skating has been a part of my life for 12 years and one thing that stands out in my mind ... were the numerous arguments I would stubbornly have with my coach.

Erin's trial was an attempt at an axel (a figure skating jump with one and one-half completed turns). Erin found that she was highly statistically significantly better at completing an axel off her right foot than an axel off her left foot.

8. **Kathy** found that she was much better at successfully completing a cartwheel if she led with her right hand rather than her left.

9. When signing the alphabet, it is standard to use one hand as the primary hand and the other as the assistor. **Diana** found that choosing her right hand as primary made her a better signer than when her left hand was primary, but the difference just failed to achieve statistical significance.

10. **Lisa S.** found that she was a much better lacrosse shooter with her right hand than with her left.

11. **Mike** enjoyed riding his personal water craft very fast and making sharp turns. His pleasure was diminished, however, whenever he would be thrown from the craft and land 30 feet away from it. Mike found that he was much better at staying on-board if he turned left than if he turned right.

In the next section I will present projects with a numerical response. Before turning to them, I want to share a bit of what my students and I have learned from projects like those above.

Over the past few years, I have graded thousands of student projects. A small number of the project-topics appears to have been chosen to complete the assignment with as little thought and effort as possible. For example, a study of the effect of the hand used on the outcome of the toss of a coin would be of this type. I make it clear to my students that it is not necessary for me to consider the topic to be interesting; it is necessary, however, that the project report convincingly explains why the topic is of interest to the student.

The great majority of the projects are creative and interesting, and not qualitatively different from the ones described above. Students show great interest in studying ambidexterity, and various sports and games, especially darts, golf, basketball, archery and sharpshooting.

Analyzing their own data makes students appreciate the importance of the P-value. Obtaining a very small P-value seems to make them think, "Yes! I have achieved results that standard scientific practice says are real!" When a difference that is large enough to be important is not statistically significant, most students realize in a very personal way the advantages of collecting more data. Unfortunately, some students misinterpret P-values larger than 0.05 as *proving* that the treatments are identical.

I learn more about what my students really understand by reading what they write freely, instead of relying strictly on responses to exam questions. Sometimes they display ignorance or misconceptions in areas I might never think of

examining. Also, occasionally a student will make it quite clear that even though he or she understands what the data and P-value signify, no study is going to change the student's view of the world! For example, a male student's data revealed that male subjects lied about their age more than female subjects did, but the difference was not statistically significant (assuming random samples, which was invalid). The researcher wrote, "I don't care what the data say, we all know that women lie about their ages more than men do."

Thirteen Projects with a Numerical Response

One of the pleasures of a numerical response is that we can draw pictures of our data and see what the pictures reveal. Unfortunately, space limitations prevent me from drawing pictures for all of the projects of this section.

12. **Sara** enjoyed playing golf. Like many novice golfers, Sara wondered whether she was more effective at hitting a golf ball from a fairway lie with a three-wood or with a three-iron.

13. **Brian** was a student in the ROTC program. As part of his training, Brian was required to run in combat boots and in jungle boots. Brian wondered whether the type of boot affected his running.

Figure 2 presents stem-and-leaf plots of the distance, in yards, that Sara hit a golf ball, by club. Sara's data with the three-wood could be described as moderately skewed to the left, whereas her data with the three-iron are not so well-behaved. I would argue that there are three distinct

	Three-Wood		Three-Iron
2	2	2	7
3	28	3	
4		4	
5	68	5	23789
6		6	888
7	7	7	
8	1	8	248
9	39	9	22227789
10	111477899	10	01577789
11	0134568	11	068
12	22778889	12	7
13	11799	13	22667899
14	07		

FIGURE 2
Stem-and-leaf Plots of the Distance, in Yards, Sara Hit a Golf Ball, by Type of Club.

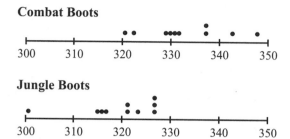

FIGURE 3
Dot Plots of the Time, in Seconds, Required for Brian to Run One Mile, by Footwear.

groups of observations plus a small outlier. The reader, of course, can reasonably disagree with my interpretation.

Figure 3 presents dot plots of the time, in seconds, Brian required to run one mile, by footwear. Although the distributions overlap, it is clear (descriptively) that Brian ran faster while wearing jungle boots than he did while wearing combat boots. The distribution of the combat boot data is approximately symmetric, but for the jungle boots it is skewed to the left with a small outlier.

It is my experience that students find examining pictures of data to be more interesting, and they are better at it when they have a personal interest in the data. In addition, typically it is easier and more meaningful to compare and contrast two related pictures than to evaluate one picture in isolation.

Brian's mean and standard deviation are 333.0 and 8.18 wearing combat boots, and 319.5 and 7.93 wearing jungle boots. Sara's mean and standard deviation are 106.87 and 29.87 with the three-wood, and 98.18 and 28.33 with the three-iron. Either Brian's or Sara's data can be used to illustrate various inference formulas. Notice that exercises of this type would naturally be of the willing variety. These data provide excellent opportunities for a consideration of issues like robustness. For these data, the randomization distribution and t-distribution procedures give qualitatively the same answers. For Brian, the jungle boots are significantly faster (mean) than the combat boots. For Sara, the difference (of means) between the clubs is not large enough to achieve statistical significance. (Note: Because both studies are balanced and have nearly equal sample standard deviations, all the usual two sample t formulas give essentially the same quantitative answer.)

Below I will list 11 more student projects. Because of space limitations, I will not discuss the results of the data analysis.

14. Maria was a member of the UW varsity soccer team. Her team had two games per week, every Friday evening

and Sunday morning. Maria wondered whether she played better in the evening or morning. As an indirect way of measuring this, she performed a study to see whether her ability to juggle a soccer ball was influenced by the time of day.

15. Jennifer E. was a softball player and wanted to investigate whether the type of bat, aluminum or wood, influenced how far she could hit a pitched ball.

16. Doug performed a study to investigate whether the type of dart he used, "bar darts" or his personal set, influenced how many rounds he required to complete the game "301."

17. Kymn was a member of the women's varsity crew and frequently worked out on a rowing simulation machine called an ergometer. She wanted to investigate whether the setting of the machine, there are two, influenced the time required to row a simulated 2,000 meters. No doubt because of her superb conditioning, Kymn's times on each setting showed little variation.

18. Mei Lan, Sin Fai, and **Todd** performed a study to investigate whether having a car's windows open or closed influenced the time required to accelerate from 40 to 65 miles per hour.

19. Damion performed a study to determine whether his smoking a cigarette or not influenced how long it took him to climb Bascom Hill on the Madison campus.

20. Lisa J., a former horticulturist in my class, performed a study to investigate the effect of temperature on the growth of Rhizoctonia solani fungus.

21. Jennifer C. swam competitively in college and was a high school swimming coach when she enrolled in my course. She performed a study to compare two methods of starting a freestyle swimming race. She found that, for her, the traditional start was superior to the new "track start."

22. Eric was a punter on the varsity football team and performed a project to estimate how much farther he would punt the ball with two steps (before kicking) rather than one step.

Most projects with a numerical response are concerned with the center of the distribution; either larger or smaller is better. The next two projects provide examples in which spread is more important than center. The first project is an example that deals with variation from a fixed target and the second deals with the more common statistical problem of variation without a fixed target.

23. Paul and **Leslie** enjoyed playing the dart game Cricket, with each claiming to be the superior player. Hitting the twenty wedge on the dart board is particularly important for a successful game of Cricket. Each person attempted 78 throws, with each toss aimed at the 20 wedge. A response of 0 was noted if the throw hit the target wedge of 20. If the throw landed one wedge to the right of 20, the response was +1; if it landed two wedges to the right of 20, the response was +2, and so on. Darts that landed to the left of 20 gave responses of −1, −2, and so on, in the analogous manner. These data contained a wealth of information. Viewed as a dichotomy, Paul was better at hitting the 20, by a score of 36 to 10. (This pretty much settled who was the better player.) Paul's mean response was 0.31 and Leslie's was 0.65, indicating that both had a tendency to shoot to the right. Finally, Paul's mean absolute response was 0.62 and Leslie's was 1.71, indicating a substantial difference in variation.

24. **Kim** wanted to compare the distributions of the distance obtained when hitting a golf ball with two seven-irons; one made of steel and one of graphite. In golf, consistency with a seven-iron is more important than distance; if you want to hit the ball farther, use a six-iron. By examining dot plots, histograms, and various measures of spread, Kim concluded that there was no substantial difference in the spreads of the two distributions.

Most students have no trouble selecting appropriate trials for their projects, but a significant minority make a particular error; namely, they make the trials "too small." This error is particularly common for students studying darts or bowling. For example, a bowler might want to know whether the weight of the ball influences performance. What should the trial be: a frame or a game? Unfortunately, some students seem to reason as follows. More data gives us better answers, and defining a trial as a frame will yield more data than defining a trial to be a game. Therefore, I will have more data if the trial is a frame. Let us ignore the important issue that for trial-equal-to-frame, there is no sensible way to measure the response—a ten and an eight are clearly much better than two nines, and a ten on one ball, a strike, is better than a spare. This is where randomization can help the student see his or her error. If the trial is a frame, then when one randomizes it is likely that the bowler frequently will be forced to switch from one ball to the other. But no serious bowler would do that! (Similarly, a dart player would not change darts after every throw.) My advice to students is to let the goal of the study determine the size of the trial and be careful not to make the trial too small. For example, a bowler is interested in the score in a game of bowling, so any trial smaller than a game would be wrong. (In fact, a league bowler might be interested in the score for three games and choose three games to be the unit.)

Examining Assumptions

See [6] for a more detailed discussion of the ideas in this section.

As discussed in Section 2, for population inference to be valid, one needs to assume that the units are obtained by random sampling. If the units are trials, then random sampling means that the trials are independent and identically distributed (i.i.d.). For a dichotomous response, i.i.d. trials are called Bernoulli trials. In this section I discuss student projects that examine whether a sequence of dichotomous responses can be viewed as Bernoulli trials. If the trials are Bernoulli trials, then population inference is valid. Note that, unlike earlier projects that compared data from two groups, the studies of this section have data from only one source.

The idea of a mathematical model for the outcomes of trials is difficult for many of my students to understand. For example, if I tell them that a random sample of 100 persons from a population yields 70 successes, they understand that $\hat{p} = 0.70$ might not be the same number as p, the population proportion. If, however, I say that a basketball player's successive free throws are Bernoulli trials and that she makes 70 out of 100 shots, many of my students conclude that $p = 0.70$. It is strange; if $n = 1$ students readily understand that p need not be 1 or 0 (the two possible values of $\hat{p}$), but somehow as n grows the distinction between $\hat{p}$ and p disappears, faster and more completely than the law of large numbers indicates.

Even though it is difficult to teach students a better understanding of Bernoulli trials, I believe that it is an important topic. Many sciences rely critically on mathematical models, and I believe there is value in helping students obtain a better understanding of such models, even in the simple form of Bernoulli trials.

Below are some examples of sequences of dichotomous trials observed or obtained by my students.

25. **Mieke** defined a trial to be her playing a B-flat on her clarinet into a tuner. The tuner classified the note as sharp, flat, or perfectly in tune. A perfectly in tune note denoted a successful trial, while either of the other two classifications was labeled a failure.

26. **Mary** defined a trial to be her father's morning wait for the bus. If the bus arrived within two minutes of the scheduled time, the trial was a success; otherwise, it was a failure.

27. **Matthew** defined a trial to be a live birth at a local hospital; female babies were successes and males were failures.

28. **Mark** and **Justin** defined a trial to be a bicyclist riding through a busy intersection in Madison. A rider with a helmet was a success and a rider without a helmet was a failure.

29. **Kristin** defined a trial to be rolling two small balls across the floor in her living room. A trial was a success if her dog, Muffin, fetched the red ball and a failure if she fetched the blue ball.

30. There have been numerous projects in which the trials are golf putts, basketball free throws, dart tosses, and other game activities.

I suggest two simple-minded ways to investigate the validity of the two assumptions of Bernoulli trials. First, compare the proportion of successes in the first and second halves of the study. Second, look at the 2×2 table that relates the current outcome to the previous outcome. The first comparison gives some insight into whether p remains constant and the second provides some insight into whether the trials have memory.

The dichotomous trials projects have been quite successful. The only serious problem was that, initially, my students chose really boring trials—tossing a coin, casting a die, throwing paper wads in a basket. It turned out that they had misinterpreted my instructions. They thought that I wanted them to be sure they had Bernoulli trials. Quite the contrary, often it can be very interesting to discover memory or a time trend in a process.

Conclusion

Confucius taught,

> I hear, I forget.
> I read, I remember.
> I do, I understand.

I encourage you to include more "doing" in your introductory statistics classes. For me, assigning small student projects has been a very successful and rewarding way to incorporate more active learning into an introductory statistics course. An added bonus is that students get additional practice at writing.

If you decide to include small student projects in your course, I hope that the examples and comments in this paper will prove useful.

References

1. Ramsey, F.L. and Schafer, D.W., *The Statistical Sleuth: A Course in Methods of Data Analysis,* 1996, Duxbury Press, Pacific Grove, CA.
2. Rossman, A., "Book Review of *Statistics: Learning in the Presence of Variation,*" *The American Statistician,* **49**(2), 1995, 237–238.
3. Wardrop, R., "A Radically Different Approach to Introductory Statistics," University of Wisconsin–Madison, Department of Statistics Technical Report No. 889, 1992.
4. ——, "Guest Editorial: A New Approach to Introductory Statistics," *The Journal of Undergraduate Math and Its Applications,* **16**(1), 1995, 1–8.
5. ——, "Student Sports Projects in a Statistics Course," An invited paper presented at the Joint Statistical Meetings, Section on Statistics in Sports, 1996, Chicago.
6. ——, "Bernoulli Trials: Do They Exist?" A contributed paper presented at the Joint Statistical Meetings, Section on Statistical Education, 1996, Chicago.

Motivating, Monitoring, and Evaluating Student Projects†

Katherine T. Halvorsen
Smith College

Thomas L. Moore
Grinnell College

Introduction

Student projects can teach students concepts not usually encountered in introductory or second-level statistics courses. Questions about study design, study protocols, questionnaire construction, informed consent confidentiality, data management, data cleaning, and handling missing data may arise when students deal with collecting and analyzing their own data. Projects can teach technical writing. Few students receive instruction specifically focused on writing about numbers, and the statistics research project offers a unique opportunity to do this. Projects also give instructors a chance to discuss a wide variety of graphical methods for presenting quantitative information.

Projects can teach oral presentation skills. Instructors may wish to discuss with students issues such as organizing the material, practicing the talk, or making and using handouts and visual aids. Additionally, student projects can teach group dynamics and methods for working effectively with others.

This paper describes student projects we have used in both introductory and in second-level statistics classes. It addresses the issues of motivating, monitoring, and evaluating student projects, and it discusses some special considerations that student projects present for instructors using them.

Structuring Student Projects

The student projects described here may be used in a variety of courses: an introductory applied statistics course (with or without a calculus prerequisite); a second-level applied statistics course in regression analysis, analysis of variance, or linear models; or the standard probability, mathematical statistics sequence. These projects have been used successfully in courses taken by mathematics majors and in-service courses for non-majors.

The project structure we use was originally designed by Professor Douglas Zahn for an introductory business statistics course for MBA's at Florida State University. We modified his instructions to fit the needs of undergraduate statistics students in liberal arts colleges, and to meet the special needs of particular courses. Readers can modify these instructions to better fit their own circumstances, goals, or constraints.

Our project consists of a written proposal, due early in the semester (from the third to the sixth week of the semester depending on the course); a short oral presentation of the proposal, given to the class after the proposal is approved; a short, written, progress report due at midsemester; an oral report of results, given during the last

† An earlier version of this article appeared in the *Proceedings of the Section on Statistical Education,* 1991, American Statistical Association, 20–25.

week of classes; and a written final report, due on the last day of class. Depending on the time available and on the needs of the class, the instructor may require an extra oral progress report at the time the written progress report is due.

Motivating Projects.   We believe that projects must be an integral part of the required work for the course to make them an effective learning experience for students. Thus, our students initially learn about their project in the course syllabus handed out on the first day of class. The syllabus has a separate section describing the project, and the course-work timetable given in the syllabus lists the due dates for each part of the project along with the dates for readings, homework, and exams. This gives students who are "shopping" for courses full information about the amount of work expected of them in the course. The syllabus also tells students how much weight their project performance will have in their course grade. This has varied from 10 to 30 percent in our classes.

Students receive an additional handout that gives detailed instructions for preparing the project proposal, and we spend a class period discussing it. The discussion includes examples of possible projects and information about projects that previous students have completed. In this first class, you might ask students to introduce themselves, giving their names, class years, majors, and their interests or hobbies, and what they want to get out of the course. This promotes an atmosphere of open discussion and helps students find compatible team members with similar interests.

Project Teams.   Two to five students work together on a project. Students select their team members themselves and together decide on the research question they will study. Groups prepare a written working agreement that specifies how they will allocate tasks, and each group member signs the agreement. If a project involves expenses, the working agreement should explain how students will cover the costs.

Project Proposals.   The first stage of the project requires students to choose a research topic and write a project proposal. The proposal is a detailed plan stating what research question they will investigate and how they will carry out the research. Teams meet with the instructor to discuss their ideas for projects before writing the proposal, or they may hand in drafts for comments from the instructor if they allow adequate time before the due date for completed proposals. Students may not begin data collection until the instructor has approved the project proposal. Projects that

are not approved must be revised until the group produces an acceptable proposal.

Projects may be observational or experimental. Many groups choose surveys of the school population, and some plan surveys of local townspeople. In either situation, these proposals must gain the approval of the college's committee on research on human subjects. The committee primarily ensures that subjects are properly informed, that they are treated fairly, and that their privacy is protected.

The project need not involve collecting original data. Many popular publications regularly publish extensive data sets. For example, *Fortune* and *Business Week* often have financial data. *U.S. News and World Report* publishes annually *America's Best Colleges* [3], a magazine that gives vital statistics for more than 1350 U.S. colleges and universities. Newspapers in large metropolitan areas, for example, *The New York Times* or *The Boston Globe*, often publish usable data. Students also may use data previously published in research journals. Singer and Willett [16] provide references for a collection of articles that contain original data. They describe each data set and give suggested analyses for some. They note that articles published in the early volumes of journals in psychology, education, agriculture, and life sciences often contain original data. Case books can provide good project data, especially the open-ended cases. (See Sharpe's article—"Curriculum in Context: Teaching with Case Studies in Statistics Courses"—in this volume, for more on case studies and resources for case studies.)

Another source of existing data that students are eager to access is the internet. Robin Lock's article—"WWW Resources for Teaching Statistics"—in this volume describes particularly good internet sources for data sets. If students use data available on the internet, the teacher may require that it be data that does not come with suggested analyses.

After teams select a research question they focus on the statistical questions: What is the population they will study? What is an element of the population? How big is the population? What variables will they measure on each element? How will each variable be used to answer their research question? Teams must outline their plans for data collection in the project proposal. They must use random (or approximately random) sampling if they are conducting a survey or random allocation if they are performing an experiment. They must describe in sufficient detail how this will be done so that another person could carry out their plans without further instructions. They also must state the sample size(s) they plan to collect. If they plan to interview subjects, they must provide the script they will use to inform potential subjects about the nature of the study and to give them the opportunity to choose whether to participate.

They also need to include a copy of the questionnaire or study protocol. They must write operational definitions for each variable they intend to measure and construct a codebook for the data set that includes variable names, columns required in the data file, and expected ranges or codes for each variable.

They must describe data analysis plans in the proposal in some detail. Their analysis should include examining distributions and reporting summary statistics for each continuous variable and should include frequency tables for each categorical variable. The proposal should describe the graphs, tables, and statistics that the students plan to use to examine bivariate or multivariate relationships. If they plan to use regression analysis, then they should give the initial model they intend to test, and they should specify how they plan to check the fit. One of us requires that the last section of the proposal provide a budget for the project. Teams estimate how much time each task will require and how much time each team member will spend on each task. They also estimate their requirements for any other resources and state who will supply them.

Progress Reports.   At about midsemester, usually two or three weeks after the proposals have been approved, teams hand in a short report on their progress. They discuss any unexpected problems that have come up and how they have resolved those problems, any changes that were needed in the proposal and why they were needed, and they re-estimate the project timetable and budget.

Final Reports.   Students hand in the project final report on the last day of class. This document consists of a one page executive summary and a much longer statistical summary. The executive summary must be written in non-technical language for the reader who may have an interest in the research question but does not have any statistical training. It must state briefly: (1) the research question and why it is important; (2) the methods used to study the question; (3) the findings and what they mean; and (4) what action they recommend on the basis of their findings. The statistical summary has the form of a science research paper and includes introduction, methods, results, and discussion sections accompanied by tables and graphs illustrating the results. Students have to comment on what they have learned from this project that will influence their approach to similar problems in the future.

Oral Presentations.   Student projects provide an opportunity for students to develop oral-presentation skills. At least three oral-presentation opportunities exist within the project timeline: right after the proposals have been accepted, shortly after the data have been collected, and at the end of the semester.

When groups give brief oral reports to the class after their proposals have been accepted, they describe the project and answer questions from the class. In smaller classes we have also asked groups to make oral progress reports after they turn in the written progress report and have their data in hand. The oral report given at the end of the semester is more extensive than the other two and may include visual aids and handouts. In some classes, visitors, other faculty, or college staff attend these presentations.

Following the presentation and question period, each member of the audience and each member of the presenting group may be asked to complete a short (5 questions) evaluation form about the talk. The presenting group receives these after the instructor has read them, usually later the same day.

Besides teaching individual skills, oral presentations create a sense of intellectual community in the class— students appreciate hearing about other projects and the class discussion can improve the overall quality of the projects.

Evaluating Projects.   The instructions for the project proposal include information about how the credit for the class project will be distributed over the parts of the project; the proposal, the team working agreement, the progress report, the oral presentations, and the final report should all count for a percentage of the final project grade. Consult Garfield's assessment paper in this volume—"Beyond Testing and Grading, etc."—for suggestions on how to evaluate components of the project through the use of a rubric.

Results: Student Generated Projects

Introductory Statistics Classes.   The most challenging problem we encounter in asking introductory statistics students to write a project proposal is the students' lack of experience in formulating a tractable research question. Students also need time to become familiar with statistical language and to become comfortable using the computing software for the course. Regularly allocating class time to answer questions about the proposal during the proposal writing stage of the project helps the students learn more quickly and emphasizes the importance of the project to the course. If the course begins with descriptive statistics, then by the time the proposal is due they have learned rudimentary graphical methods for displaying data and some summary statistics for describing distributions. Additionally, we use few technical terms in describing the proposal. Discussions between the instructor and individual groups also help to allay fears. Instruction and practice in the use of the software as early as the second class period also helps.

Students find it difficult to write statistically and so we give them opportunities to practice writing throughout the semester. We do not want the final report to be their first attempt. These opportunities can take the form of periodic data analysis labs, a small mini-project on data description using existing data, or take-home exams where writing is part of the evaluation.

Our students in introductory courses have examined the following research questions:

1) Do Smith College students eat a balanced breakfast? The investigators surveyed students and concluded that 29 percent of the students do not consume any food or beverage before 10:00 AM. Among the 70 percent who eat breakfast, only 29 percent of them eat a nutritionally balanced meal. [7]

2) Do the busses from Smith to Amherst College and The University of Massachusetts run on schedule? The investigators observed the bus pull out from the bus stop at J.M. Green Hall at Smith four times a day on weekdays for two weeks. They recorded the actual time of departure for each bus and computed the difference between the scheduled departure time and the actual departure time. They found that a 95 percent confidence interval for the difference included zero, and they concluded that, on average, the busses leave on schedule. [10]

3) Does the attire worn by Grinnell College students when they go to the shower depend on the sex of the students and on the type of floor they live on—single sex floor versus coed floor? The investigators used a stratified sample (of the four combinations of sex by floor type) and a telephone survey to collect the data. They found that males behave independently of floor type, but females' dress depends upon floor type. The table below gives the data. [6]

4) Do lost letters get mailed? Using a "lost-letter" technique learned from [12], two students intentionally "lost" letters in three general locations: the city of Des Moines, the town of Grinnell, and the campus of Grinnell College. The students addressed half of the letters to a fictitious, overtly conservative organization (Friends of the Confederacy) and the others to a fictitious, overtly liberal organization (Iowa Peaceworks). They wanted to estimate an overall proportion of lost letters that would be returned and whether the proportion would depend upon the address. About 59% of the letters were re-

Males:		Attire		
		Towel	Robe	Other*
Floor	Coed	5	7	3
	Single Sex	4	5	6

Females:		Attire		
		Towel	Robe	Other*
Floor	Coed	0	8	7
	Single Sex	3	11	1

*"Other" includes responses from 'underwear' to fully clothed.

turned and a statistically significant greater proportion were returned to Iowa Peaceworks. [9]

Second-Level Statistics Courses. At this level we expect students to be familiar with some graphical and arithmetic methods for summarizing data and with elementary inferential techniques for constructing confidence intervals and hypothesis tests. They may also have used simple linear regression. Often these students have a better understanding of the requirements of the project proposal than students in introductory courses, but they may choose more ambitious projects that make finding appropriate data somewhat more difficult.

Our students in second-level courses have examined the following research questions:

1) One group used data from *U.S. News and World Report* to predict the percentage of college freshmen who were in the top ten percent of their high school class. They used average SAT score, percentage of applicants accepted by the college, percentage of faculty with PhD's, student-faculty ratio, and instructional budget per student as explanatory variables. They found that SAT score and acceptance rate explained 72.5 percent of the variation in the dependent variable. [4]

2) Another group used *Boston Magazine* data on Massachusetts public schools. They found that the percentage of high school seniors who go on to four-year colleges could best be predicted by average teacher's salary in the district and percentage of high school graduates in the district. The R^2 value was 55 percent. [2]

3) Are bridge hands random? The investigators regularly played tournament bridge at two locations in Iowa and looked at sampled hands from these two locations as well as at samples of computer-generated hands from a bridge journal. They discovered that the hand-shuffled bridge hands at Marshalltown, Iowa, were not at all ran-

dom, whereas they could not detect non-randomness in the Grinnell or computer-generated hands. [1]

4) What factors influence whether a Smith College student takes a mathematics course when she is not required to? The investigator for this class project asked 50 seniors to complete a survey about their attitudes towards mathematics and their previous experience with mathematics. She used discriminant analysis to analyze the data and concluded that only two variables were associated with the student taking mathematics in college: her experience with mathematics in high school and her major in college. Students with more positive experiences with mathematics in high school and students with majors in mathematics and the sciences were more likely to take mathematics classes in college. [17]

5) Is there a preferred location of bidding position on the T.V. game show "The Price is Right?" Students watched several weeks' worth of shows. They found that the person bidding last (fourth) had a significantly better chance to win and that the person bidding first is least likely to win. Probably since the first round of each day has the person seated on the right end bid first, this stage position is the least successful of the four. [13]

6) Do adverbs multiply adjectives at Grinnell College? In a famous linguistical study of the 1950's, Norman Cliff quantified the effect that adverbs have when combined with adjectives. For example, the adjective "pleasant" might have a numerical rating of 2.18 on a "scale of favorableness" (which goes from -5 to 5) and the adverb "somewhat" might have an intensifying effect of .66, so that the combination "somewhat pleasant" has a value of 1.44 (=2.18 × .66) on the favorableness scale, while the adverb "very" has an intensifying effect of 1.25 so that "very pleasant" occupies a position of 2.725 on the favorableness scale. [See [5] for a fuller description of the original study.]

This study was replicated by Grinnell College students using classmates as subjects. The multiplicative effect that adverbs had on adjectives at Grinnell fit the original model very well. Students also investigated gender differences and found none, except for the effect the adverb "pretty" had when combined with various adjectives. [15]

Discussion

Research on Learning.   Research suggests that learning is a constructive process. Students learn by active involvement with the material, and they learn to do well only what they practice [8]. To involve students with statistical is-

sues, educators recommend "data-driven" courses that rely on real research questions and the data gathered to answer those questions [14, p. 81 and 16]. Student projects foster active learning through their involvement in the practical, day-to-day issues statisticians confront in doing their work. Students maintain interest in their projects because they choose the questions they want to answer. They decide what data they need to answer these questions, and they decide how to collect and analyze the data. Projects give students one problem to solve that actually consists of many small and not-so-small problems: what data would address this problem? how do we get the data? how do we extract the answer from the data after we collect it? how can we convince others that we have the answer? We have found that students who were initially afraid of taking statistics and take the course only because they have to, begin to relax and enjoy the work when they see that they really can grasp, and even make contributions toward, answering the particular questions involved in a student research project.

Implications for Statistics Teaching.   Using projects requires some restructuring of class time. Instructors will lecture less because they spend some class time on project discussions or oral presentations. Instructors may devote more office hours or more time before and after class to students' project-related questions. Students frequently have questions not typically covered in the standard textbook, for example: "Is the sample random if we ask every one who comes in the door between 7 and 9 tonight to answer our survey?"; "What do I do if someone leaves a question blank?"; or the panic call, "We just deleted our data set, how can we get it back?" Giving students feedback changes from grading 30 sets of nearly identical homework papers or exams to giving your responses to 15 (or fewer depending on team size) varied papers on topics that most students felt excited about. Instructors sometimes begin to feel like a partner in the students' research, especially if the instructor is willing to read and comment on drafts for students. Statistics faculty need to learn new skills. We now have to grade grammar and writing style as well as statistical thinking. Many colleges offer workshops for faculty in writing-across-the-curriculum and these may be useful to us.

Student Response to Projects.   The time and effort required to make these changes in the undergraduate statistics courses produce large benefits. The Harvard Assessment *Report on College Teaching* [11] found that students like the opportunity to try out new techniques, get feedback, and then be allowed to revise before handing things in for grading. Students believe they learn more this way. In our experience, students usually conclude that the project was one of the most useful parts of the course. Some students comment that the project made them apply everything they learned as soon as they learned it. Most say it was a lot of work. For some it is the first time they have stood in front of an audience to present their work. On the whole we encourage other faculty to use this kind of project in their classes.

References

1. Ahmann, Tom and James Abbott, "Bridge Distributions," Math 336 course paper, Grinnell College, Department of Mathematics.

2. Allen, Jane M., Heather C. Fennell, and Kim M. Howard, "Final Project," MTH 247 course paper examining factors that influence the percentage of seniors from Massachusetts public high schools that go on to four-year colleges, May, 1991, Smith College, Department of Mathematics.

3. "America's Best Colleges, 1991 College Guide," *U.S. News and World Report*, Washington, D.C.

4. Bond, Julia, Charole Chun, Sihame Kairovani, and Catherine Moye, "A Regression Analysis of Colleges and Universities," MTH 247 course paper, May, 1990, Smith College, Department of Mathematics.

5. Cliff, Norman, "Adverbs Multiply Adjectives," in *Statistics: A Guide to the Unknown,* by Tanur, J., F. Mosteller, W. Kruskal, R. Link, R. Pieters, and G. Rising (eds.), 1972, Holden-Day, San Francisco, 176–184.

6. Doerre, Sharon, and Sarah Clatanoff, "Journeying to the Shower Attire: A Brief Study of Grinnell Dorm Life," Math 115 course paper, December, 1986, Grinnell College, Department of Mathematics.

7. Fleischman, Jennifer, Nancy Karella, and Sobhana Retnasami, "A Study of Morning Food and Beverage Consumption Habits of Smith College Students," MTH 107 course paper, May, 1990, Smith College, Department of Mathematics.

8. Garfield, Joan B., "Helping Students Learn," Appendix A in George Cobb's "Teaching Statistics," article in *Heeding the Call for Change: Suggestions for Curricular Action,* MAA Notes No. 22, edited by L. Steen, 1992, Mathematical Association of America, 24–25.

9. Gratch, Adam and Laure Muir, "The Lost-Letter Technique: Political Alignment and Civic Duty," Math 115 course paper, May, 1999, Grinnell College, Department of Mathematics.

10. Haney, Lisa, Juliana Hsu, and Janice Lee. "Does the UMASS Bus Leave On Time?", MTH 245, Introduction to Probability and Statistics, class project, December, 1994.

11. *The Harvard Assessment Report on College Teaching*, edited by Richard Light, 1990, Harvard Graduate School of Education.

12. Milgram, S., "The Lost Letter Technique," *Public Opinion Quarterly,* **29** (1965), 437–438.

13. Monaco, David G., and James C. Lin, "A General Studies on the Game Show 'The Price is Right'," Math 336 course paper, May, 1991, Grinnell College, Department of Mathematics.

14. Moore, Thomas L. and Rosemary A. Roberts, "Statistics at Liberal Arts Colleges," *The American Statistician,* **43**(2), 1989, 80–85.

15. Shierholz, Heidi, "Statlinguistic Analysis of Adjective and Adverbs," *STATS,* Number 16, Winter 1996, 25–27.

16. Singer, Judith D., and John B. Willett, "Improving the Teaching of Applied Statistics: Putting the Data Back into Data Analysis," *The American Statistician,* **43** (1990), 223–230.

17. Maria Termini, "What Factors Influence Whether a Smith College Student Takes a Math Course When She is Not Required To?," MTH 247, Regression Analysis, Class Project, May, 1997.

18. Zahn, Douglas, "Student Projects in a Large Lecture Introductory Business Course," *Proceedings of the Section on Statistical Education of the American Statistical Association,* 1992, 147–154.

Bibliography on Student Projects

Burrill, G., J. C. Burrill, P. Coffield, G. Davis, J. de Lange, D. Resnick, and M. Siegel, *Data Analysis and Statistics Across the Curriculum*, 1992, The National Council of Teachers of Mathematics, Reston, VA.

Includes a 10 page chapter on student projects and a list of 35 samples.

Fillebrown, Sandra, "Using Projects in an Elementary Statistics Course for Non-Science Majors," *Journal of Statistics Education*, http://www.amstat.org/publications/jse/v2n2/fillebrown.html (on-line), 2(2), 1994.

The author describes using projects in an introductory course for non-science students. She gives practical advice on managing the projects and also includes sample student project summaries.

Hunter, William G., "Some Ideas About Teaching Design of Experiments with 2^5 Examples of Experiments Conducted by Students," *The American Statistician*, **31** (1977), 12–17.

This may be the seminal paper on the use of student projects for teaching statistics and it is still a fun read.

Ledolter, Johannes, "Projects in Introductory Statistics Courses," *The American Statistician*, **49** (1995), 364–367.

Ledolter describes using student projects in a large introductory course for business students.

Macisack, Margaret, "What is the Use of Experiments Conducted by Statistics Students?" *Journal of Statistics Education*, http://www.amstat.org/publications/jse/v2n1/mackisack.html, 2(1), 1994.

Here the course is one for science and mathematics students. Projects are experiments. The author beautifully examines the educational motivations for assigning projects. Even if you aren't teaching lots of experimental design, this paper is a "must read" if you are considering student projects in your teaching.

Moore, Thomas L., "Using Student Projects in an Introductory Course for Liberal Arts Students," *Communications in Statistics*, **25** (1996), 2647–2661.

While the advice in this paper is ostensibly for the liberal arts setting, the paper gives both rationale and practical advice that should be useful to any projects setting.

Roberts, Harry V., "Student-Conducted Projects in the Introductory Statistics Course," in *Statistics for the Twenty-First Century*, MAA Notes No. 26, edited by Florence Gordon and Sheldon Gordon, 1992, The Mathematical Association of America, 109–121.

To the query, "How can inexperienced teachers get started on projects," Roberts answers, "Just jump in and do them, and learn as you go." Fortunately this article gives you some solid advice backed by Roberts's many years teaching introductory statistics, primarily to MBA students. Roberts figures course grades solely on student projects.

Sevin, Anne, "Some Tips for Helping Students in Introductory Statistics Classes Carry Out Successful Data Analysis Projects," *Proceedings of the Section on Statistical Education of the American Statistical Association*, 1995, 159–164.

Sevin give's some excellent advice for managing student projects, including the use of interim reports, frequent feedback, and peer review. She also gives samples of actual assignments.

Short, Thomas H. and Joseph G. Pigeon, "Protocols and Pilot Studies: Taking Data Collection Projects Seriously," *Journal of Statistics Education*, `http://www.amstat.org/publications/jse/v6n1/short.html`, **6**(1), 1998.

Short and Pigeon describe ways to engage students in the often-overlooked planning stages of a study. They describe both short assignments and student projects more in the mold of other works in this bibliography.

Zahn, Douglas, "Student Projects in a Large Lecture Introductory Business Course," *Proceedings of the Section on Statistical Education of the American Statistical Association*, 1992, 147–154.

If you write to Zahn, he will send you (for copying costs) an annotated bibliography of resources and his extensive instructions, including a 33 page set of instructions for term projects. Dept. of Statistics, Florida State University, Tallahassee, FL 32306-3033.

Curriculum in Context: Teaching with Case Studies in Statistics Courses†

Norean Radke Sharpe
Babson College

Introduction

The Harvard Business School has used case studies as its primary teaching tool ever since their first appearance in 1920 [4], and now produces between 600–700 cases (including field-based cases and "case-related" teaching materials) each year [23]. In the past decade, the success of using cases to teach has transcended the traditional business disciplines and case studies are now used to teach courses in statistics at a variety of levels. This increased interest in non-business oriented cases has generated several new casebooks that provide teaching alternatives, with a wide array of application areas at multiple levels of difficulty.

Although most business disciplines have been actively using and producing case studies as part of their standard curriculum, cases have not been considered an integral part of the undergraduate statistics curriculum. Thus, I began experimenting with the case method a few years ago in an effort to find pedagogical tools that could be used to discuss statistical concepts in a real context. After using cases now at all levels—introductory, intermediate, and advanced—in our undergraduate applied statistics sequence, we are now writing cases for our integrated curriculum (with finance and marketing). Cases motivate students to learn about the subject of statistics, challenge students to think critically and creatively about open-ended problems, and help students to visualize and apply statistical concepts in other disciplines. In this paper, I reinforce how the case study approach complements suggested reforms in statistics education, such as using real data, motivating active learning, and improving written work. I also share insights into teaching with cases and provide an annotated bibliography of current casebooks in statistics.

Why Use Case Studies?

Cases Use Real Data in Context. Statisticians widely believe that statistics should be taught using real data (see, for example, Bradstreet [2]; Cobb [8]; Lock [12]; Moore [13]; and Singer and Willett [22]). In a benchmark summary of statistics education reform, Cobb recommends using "More Data and Concepts: Less Theory, Fewer Recipes" [8, p. 7]. Cobb bases these recommendations on the belief that working with real data helps students learn statistical concepts and that students learn by constructing, doing, and reapplying [8]. From these assumptions about learning, we conclude that students need to spend time constructing databases and applying statistical methods in real situations. The appropriate application of statistical procedures depends on the data, the context in which the data were collected, and the context in which

† This article is based on a working paper prepared and submitted for publication in September, 1997.

the data are to be interpreted. Thus, to fully appreciate both the power and limitations of data, data analyses need to be conducted in context.

Cases require analysis and interpretation of data in context. Cases provide a description of a problem in industry that requires data analysis. The focus is on decision making, and the application area of the problems is varied; the industries represented include financial, medical, pharmaceutical, manufacturing, and transportation. A description of the primary data source, data collection process (e.g., surveys, site visits, etc.), and variable definitions is included in the case along with the data. Cases vary in levels of complexity and stages of completion: (1) the "fully-analyzed" cases describe the appropriate paradigm for descriptive and inferential analysis in detail; (2) the "proscriptive" cases provide specific questions to guide the student through the analysis; and (3) the "open-ended" cases require the student to select a set of statistical procedures appropriate for analyzing the data and making a decision. All of these cases encourage an appreciation for the context (time frame, limitations, assumptions, etc.) of the data and teach the implications of choosing suitable tools in different decision making contexts.

Cases Motivate Student Involvement. Students learn better if they are actively involved in the learning process [17]. If students are actively working with information, rather than passively receiving it, they have a better chance of understanding it. Cobb recommends that we "Foster Active Learning" [8, p. 10]. More specifically, Garfield [9] suggests that students should involve themselves in the learning process, practice doing, receive feedback, and "confront their own misconceptions" [9, p. 24]. Students need the opportunity to read about concepts, experiment with their interpretation of these concepts, raise questions about these interpretations, and participate in constructive interactive exchanges about their questions. Moore [15] describes a model that strives to achieve the goals of statistics education reform as a model in which students learn through activities, and teachers guide—as opposed to provide—student learning.

Cases motivate student preparation and active student involvement in data analysis and interpretation. To accomplish the goal of actively involving students in the analysis process, we use all three types of cases—fully-analyzed, proscriptive, and open-ended—in a sequence of increasing difficulty. First, students read and discuss good examples of data analysis required for consulting: method selection, output interpretation, and a decision-oriented recommendation. Second, students complete unfinished cases, optimally

as part of an interactive laboratory component, and accompany their results with a written report. Third, students answer an open-ended question for a "client," given only the objective, the data, and background information on the data. To effectively complete this series of cases, students need to be active analysts—determining, conducting, and interpreting the analysis in the context of the data.

Cases Encourage Oral and Written Communication. As the writing-across-the-curriculum movement was gaining momentum in the early nineties, statistics educators recognized the importance of strong oral and written communication skills for their students (see, for example, Cobb [8]; Iversen [10]; Radke-Sharpe [21]). A pedagogical approach that emphasizes these communication skills with statistical concepts is essential; a statistician must be prepared to convey statistical results and conclusions to clients in industry—including both practitioners and non-practitioners of statistics. In recent talks on this subject, Moore [14, 15] has emphasized the importance of communication and cooperation in relationship to introducing students to statistics in practice. If we assume that students are going to use statistics in an applied context, then the importance of communication is clear. Students need experience with communicating their own questions to instructors and other students, communicating their interpretations as a team member to other members of the team, and communicating their conclusions to an audience outside the statistical community. In a recent discourse on the impact of technology on statistics education, the themes of human interaction, facilitation, and feedback were defended as important aspects of the educational process [16].

Cases enrich the educational process by providing templates of good writing in the discipline and by providing opportunities for oral discourse on statistical issues. The fully-analyzed cases provide templates of writing about statistics. More specifically, these templates demonstrate appropriate use of tables and figures, mathematical expressions, and prose. They also provide examples of how to structure a report based on statistical analysis. When students are required to produce reports for the open-ended cases, their own documents improve over time after repeated revisions and exposure to other exemplary reports (obtained from both the casebook and other students). In addition to increasing emphasis on written work, cases stimulate class discussion. Because cases present the data in the context of a real issue in industry, most students find them intrinsically interesting, and sometimes even controversial. This increased level of interest among the students seems to generate enthusiasm for the class discussions, as well as for the statistical concepts themselves.

One Approach to
Teaching Statistics with Cases

Just as with other teaching materials, different pedagogical approaches are possible with case studies, and several casebooks are now available (see Appendix). We chose to use a casebook [6] in conjunction with a standard business statistics textbook [1]. I required my students to purchase both books and have not received negative feedback regarding the cost. In fact, students have used their textbook as a "reference" book and their casebook as the primary reading material for the course (their casebooks were visibly used—marked up and worn). More recently, in an effort to provide students with a shorter and less expensive casebook, I have had success in working with a publisher to combine a few of my own cases with previously-published cases to create a customized casebook (see [7]). Both our introductory and intermediate courses are required of all undergraduates and thus are offered multiple times every semester. The first course is an intensive one-semester survey of descriptive and inferential statistics that concludes with simple regression. The second course is a continuation of these topics and includes multiple regression, time series, forecasting, quality control, simulation, and decision analysis. Our students typically have a wide range of academic ability, from second-year students who failed previous semesters of statistics to first-year students who placed out of calculus by taking the AP exam. Here, I attempt to summarize a few insights into teaching with cases. Since the case method has been growing in popularity, there are many academics with experience in this approach, who are able to provide guidance. New case instructors might consider attending workshops and reading the case literature (see, for example, Parr and Smith [18], who provide a detailed template for developing a case-based course). In addition, the more recent casebooks (see Appendix) include excellent teaching notes.

Assign cases in advance for preparation for class discussion. Requiring advance preparation raises expectation and performance. We expect students to read, understand, interpret, and explain the concepts they encounter in the cases. For fully-analyzed cases, we expect students to explain why a specific statistical technique was chosen, to interpret the results, and to agree or disagree with the conclusions of the author. By initially using cases that are fully analyzed, we provide students with a written model of the relationship between the data, the analysis, and the conclusions. We encourage them to explore their understanding of concepts, raise questions about these interpretations, and comment on other students' interpretations. The ex-

pectation of prior preparation by students increases their self-reliance and self-discipline, enhances teamwork skills among the students, and encourages students to become more responsible for their own learning. The focus of the responsibility for the learning experience is removed from the instructor and returned to the student. Moore [15, p. 254] suggested this idea recently when he said:

> The teacher's task is to encourage and guide construction of correct mathematical understanding. Telling does not do this. Students must be active participants in learning.... Within this environment, the teacher serves more as a consultant and moderator than as a presenter.

Case studies motivate, encourage, and demand that students be active participants in the learning process—both in small study groups prior to class and in the class itself during discussions.

Ask students to introduce cases, ask and answer questions about cases, and respond to other students' questions. Case discussions emphasize oral communication of statistical questions, ideas, and interpretations. This approach also encourages interaction between the instructor and other students. To create an encouraging environment for class discussion, we try to consistently provide every student an opportunity to comment on the case over the period of two case discussions. Probably more important from the student perspective, we have instituted a reward structure for class participation on case discussion days. The dynamic of an active class discussion, as opposed to a discourse on the topic by the instructor, motivates the students to learn more about the application of statistics to other functional areas. The encouragement to participate also seems to raise questions that are less frequently asked, internally confusing, and more interesting. Frequent oral discussions in which the students are expected to participate enhance the interest level, intellect, and insightfulness of the students in the class.

Ask students to produce statistical output on line in class, bring prepared output to class, or complete cases as laboratory projects. As the students become comfortable with the case method, we expect them to prepare open-ended cases, as if they were a consultant in industry. Students access databases on their own outside of class and either bring their output to class, or are prepared to create it using the technology in the classroom. We also use cases as laboratory assignments followed by required written lab reports. A popular final project is one in which teams of students obtain and analyze a unique dataset and write their own case study. We have even revised and rewritten some of these projects for use as later case studies. As with most teaching materials, instructors should customize the use of cases to their own course topics, classroom dynamics, class size, student academic abilities, and student communication skills. When students choose their own datasets, conduct their own analyses, and write their own case studies, they learn more about the practice of statistics, gain experience working in a team, and feel a greater sense of accomplishment.

Student Feedback

At the end of prior semesters, I have distributed a case evaluation survey and asked for student opinion on: (1) the effectiveness of the cases in helping to explain statistical concepts and techniques, (2) the strength of student recommendations to continue using cases in the course, and (3) the usefulness of the fully-analyzed cases. The results were extremely positive: approximately 80% of students responded that the cases were effective at explaining concepts and "techniques covered in class." More impressively, approximately 90% responded that they would "recommend . . . the use . . . [of] cases again in this statistics course." When asked if they would recommend "the use of *more* cases in the statistics course," student responses were mixed. My interpretation of these mixed responses is that our introductory statistics course is densely packed with material—if more cases are added, then something else must be subtracted. (Many institutions may have similarly packed courses and share the dilemma of how to experiment with pedagogical innovations, while still covering the required set of topics—breadth vs. depth.) Finally, on the question about the usefulness of fully-analyzed cases, approximately 90% found the cases to be "helpful."

From the questions on the survey that required a written response, I have concluded that the most effective and most popular cases were those on regression. I should also note that some students wrote that they would *not* have understood a particular statistical concept (e.g., The Central Limit Theorem) without the associated discussion motivated by the case. Over the past few years, several comments on cases have appeared on my standard college student opinion surveys. No negative remarks about cases have appeared on any of my opinion surveys and only one individual asked for fewer cases, because of the "fast-pace" of the course. Below is a sample of these unsolicited comments:

"The cases were good at explaining the information in the class."

"[Use] more cases studies—that's how . . . everyone learned the material."

"[Use] more cases with detailed, maybe two-day discussions, and with homework questions."

"Cases were excellent in helping me understand the course. Maybe the whole class can turn into a case-based class."

"The use of cases was very helpful, especially since it showed how the statistical material was applied in real situations. I think cases should be used more frequently."

"The cases helped a lot and gave an interesting twist to the course."

"Very relevant to the real world—I liked the cases and the review of the cases was very helpful in understanding the material."

Conclusion

In summary, cases facilitate recent reforms in statistics education such as using real data, motivating student involvement, and providing examples and opportunities for written work. In addition, cases encourage class discussions and motivate the use of databases for a laboratory component of the course. Finally, student feedback suggests that cases help students learn statistical concepts and techniques. As a result of the training cases provide in decision making, students, faculty, practitioners, and employers in industry should all benefit.

Acknowledgment.   The author would like to acknowledge George Cobb for his thoughtful and insightful comments on an earlier version of this manuscript.

References

1. Berenson, M.L., and D.M. Levine, *Basic Business Statistics,* 6th edition, 1996, Prentice Hall, Englewood Cliffs, NJ.
2. Bradstreet, T.E., "Teaching introductory statistics courses so that nonstatisticians experience statistical reasoning," *The American Statistician*, **50** (1), 1996.
3. Bryant, P.G., and M.A. Smith, *Practical Data Analysis: Case Studies in Business Statistics*, Volumes I and II, 1995, Irwin, Inc., Chicago, IL.
4. Budman, M., "The Business of Cases," *Across The Board*, **32** (2), 1995.
5. Carlson, W.L., *Cases in Managerial Data Analysis*, 1997, Duxbury Press, Belmont, CA.

6. Chatterjee, S., M.S. Handcock, and J.S. Simonoff, *A Casebook for a First Course in Statistics and Data Analysis*, 1995, John Wiley and Sons, NY.

7. Chatterjee, S., M.S. Handcock, and J.S. Simonoff, (selected cases) with additional cases by N. Radke Sharpe, *Casebook for Statistics and Data Analysis*, 1997, John Wiley and Sons, NY.

8. Cobb, G., "Teaching Statistics," in L.A. Steen (ed.), *Heeding the Call for Change*, MAA Notes **22**, 1992, Mathematical Association of America, Washington, DC.

9. Garfield, J., "Helping Students Learn" in "Teaching Statistics," in L.A. Steen (ed.), *Heeding the Call for Change*, MAA Notes **22**, 1992, Mathematical Association of America, Washington, DC.

10. Iversen, G., "Writing Papers in a Statistics Course," *Proceedings of the Section on Statistical Education*, American Statistical Association, 1991.

11. Klimberg, R., P. Arnold, and P. Berger, *Cases in Business Statistics*, 1994, Allyn and Bacon, Boston, MA.

12. Lock, R.H., "Alternative Introductions to Applied Statistics for Mathematics Students," *SLAW Technical Report 90-008*, 1990, Pomona College, Pomona, CA.

13. Moore, D.S., "Teaching Statistics as a Respectable Subject," *SLAW Technical Report 91-002*, 1991, Pomona College, Pomona, CA.

14. Moore, D.S., "Current Trends in Statistics Education" (Invited Talk) at Conference for Isolated Statisticians, 1995, Chaska, MN.

15. Moore, D.S., "Teaching Statistics" (Keynote Presentation) at Trends in Introductory Applied Statistics Courses: Topics, Techniques, Technology, 1996, Framingham State, Framingham, MA.

16. Moore, D.S., G. Cobb, J. Garfield, and W.Q. Meeker, "Statistics Education Fin de Siecle," *The American Statistician*, **49** (3), 1995.

17. National Research Council, *Everybody Counts: A Report to the Nation on the Future of Mathematics Education*, 1989, National Academy Press, Washington, DC.

18. Parr, W.C. and M.A. Smith, "Developing Case-Based Business Statistics Courses," *The American Statistician*, **52** (4), 1998.

19. Peck, R., L.D. Haugh, and A. Goodman, *Statistical Case Studies*, 1998, ASA and SIAM, Alexandria, VA and Philadelphia, PA.

20. Peters, H., and J.B. Gray, *Business Cases in Statistical Decision Making*, 1994, Prentice Hall, Englewood Cliffs, NJ.

21. Radke Sharpe, N., "Writing Papers in a Statistics Course," *The American Statistician*, **45** (4), 1991.

22. Singer, J.D., and J.B. Willett, "Improving the Teaching of Applied Statistics: Putting the Data Back into Data Analysis," *The American Statistician*, **44** (3), 1990.

23. Stern, A.L., "A Study in Diplomacy," *Across the Board*, **32** (2), 1995.

Appendix
Annotated Bibliography of
Case Study Books[†]

Bryant, P.G. and M.A. Smith, *Practical Data Analysis: Case Studies in Business Statistics*, Volumes I and II, 1995, Irwin, Inc, Chicago, IL.

Each volume of this book contains 25 cases covering a range of statistical topics (e.g., descriptive statistics, regression, confidence intervals, and nonparametric methods) as they apply to a variety of business applications (e.g., management, accounting, marketing, and finance). The instructor's edition includes both volumes I and II, and a data disk containing the data for the cases. A "custom" version of this book is available, as long as the instructor selects at least 10 cases. An advantage of this casebook is that each case is classified by level (beginning, intermediate, or advanced) and statistical technique in a matrix in the front of the book. A few discussion/assignment questions are also suggested for each case. The disadvantages of this book are the focus on business applications and the fact that the analysis presented for each case is brief.

Carlson, W.L., *Cases in Managerial Data Analysis*, 1997, Duxbury Press, Belmont, CA.

This book is one of the more recent casebooks aimed towards teachers of statistics and contains 28 cases in a variety of functional areas, including accounting, economics, finance, management, and marketing. The cases are brief (3–4 pages) and are followed by a set of questions to guide the students through the case analysis. The brevity of the cases can be an asset for a densely packed statistics course and, while the questions are specific, they are probably helpful (perhaps even necessary) for undergraduates. Each

---

[†] This appendix was written in 1997 as part of a working paper and has since been updated to reflect the books published since 1997 (i.e., Carlson (1997) and Peck, Haugh, and Goodman (1998)).

case asks the students to prepare a written report summarizing their analysis and recommendations. The most useful aspect of this casebook is the first chapter, which outlines the motivation and process for analyzing cases—a great summary for faculty and students alike. An apparent omission from this book is an index of statistical topics covered by each case to facilitate its use by instructors in conjunction with a textbook. The accompanying solutions manual contains Minitab output, as well as suggestions for the contents of the written report.

Chatterjee, S., M.S. Handcock, and J.S. Simonoff, *A Casebook for a First Course in Statistics and Data Analysis*, 1995, John Wiley and Sons, NY.

This book offers cases with datasets from a variety of areas (e.g., medicine, finance, sports, and general interest) for statistical concepts ranging from exploratory data analysis to multiple regression. The instructor has the flexibility to choose the datasets which interest the students and to choose the difficulty level of the cases; each case is classified by stage of completion—from cases that are fully analyzed, to open-ended cases that leave all the analysis to the student. Keywords at the beginning of each case identify what techniques are covered and an index helps to identify the topics and techniques used in each case. An annotated edition of this book, which contains comments on the incomplete cases, is available for the instructor. A data disk is included with the book. The advantages to this book are: (1) the organization of the cases and (2) the wide range of subject matter of the datasets. The main disadvantage of this casebook is its cost and length; in its current form, it contains many more cases (61) than an instructor would most likely use in one semester.

Klimberg, R., P. Arnold, and P. Berger, *Cases in Business Statistics*, 1994, Allyn and Bacon, Boston, MA.

This book contains 22 cases that predominantly revolve around business issues and involve an aspect of financial analysis. The style in which these cases are written is most similar to the style of traditional business cases (i.e., vignettes involving role playing) and business terminology is predominant throughout the cases. A data disk containing the datasets discussed in this book is available. However, most of the datasets are also presented as tables in the book and are small enough for the students to manually enter into their software package. An instructor's manual is available,

which presents analyses (in Minitab) and brief comments on teaching strategies. The advantage of this casebook is the suggested teaching strategies. The main disadvantages of this casebook are the lack of variety in the cases and the lack of indexing by statistical topic and technique.

Peck, R., L.D. Haugh, and A. Goodman, *Statistical Case Studies*, 1998, ASA, Alexandria, VA, and SIAM, Philadelphia, PA.

This is the most recently published casebook in this sample. Each case is the result of a collaboration between statisticians in industry and academe, which was funded by the National Science Foundation's Division of Undergraduate Education through an Undergraduate Faculty Enhancement grant. The grant supported a workshop for the participants during the summer of 1995 and subsequent site visits. The focus of these cases is on the selection and use of statistical methods to solve real problems encountered in industry. Useful cross-referenced tables are provided that categorize each case by statistical method, functional area, and level of appropriate course; most of the cases are recommended for an intermediate (second course) in statistics. The functional areas include biological/environmental, medical/pharmaceutical, marketing/surveys, and manufacturing. Brief notes for the instructor are provided at the end of each case. These cases may be used as a text in a statistical consulting course, or as a supplement in a second statistics course.

Peters, L.H. and J.B. Gray, *Business Cases in Statistical Decision Making*, 1994, Prentice Hall, Englewood Cliffs, NJ.

This book contains 18 cases which represent "several functional business areas—management, marketing, advertising,...[and] operations management." The data for the cases are contained on a data disk and have been tested by the authors with a few different statistical packages. An instructor's guide is available containing Minitab output for the cases. One notable advantage of this casebook is that each case is followed by a series of specific student questions, which can be used to focus student preparations, discussions, and assignments. In addition, the cases are caterogized by statistical topic in the Instructor's Guide. A possible limitation for "nonbusiness" academic environments may be the exclusive business focus of the datasets.

Section 3
Established Projects in Active Learning

A constant theme of the reform in teaching statistics has been the notion that students learn best through activities, many of which can and should replace some of the lectures we typically do in class. A number of books have been developed, and commercially published, that are based on this notion. We describe three of them that have proven particularly noteworthy and useful.

Allan Rossman's *Workshop Statistics* puts together in textbook form the ingredients for a course he has been teaching at Dickinson College for many years. The idea behind the course, as stated in the book's preface, is that students learn best by "doing statistics." So while the broad table of contents for *Workshop Statistics* might suggest a rather traditional and ordinary course in statistics—EDA (one and two variables), Randomness (e.g., random samples, sampling distributions, and the Central Limit Theorem), and various standard topics in Inference—the spirit of the course becomes evident as soon as one plunges into the details behind the chapter headings. The course is actually taught through an organized sequence of activities that students perform in class to generate and analyze data and learn statistical principles. Michael Seyfried, of Shippensburg University of Pennsylvania, describes in his companion piece how *Workshop Statistics* has become the sole textbook for his introductory statistics course.

Activity-Based Statistics, by Scheaffer, Gnanadesikan, Watkins, and Witmer, is less an entire course than a collection of activities that instructors can use to enhance their courses. One could build an entire course around these activities or select just a few. The activities in *Activity-Based Statistics* support the notion that data are at the heart of all statistical endeavors. In *ABS* you can find interesting activities to help teach concepts from essentially any part of the introductory statistics course. Many of the activities take substantially less than a full class period, so can be used to change the pace of class, foster a discussion on important concepts, or reinforce a lecture or text reading. Bruce King describes how he has incorporated many of the *Activity-Based Statistics* activities into his introductory courses.

Finally, the section closes with a description of the *Elementary Statistics Laboratory Manual,* by Spurrier, Edwards, and Thombs. This book describes a collection of "labs" involving statistics. The goal of the *Manual* is "... to give students examples and experiences that they will remember long after the course is over." The "labs" typically involve both data collection and data analysis and are more involved than the typical activity in the previous two collections. Sneh Gulati of Florida International describes how she uses the *Manual* as a lab component to a traditional introductory course.

Excerpts from *Workshop Statistics: Discovery with Data*[†]

Preface

> Shorn of all subtlety and led naked out of the protective fold of educational research literature, there comes a sheepish little fact: lectures don't work nearly as well as many of us would like to think.
>
> —George Cobb (1992)

This book contains activities that guide students to discover statistical concepts, explore statistical principles, and apply statistical techniques. Students work toward these goals through the analysis of genuine data and through interaction with one another, with their instructor, and with technology. Providing a one-semester introduction to fundamental ideas of statistics for college and advanced high school students, *Workshop Statistics* is designed for courses that employ an interactive learning environment by replacing lectures with hands-on activities. The text contains enough expository material to stand alone, but it can also be used to supplement a more traditional textbook.

Some distinguishing features of *Workshop Statistics* are its emphases on active learning, conceptual understanding, genuine data, and the use of technology. The following sections of this preface elaborate on each of these aspects and also describe the unusual organizational structure of this text.

Active Learning

> Statistics teaching can be more effective if teachers determine what it is they really want students to know and to do as a result of their course, and then provide activities designed to develop the performance they desire.   — Joan Garfield (1995)

This text is written for use with the workshop pedagogical approach, which fosters active learning by minimizing lectures and eliminating the conventional distinction between laboratory and lecture sessions. The book's activities require students to collect data, make predictions, read about studies, analyze data, discuss findings,

---

and write explanations. The instructor's responsibilities in this setting are to check students' progress, ask and answer questions, lead class discussions, and deliver "mini-lectures" where appropriate. The essential point is that every student is actively engaged learning the material through reading, thinking, discussing, computing, interpreting, writing, and reflecting. In this manner students construct their own knowledge of statistical ideas as they work through the activities.

The activities also lend themselves to collaborative learning. Students can work together through the book's activities, helping each other to think through the material. Some activities specifically call for collaborative effort through the pooling of class data.

The text also stresses the importance of students' communication skills. As students work through the activities, they constantly read, write, and talk with one another. Students should be encouraged to write their explanations and conclusions in full, grammatically correct sentences, as if to an educated layperson.

Conceptual Understanding

Almost any statistics course can be improved by more emphasis on data and on concepts at the expense of less theory and fewer recipes.   —David Moore (1992)

This text focuses on the "big ideas" of statistics, paying less attention to details that often divert students' attention from larger issues. Little emphasis is placed on numerical and symbolic manipulations. Rather, the activities lead students to explore the meaning of concepts such as variability, distribution, outlier, tendency, association, randomness, sampling, sampling distribution, confidence, significance, and experimental design. Students investigate these concepts by experimenting with data, often with the help of technology. Many of the activities challenge students to demonstrate their understanding of statistical issues by asking for explanations and interpretations rather than mere calculations.

To deepen students' understandings of fundamental ideas, the text presents these ideas repetitively. For example, students return to techniques of exploratory data analysis when studying properties of randomness and also in conjunction with inference procedures. They also encounter issues of data collection not just when studying randomness but also when investigating statistical inference.

Genuine Data

We believe that data should be at the heart of all statistics education and that students should be introduced to statistics through data-entered courses.
                                          —Thomas Moore and Rosemary Roberts (1989)

The workshop approach is ideally suited to the study of statistics, the science of reasoning from data, for it forces students to be actively engaged with genuine data. Analyzing genuine data not only exposes students to the practice of statistics; it also prompts them to consider the wide applicability of statistical methods and often enhances their enjoyment of the material.

Some activities ask students to analyze data about themselves that they collect in class, while most present students with genuine data from a variety of sources. Many questions in the text ask students to make predictions about data before conducting their analyses. This practice motivates students to view data not as naked numbers but as numbers with a context, to identify personally with the data, and to take an interest in the results of their analyses.

The data sets in *Workshop Statistics* do not concentrate on one academic area but come from a variety of fields of application. These fields include law, medicine, economics, psychology, political science, and education. Many examples come not from academic disciplines but from popular culture. Specific examples therefore range from such pressing issues as testing the drug AZT and assessing evidence in sexual discrimination cases to less crucial ones of predicting basketball salaries and ranking *Star Trek* episodes.

Use of Technology

Automate calculation and graphics as much as possible   —David Moore (1992)

This text assumes that students have access to technology for creating visual displays, performing calculations, and conducting simulations. The preferable technology is a statistical software package, although a graphing calculator can do almost as well. Roughly half of the activities ask students to use technology. Students typically perform small-scale displays, calculations, and simulations by hand before letting the computer or calculator take over those mechanical chores.

This workshop approach employs technology in three distinct ways. First, technology performs the calculations and presents the visual displays necessary to analyze genuine data sets which are often large and cumbersome. Next, technology conducts simulations which allow students to visualize and explore the long-term behavior of sample statistics under repeated random sampling.

The most distinctive use of technology with the workshop approach is to enable students to explore statistical phenomena. Students make predictions about a particular statistical property and then use the computer to investigate their predictions, revising their predictions and iterating the process as necessary. For example, students use technology to investigate the effects of outliers on various summary statistics and the effects of sample sizes on confidence intervals.

Activities requiring the use of technology are integrated throughout the text, reinforcing the idea that technology is not to be studied for its own sake but as an indispensable tool for analyzing genuine data and a convenient device for exploring statistical phenomena.

Specific needs of the technology are to create visual displays (dotplots, histograms, boxplots, scatterplots), calculate summary statistics (mean, median, quartiles, standard deviation, correlation), conduct simulations (with binary variables), and perform inference procedures (z-tests and z-intervals for binary variables, t-tests and t-intervals for measurement variables).

Organization

Judge a statistics book by its exercises, and you cannot go far wrong.   —George Cobb (1987)

For the most part this text covers traditional subject matter for a first course in statistics. The first two units concern descriptive and exploratory data analysis, the third introduces randomness and probability, and the final three delve into statistical inference. The six units of course material are divided into smaller topics, each topic following the same structure:
- *Overview*: a brief introduction to the topic, particularly emphasizing its connection to earlier topics;
- *Objectives*: a listing of specific goals for students to achieve in the topic;
- *Preliminaries*: a series of questions designed to get students thinking about issues and applications to be studied in the topic and often to collect data on themselves;
- *In-class Activities*: the activities that guide students to learn the material for the topic;
- *Homework Activities*: the activities that test students' understanding of the material and ability to apply what they have learned in the topic;
- *Wrap-up*: a brief review of the major ideas of the topic emphasizing its connection to future topics.

In keeping with the spirit of the workshop approach, hands-on activities dominate the book. Preliminary questions and in-class activities leave enough space for students to record answers in the text itself. While comments and explanations are interspersed among the activities, these passages of exposition are purposefully less thorough than in traditional textbooks. The text contains very few solved examples, further emphasizing the idea that students construct their own knowledge of statistical ideas as they work through the activities.

While the organization of content is fairly standard, unusual features include the following:
- Probability is not treated formally but is introduced through simulations. The simulations give students an intuitive sense of random variation and the idea that probability represents the proportion of times that

something would happen in the long run. Because students often have trouble connecting the computer simulation with the underlying process that it models, the text first asks students to perform physical simulations involving dice and candies to help them understand the process being modeled.

- The Central Limit Theorem and the reasoning of statistical inference are introduced in the context of a population *proportion* rather than a population *mean*. A population proportion summarizes all of the relevant information about the population of a binary variable, allowing students to concentrate more easily on the concepts of sampling distribution, confidence, and significance. These ideas are introduced through physical and computer simulations which are easier to conduct with binary variables than with measurement variables. Dealing with binary variables also eliminates the need to consider issues such as the underlying shape of the population distribution and the choice of an appropriate parameter.

- Exploratory data analysis and data production issues are emphasized throughout, even in the units covering statistical inference. Most activities that call for the application of inference procedures first ask students to conduct an exploratory analysis of the data; these analyses often reveal much that the inference procedures do not. These activities also guide students to question the design of the study before drawing conclusions from the inference results. Examples used early in the text to illustrate Simpson's paradox and biased sampling reappear in the context of inference, reminding students to be cautious when drawing conclusions.

Acknowledgments

I am privileged to teach at Dickinson College, where I enjoy an ideal atmosphere for experimenting with innovative pedagogical strategies and curriculum development. I thank my many colleagues and students who have helped me in writing this book.

Nancy Baxter Hastings has directed the Workshop Mathematics Program—of which *Workshop Statistics* forms a part—with assistance from Ruth Rossow, Joanne Weissman, and Sherrill Goodlive. Barry Tesman, Jack Stodghill, Peter Martin, and Jackie Ford have taught with the book and provided valuable feedback, as have Barr von Oehsen of Piedmont College and Kevin Callahan of California State University at Hayward. Students who have contributed in many ways include Dale Usner, Kathy Reynolds, Christa Fratto, Matthew Parks, and Jennifer Becker. I also thank Dean George Allan for his leadership in establishing the productive teaching/learning environment that I enjoy at Dickinson.

I appreciate the support given to the Workshop Mathematics Program by the Fund for the Improvement of Post-Secondary Education, the U.S. Department of Education, and the National Science Foundation, as well as by Dickinson College. I also thank Springer-Verlag for their support, particularly Jerry Lyons, Liesl Gibson, and Steven Pisano. I thank Sara Buchan for help with proofreading.

Much of what I have learned about statistics education has been shaped by the writings from which I quote above. I especially thank Joan Garfield, George Cobb, Tom Short, and Joel Greenhouse for many enlightening conversations.

Finally, I thank my wonderful wife Eileen, without whose support and encouragement I would not have completed this work. Thanks also to my feline friends Eponine and Cosette.

— Allan J. Rossman

References

Cobb, George W. (1987), "Introductory Textbooks: A Framework for Evaluation," *Journal of the American Statistical Association*, 82, 321–339.

Cobb, George W. (1992), "Teaching Statistics," in *Heeding the Call for Change: Suggestions for Curricular Action*, ed. Lynn Steen, MAA Notes Number 22, 3–43.

Garfield, Joan (1995), "How Students Learn Statistics," *International Statistical Review*, 63, 25–34.

Moore, David S. (1992), "Teaching Statistics as a Respectable Subject," in *Statistics for the Twenty-First Century*, eds. Florence and Sheldon Gordon, MAA Notes Number 26, 14–25.

Moore, Thomas L., and Rosemary A. Roberts (1989), "Statistics at Liberal Arts Colleges," *The American Statistician*, 43, 80–85.

Contents

Topic 3: MEASURES OF CENTER

Overview

You have been exploring distributions of data, representing them graphically, and describing their key features verbally. For convenience, it is often desirable to have a single numerical measure to summarize a certain aspect of a distribution. In this topic you will encounter some of the more common measures of the center of a distribution, investigate their properties, apply them to some genuine data, and expose some of their limitations.

Objectives

- To learn to calculate certain statistics (*mean, median, mode*) for summarizing the center of a distribution of data.
- To investigate and discover properties of these summary statistics.
- To explore the statistical property of *resistance* as it applies to these statistics.
- To develop an awareness of situations in which certain measures are and are not appropriate.
- To recognize that these numerical measures do not summarize a distribution completely.
- To acquire the ability to expose faulty conclusions based on misunderstanding of these measures.

Preliminaries

1. Take a guess as to how long a typical member of the U.S. Supreme Court has served.
2. Take a guess concerning the distance from the Sun for a typical planet in our solar system.
3. Make guesses about the closest and farthest a student in your class is from "home." Also guess the distance from home of a typical student in the class.
4. Record in the table below the distances from home (estimated in miles) for each student in the class.

Student	Distance	Student	Distance
1		13	
2		14	
3		15	
4		16	
5		17	
6		18	
7		19	
8		20	
9		21	
10		22	
11		23	
12		24	

IN-CLASS ACTIVITIES
Activity 3-1: Supreme Court Service

The table following lists the justices comprising the Supreme Court of the United States as of October 1994. Also listed is the year of appointment and the tenure (years of service) for each.

Supreme Court Justice	Year	Tenure
William Rehnquist	1972	22
John Paul Stevens	1975	19
Sandra Day O'Connor	1981	13
Antonin Scalia	1986	8
Anthony Kennedy	1988	6
David Souter	1990	4
Clarence Thomas	1991	3
Ruth Bader Ginsburg	1993	1
Stephen Breyer	1994	0

(a) Create a dotplot of the distribution of these years of service.

(b) What number might you choose if you were asked to select a single number to represent the center of this distribution? Briefly explain how you arrive at this choice.

We will consider three commonly used measures of the center of a distribution:

- The *mean* is the ordinary arithmetic average, found by summing (adding up) the values of the observations and dividing by the number of observations.
- The *median* is the middle observation (once they are arranged in order); you will construct a formula that will help you to calculate medians.
- The *mode* is the most common value; i.e., the one that occurs most frequently.

(c) Calculate the *mean* of these years of service. Mark this value on the dotplot above with an "x."

(d) How many of the nine people have served more than the mean number of years? How many have served less than the mean number of years?

(e) Calculate the *median* of these years of service. Mark this value on the dotplot above with an "o."

(f) How many of the nine people have served more than the median number of years? How many have served less than the median number of years?

It is easy enough to pick out the median (the middle observation) in a small set of data, but we will try to come up with a general rule for finding the *location* of the median. The first step, of course, is to arrange the observations *in order* from smallest to largest. Let n denote the *sample size*, the number of observations in the data set.

(g) With the data you analyzed above (where $n = 9$), the median turned out to be which ordered observation (the second, the third, the fourth,...)?

(h) Suppose that there had been $n = 5$ observations; the median would have been which (ordered) one? What if there had been $n = 7$ observations? How about if $n = 11$? How about if $n = 9$? What about if $n = 13$?

$n = 5 :$ $n = 11 :$

$n = 7 :$ $n = 13 :$

$n = 9 :$

(i) Try to discover the pattern in the question above to determine a general formula (in terms of the sample size n) for finding the *location* of the median of an odd number of ordered observations.

Activity 3-5: Students' Distances from Home

Consider the data collected above in the "Preliminaries" section of this Topic, concerning students' distances from home.

(a) Enter the data into the computer and have the computer produce a dotplot and a histogram of the distribution.

(b) Would you say that the distribution of distances from home is basically symmetric or skewed in one direction or the other?

(c) Based on the shape of the distribution, do you expect the mean distance from home to be close to the median distance, smaller than the median, or greater than the median?

(d) Have the computer calculate the mean and median distances from home, recording them below. Comment on the accuracy of your expectation in (c).

(e) What is your own distance from home? Is it above or below the mean? How does it compare to the median? About where does your distance from home fall in the distribution?

(f) If you could not look at the dotplot and histogram of these distances but were only told the mean and median distance, would you have a thorough understanding of the distribution of distances from home? Explain.

Activity 5-1: Shifting Populations

The following table lists the percentage change in population between 1990 and 1993 for each of the 50 states.

(a) Indicate in the table whether the state lies mostly to the east (E) or to the west (W) of the Mississippi River.

State	% change	Region	State	% change	Region	State	% change	Region
Alabama	3.6		Louisiana	1.9		North Dakota	−0.6	
Alaska	8.9		Maine	0.9		Ohio	2.3	
Arizona	7.4		Maryland	3.8		Oklahoma	2.7	
Arkansas	3.1		Massachusetts	−0.1		Oregon	6.7	
California	3.7		Michigan	2.0		Pennsylvania	1.4	
Colorado	8.2		Minnesota	3.3		Rhode Island	−0,3	
Connecticut	−0.3		Mississippi	2.7		South Carolina	4.5	
Delaware	5.1		Missouri	2.3		South Dakota	2.8	
Florida	5.7		Montana	5.1		Tennessee	4.5	
Georgia	6.8		Nebraska	1.8		Texas	6.2	
Hawaii	5.7		Nevada	15.6		Utah	7.9	
Idaho	9.2		New Hampshire	1.4		Vermont	2.3	
Illinois	2.3		New Jersey	1.9		Virginia	4.9	
Indiana	3.0		New Mexico	6.7		Washington	8.0	
Iowa	1.3		New York	1.1		West Virginia	1.5	
Kansas	2.1		North Carolina	4.8		Wisconsin	3.0	
Kentucky	2.8					Wyoming	3.7	

In a *side-by-side stem plot,* a common set of stems is used in the middle of the display with leaves for each category branching out in either direction, one to the left and one to the right. The convention is to order the leaves from the middle out toward either side.

(b) Construct a side-by-side stemplot of these population shift percentages according to the state's region; use the stems listed below.

West		East
	−0	
	0	
	1	
	2	
	3	
	4	
	5	
	6	
	7	
	8	
	9	
	10	
	11	
	12	
	13	
	14	
	15	

Remember to arrange the leaves in order from the inside out:

West		East
	−0	
	0	
	1	
	2	
	3	
	4	
	5	
	6	
	7	
	8	
	9	
	10	
	11	
	12	
	13	
	14	
	15	

(c) Calculate the median value of the percentage change in population for each region.

(d) Identify your home state and comment on where it fits into the distribution.

(e) Does one region (east or west) *tend* to have higher percentage changes than the other? Explain.

(f) Is it the case that every state from one region has a higher percentage change than every state from the other? If not, identify a pair such that the eastern state has a higher percentage change than the western state.

(g) If you were to randomly pick one state from each region, which would you expect to have the higher percentage change? Explain.

You have discovered an important (if somewhat obvious) concept in this activity—that of *statistical tendency*. You found that western states *tend* to have higher percentage changes in population than do eastern states. It is certainly not the case, however, that *every* western state has a higher percentage change than every eastern state.

Similarly, men *tend* to be taller than women, but there are certainly some women who are taller than most men. Statistical tendencies pertain to average or typical cases but not necessarily to individual cases. Just as Geena Davis and Danny DeVito do not disprove the assertion that men are taller than women, the cases of California and Georgia do not contradict the finding that western states *tend* to have higher percentage changes in population than eastern states.

Topic 17: CONFIDENCE INTERVALS II

Overview

In the previous topic you began a study of the important and widely used technique of *confidence intervals*. These procedures use a sample statistic to estimate a population parameter with an interval of values and a certain confidence level. This topic asks you to continue this study by considering sample survey results and the connection between confidence intervals and the commonly used expression "*margin of error.*" You will also investigate some of the limitations of confidence intervals, encountering some situations in which one must be wary of applying them thoughtlessly.

Objective

- To understand the use of the term "*margin-of-error*" as it relates to sample surveys.
- To discover how to choose a sample size in order to achieve a confidence interval of a prespecified width at a certain confidence level.
- To appreciate the effect (or lack thereof) of the size of the population on confidence intervals.
- To learn to recognize situations in which confidence intervals cannot be applied meaningfully.
- To recognize the importance of random sampling in the context of confidence intervals.

Preliminaries

1. Tally below the responses of students to the question of whether or not they have their own credit card. Tally separately for men and women.

Men, yes	Men, no	Women, yes	Women, no

2. Count the sample *total* who do and who do not have their own credit card.
3. If a polling organization wants to estimate the proportion of all adult Americans who agree with a certain proposition to within ± 0.04 with 95% confidence, guess how many people they would have to sample.
4. If this same polling agency needed to be more confident that the sample proportion would fall within ± 0.04 of the population proportion, would they need to sample more or fewer people than in question 3?

5. If this same polling agency wants to estimate the population proportion to within ±0.02 with 95% confidence, would they need to sample more or fewer people than in question 3?

6. Guess what proportion of adult Americans would answer in the affirmative to the question of whether "most U.S. representatives deserve to be re-elected."

7. Think about your local telephone book and take a guess as to the proportion of the individual listings that contain women's names.

IN-CLASS ACTIVITIES

Recall from the previous topic that a confidence interval for a population proportion θ is formed from a sample proportion $\hat{p}$ through the expression

$$\hat{p} \pm z^* \sqrt{\frac{\hat{p}(1-\hat{p})}{n}}$$

where n is the sample size and z^* the critical value from the standard normal distribution for the confidence level desired.

Activity 17-1: American Moral Decline (*cont.*)

Recall from Activity 12-7 that a survey conducted by *Newsweek* on June 2–3, 1994 asked adult Americans, "Do you think the United States is in a moral and spiritual decline?" Of the 748 adults surveyed, 76% answered yes.

(a) Use this sample result to produce (by hand) a 95% confidence interval for θ, the true proportion of *all* adult Americans who would have answered "yes" to the question about moral decline.

(b) What are the formal assumptions which underlie the validity of this procedure?

(c) What is the half-width of this confidence interval?

(d) The *Newsweek* article states that the survey's margin of error is ±3 percentage points. Can you figure out where this number comes from?

The *margin-of-error* of a sample survey refers to (usually, at least) the half-width of a 95% confidence interval for the population proportion of interest.

(e) Remembering the comments about interpreting confidence intervals listed in Topic 16, identify each of the following statements as true or false:
   • The survey's margin-of-error *guarantees* that the population proportion θ is within ±.03 of .76.
   • The probability is .95 that θ falls within the confidence interval.
   • If one repeatedly took random samples of 748 adult Americans, asked them the survey question, and formed confidence intervals in this same manner, then in the long run 95% of the intervals so generated would contain the true value of the population proportion θ.
   • If one repeatedly took random samples of 748 adult Americans, asked them the survey question, and formed confidence intervals in this same manner, then in the long run 95% of the intervals so generated would contain the value .76.

(f) Would you expect a survey's margin of error to increase or to decrease as the sample size increases?

(g) Evaluate your conjecture by determining (by hand) the margin-of-error for the survey above if 2000 adult Americans had been interviewed (and assuming that 76% was still the sample proportion of "yes" responses). Then repeat for a sample size of 400.

(h) Do you need to modify your conjecture based on these findings?

(i) If you want to use this survey's results to estimate the proportion of all adult American *men* who would have answered "yes" to the question about moral decline, would the margin-of-error for this proportion be greater or less than ±3%? Explain your answer.

(j) If you want to use this survey's results to estimate the proportion of all adult American male *college graduates* who would have answered "yes" to the question about moral decline, would the margin-of-error for this proportion be greater or less than that for the previous question? Again explain your answer.

These last questions reveal that a survey's margin-of-error increases when one considers subgroups of the population.

Activity 17-3: Female Senators (*cont.*)

Suppose that an alien lands on Earth, notices that there are two different sexes of the human species, and wants to estimate the proportion of all humans who are female. If this alien were to use the members of the 1994 United States Senate as a sample from the population of human beings, it would have a sample of 7 women and 93 men.

(a) Use this sample information to form (either by hand or using the computer) a 95% confidence interval for the actual proportion of all humans who are female.

(b) Is this confidence interval a reasonable estimate of the actual proportion of all humans who are female?

(c) Explain why the confidence interval procedure fails to produce an accurate estimate of the population parameter in this situation.

(d) It clearly does not make sense to use the confidence interval in (a) to estimate the proportion of women in the world, but does the interval make sense for estimating the proportion of women in the U.S. Senate in 1994? Explain your answer.

This example illustrates some important limitations of the widely used technique of confidence intervals. First, confidence intervals do not compensate for the problems of a biased sample. If the sample is selected from a population in a biased manner, the ensuing confidence interval will be a biased estimate of the population parameter of interest.

A second important point to remember is that confidence intervals use *sample* statistics to estimate *population* parameters. If the data at hand constitute the entire population of interest, then constructing a confidence interval from the data is meaningless.

United States Senators are clearly not a random sample of the world population. Moreover, these 100 Senators cannot be considered a sample of Senators because they comprise the entire *population* of Senators. One knows precisely that the proportion of women in the population of 1994 U.S. Senators is .07, so it is senseless to construct a confidence interval from these data.

A Companion Piece to *Workshop Statistics*

Michael D. Seyfried
Shippensburg University of Pennsylvania

Introduction

I teach at Shippensburg University of Pennsylvania, a medium sized, state supported university located in south-central Pennsylvania. I teach a wide variety of courses including MAT 102: Introduction to Statistics. At Shippensburg, many students take this course as either a course to fill a general education requirement or to fulfill a program specific requirement. We teach statistics to history majors, English majors, elementary education majors, as well as certain biology majors. In short, this course is one that a broad spectrum of our students will take and we see tremendous variability in both student background and preparation. My task is to offer these students a solid, useful, and interesting introduction to statistics.

For many years we used a traditional textbook in this course. A few years ago, while attending a regional professional meeting, I had the chance to talk with Allan Rossman about an introductory statistics course and what it should include. He had some very definite ideas on this subject. He mentioned how students might work on projects in class and be actively engaged in their education. "Wow," I thought, "we could work with them as they begin to cooperatively discover some of these marvelous statistical ideas." This changed how I looked at the course. Over the next couple of years I began to add more activities and more group work and began to lecture less. The response from the students was overwhelmingly positive. They found that taking their own samples and discovering sampling variability and sampling distributions made more sense than listening to me lecture about the same topics. The students' attitudes improved, they asked better questions, and we saved a whole lot of chalk. It seemed like a win-win situation.

For the fall semester of 1997, four of the six instructors teaching sections of MAT 102 adopted *Workshop Statistics, Discovery with Data* by Allan Rossman as their text for the course. I acted as the unofficial coordinator of the course in the sense that I made sure each of the faculty members teaching the course had access to all the information found on the Workshop Statistics home page (www.dickinson.edu/~rossman/ws/). This web site has a wealth of information including topic-by-topic notes, a suggested outline, answers to the in-class activities (where appropriate), as well as links to the data sets and links to programs written for the TI-83 graphing calculator. I downloaded the information and made it available to each of my colleagues. With the information hot off the net in one hand and the textbook in the other, we were ready to begin; almost.

Based on discussions with colleagues in similar situations, I think that our situation at Shippensburg University may be unique among the institutions that have adopted Rossman's book. We teach this course in an ordinary classroom setting. We do not have a computer classroom dedicated to introductory statistics nor do we have a laboratory component to this course. Technology is an important part of the philosophy of *Workshop Statistics,* so how do we compensate? Like everyone else, we simply do the best we can with what we have. I have a statistical software program on my office computer and I use this to generate statistical plots and summary statistics where necessary. I make transparencies from this and also make copies for the students, which give the students some idea of how the computer can be used as a tool to help us understand the story the data are trying to tell. I also have access to a classroom set of TI-83 graphing calculators. I used these in the classroom a couple of times. They proved to be useful when doing some simulations. I probably could have made better use of these calculators and will the next time I teach this course. More about what I would change in my approach to this course later.

So where do we begin? With data of course! Actually, the students learn what is data and what isn't data. Many of the topics (there are 25 in all) begin by asking students to gather their own data on things such as political views, states visited, penny spinning, and so on. This accomplishes at least two things: they begin to realize that statistics deals with real things (how much sleep did you get last night?), and they begin to talk and work together. The last point is one that I feel is very important. I found that having the students work in small groups and move through an activity from premises to conclusion greatly enhanced their facility with the material, and it also helped with their confidence level. We have many students who take this class and have a very low opinion of their own quantitative skills. For most of these students, the group work seems to help with their level of comfort and so allows them to overcome this barrier to learning.

Implementation

In a typical class period I start by summarizing where we are in the overall scheme of the course and course goals and what we hope to accomplish with the day's topic. *Workshop Statistics* facilitates this by beginning each topic with both an overview and a set of objectives for that particular topic. Then I begin with the day's topic. Suppose the topic of the day is "Measures of Center" (Topic 3 in *Workshop Statistics*). Each topic is divided into two types of activities—in-class activities and homework activities. Generally there are anywhere from three to six in-class activities and from four to sixteen homework activities. "Measures of Center" has five in-class activities and eight homework activities.

After my initial overview, I ask students two of *Workshop Statistics'* preliminary questions: (a) to guess how long a typical member of the U.S. Supreme Court has served, and (b) to guess maximum, minimum, and "typical" distance from home for a student in the class. For the latter question, I find it helpful to have the students give me their own distances-from-home the previous class period, so I can prepare transparencies of the stemplots ahead of the class discussion.

I next ask the students to create a dotplot of a small data set, here the years served by current members of the U.S. Supreme Court. I then ask them to choose a single number to represent the "center" of the distribution. This question usually gets the groups to talk about what the center could mean. Next, the students see the definition of mean, median, and mode and compute each of them for this data set. They also locate them on their dotplot. Finally, I ask them to look for a pattern for finding the median with data sets of various odd sizes, and Activity 3-2 ("Faculty Years of Service") has them find a pattern with data sets of even size.

Activity 3-3 explores "Properties of Averages." The emphasis here is conceptual rather than computational. For example, in a previous activity (Activity 2.1) students created a dotplot of exam scores from three hypothetical classes. Activity 3-3 nows asks students how they would expect mean scores to compare between the three classes, and then asks likewise for median scores. These questions get students discussing the effects of shape on mean and median and allows them to discover the relationship between shape and a particular measure of center.

Activity 3-5—"Students' Distances from Home"—allows students to reinforce their understanding by applying the principle they have just discovered to the class's distance-from-home data set. Using the prepared overhead transparencies for this data set, the class tries to eyeball the center. I then provide the students with a copy of the raw data, break them into small groups (three to five students), and have half of the groups compute the mean, and half compute the median. I ask groups to supply the mean and median, which I place on the dotplot transparency. We talk about why these two numbers are different. As a class we look at the final question of the activity. This question asks whether we would have a thorough understanding of this distribution if we had only the mean and median but not the dotplot. This is an example of one of *Workshop Statis-*

tics' conceptual questions and motivates the need to study the next topic, which is variability.

Using *Workshop Statistics,* students not only "discover" the basics of descriptive statistics, they also work on ideas from inferential statistics. In Topics 16 and 17 students discover principles of confidence intervals. Topic 16 introduces students to the concept of a confidence interval through an activity where they spin a penny on its side, as opposed to tossing it in the air. The goal is to estimate the true proportion of times a spun penny will land heads up. Students realize that we may never know the true value of this parameter exactly, but we can use the sample data to make a very good guess at it. We discuss what would happen if this experiment were repeated over and over. This helps reinforce the notion of the sampling distribution and students begin to see how the sampling distribution can help us in our quest for a reasonably good value, or range of values, for the unknown parameter. Later we work on the mechanics of finding critical values. *Workshop Statistics* assumes some form of technology will be used in the course. I use what we have available. In this case I use our set of TI-83 graphing calculators to show what happens as we simulate this penny spinning experiment. I use a program written by Barr von Oehsen for the graphing calculator version of *Workshop Statistics* (this program and many others are available through the *Workshop Statistics* home page). We can look at the effect of changing the sample size or changing the confidence level. This is one of several experiments that my students really got involved with. I enjoyed watching them make conjectures about what would happen if, for example, the sample size were increased, then running the simulation again. I think this simulation did more to drive home the key ideas of estimating with confidence than a typical lecture on the same material could ever do.

Topic 17 furthers the discussion of estimating with confidence. Here we look at the margin of error, choosing an appropriate sample size, and the limitations of confidence intervals. Activity 17-1, taken from a *Newsweek* article, asks students to construct a confidence interval (reinforcing the previous topic), to determine the half-width of the interval, and to interpret the margin of error as stated in the article. Questions then follow dealing with how the margin of error is affected by changes in the sample size, and how it would change if we restricted the population of interest. There is also a very nice activity on the limitations of confidence intervals. This deals with an alien who uses the U.S. Senate as a sample of the world population and tries to estimate the true proportion of women in the world based on this sample. We had a lot of fun discussing this

activity in class. Students saw how absurd it was to use confidence intervals here. They saw how a biased sample can obliterate the good intentions of a confidence interval. Topics 16 and 17 work well together and give students an excellent understanding of confidence intervals.

Helpful Hints

I try to stick to a schedule of one topic per class, although some of the meatier topics (such as tests of significance and confidence intervals) may require a class and a half to two classes. I find that if I stick to this schedule we are able to move at a pace most of my students find comfortable.

For many topics, like sixteen and seventeen concerning confidence intervals, I talk very little and have students work in small groups. (Typically students work in groups of three to five students, although I allow a student to work alone if he or she feels more comfortable doing so.) I try to use the last ten or fifteen minutes (of a seventy five minute period) to check answers to in-class activities and wrap things up. I find that this closure helps students and gives them a bit more confidence. For some topics, I keep the feel of the text but vary the activity. For example, instead of trying to estimate the proportion of orange Reese's Pieces as in Topic 12, I used M&M's. I passed out candies in a tin and told each student to take one scoop of the candies. I knew ahead of time that a scoop would yield between 25 and 35 pieces. Once each student had taken the M&M's, I told them to make sure they had 25 on their desk top. They ate any extra candies. Then we collectively chose a color to estimate. We talked about why things were done in this order (e.g., to minimize bias), then we proceeded more or less as in the text. Each student found his or her own sample proportion of green (or whatever the chosen color was) M&M's, then we made a "post-it"-plot on the blackboard. Students could see the sampling distribution appear before their very eyes. While they analyzed the plot, describing the shape, center, and spread, I quickly did some computations and came up with the summary statistics for the data. We then talked about how close their guess of the center was to the value I computed. Also, they had to determine the proportion of the data points that were within a certain distance of their value (essentially this distance was two standard deviations). This activity was very useful in tying together many of the ideas previously discussed and in anticipating what was to come. Many students said this was their favorite activity of the course. (I'm sure the M&M's in no way influenced their decision.)

The point of the above discussion is that the text serves as a guide. Sometimes you want to follow it step-by-step.

Other times you want to go off exploring on your own with the comfort of the guide not far away. Sometimes you may ignore the guide altogether. The instructor has to decide which course of action to follow and when to follow it. While I had used individual activities from this book (and from others) in conjunction with the traditional textbook, this was the first time I used *Workshop Statistics* as a stand-alone text. I thoroughly enjoyed using this book and the overall reaction by my students was positive.

Some students remarked that, unlike so many mathematics and statistics texts, there were no examples or model problems in the book. This is correct. The *Workshop Statistics* approach is that students, in the course of doing the in-class activities, create their own examples. Some students missed this point completely, but those were mostly students who had poor attendance records. Most students (even those in my 8:00 A.M. section) quickly realized that attendance was a must.

Since this was the first time I had used the book as the sole text, I did run into some areas where things didn't go as smoothly as they did in other sections. In particular, the discussion of the normal distribution (Topic 14) was a trouble spot for us. We spent most of the semester without the burden of elaborate mathematical jargon and then, wham, out of left field comes a full classical probability statement like $\Pr(X < 100) = \Pr(Z < 1.00) = .1578$ (page 238). We ignored the notation and did the same examples emphasizing the area idea (interpreted as: the probability of an event is equal to the area it occupies under the appropriate density curve). This gave students something to visualize and almost all of them said they found that this approach made more sense to them than the one in the text. This was one instance where an alternative approach to that given in the text really helped my students.

Some students found the approach to tests of significance (Topics 18 and 19) difficult to follow and we spent more time than I had planned with this topic. I realize this is a topic many students seem to find difficult, so going slowly is probably a good idea. I think, in the end, students did understand significance tests. There were a few other rough spots during the semester, but these two were the concepts that really forced us to put aside the text for a bit and look for other approaches.

One very nice feature of the book is that Rossman has gathered together some very interesting data sets. He has information on Blockbuster movies, sports, salaries of elected officials, and many more. These are data sets that are alive and fun to work with. There's nary a boring real data set in the entire text. Sometimes I updated data sets from the text or even replaced data about Dickinson College (where Al-

lan Rossman teaches) with the appropriate data from Shippensburg University. An instructor at any other university could easily do the same.

The first time through the text I covered only nineteen of the twenty five topics in fourteen weeks. I hope to be able to cover more topics next time. I tried to cover most of the in-class activities in class (where else right?), but wasn't always successful at it. If we left out such an activity, and it did not involve using the computer to simulate something, then I made that part of the homework assignment for next time. I also assigned problems every week from the homework activities section. There are many good problems here so you have to show some measure of self control. Don't go overboard! Some of these problems take some time to do, and students have demands on their time beyond this course. I wound up grading between two and four problems per student per week. I did spend a lot of time on this, but students do appreciate the immediate feedback on their work, so I feel it was worth it.

Due to our lack of a dedicated lab for statistics, I tried to select problems that a student who had only a basic statistical calculator could handle. Fortunately, there are enough problems of this type in the textbook. Some students used graphing calculators and some used spreadsheets. Those with access to technology were encouraged to use it. The majority used a basic calculator and got along fine. Flexibility is a key feature of this text.

Because time is always short, decisions about what to cover are inevitable. I chose to leave out some topics concerning two variable associations (the formalities of simple linear regression) as well as some topics dealing with comparing two proportions. In place of these topics, I spent the last part of the semester looking at inferences from measurement data. Here they were introduced to the t-distribution and saw estimation and tests of significance in this setting. It would be nice to cover the entire book, but it may be more important to cover enough so that students come out with a good understanding of the basic principles of statistics.

As far as some general guidelines for using the text I would have to say that first and foremost you should be committed to the ideas of active learning and group work. These are fundamental to having a successful experience with this text. Taking control of the class is also important. It is easy to simply say to students "OK, today we do Topic 18. Go to it." then not provide any guidance or direction in the class. Know when you need to lecture and when you can simply have students go at a topic on their own. For example, I lectured on the normal distributions and the t-distributions, while I let the students have a go at comparing distributions and random sampling (Topics 5 and 11 respectively). You need to use your own judgement here. In part, this is a function of your students. If I notice that the room gets quiet and no one is writing anything, I know something is not getting across. Then it is time to regroup and do a mini-lecture on the topic. In short, be attentive to the needs and abilities of your students and have fun with this book.

Conclusion

So next semester when I teach this course, what will I do differently? That is the question I first asked myself while my students were taking their final examination. I will have a better plan for incorporating technology into the course. I plan to make better use of our TI-83's. I hope to use them for the initial part of the course dealing with descriptive statistics and for help with more simulations. I may also try to set up a home page and put course information there for the students. I may also suggest that they submit questions to me via e-mail if they so choose. I plan to experiment in this area.

I was anxious to get student feedback on this new approach. Starting very early in the semester I asked any of my students who came near my office for their opinion on the text. At the end of the course the students filled out written evaluations and I asked them to comment on the text there. The vast majority of the comments I received were positive about the text and the approach. The comment most heard was that they weren't simply memorizing a bunch of formulas. They were gaining some insight as to where the information they read about in the paper—political polls and so on—came from. Many told me that they didn't realize that math could be fun. I can't recall students having a more positive attitude towards this class.

Many of the students thought that the group work was great. They were able to split up the chores in the activities and then piece together this information to formulate (and many times debate) responses to the questions. One brief example of this came about in Activity 5-1. Students were given information on the percentage change in population between 1990 and 1993. The question is to compare the eastern states and the western states. The groups had great fun deciding which states fell into which region; some even pulled out their daily planners to check maps. This was fun but don't let the geography lesson run too long here! After about ten minutes or so, we pooled our information and decided on the number of states in each category. The groups, armed with the correct placement of the states, then set about to construct side-by-side stem-and-leaf plots. They then answered the questions from the text.

As I stated earlier, four of the six instructors for our course adopted *Workshop Statistics* as the sole text. (Two decided that the format would not work for them and elected to use another text.) Of these four, two have continued using *Workshop Statistics* and two have switched to another text. The primary reason for not staying with *Workshop Statistics* is that the format proved not to fit the instructor's style. However, these instructors like the activities and, in fact, use some activities in their subsequent courses, but they feel more comfortable with a more traditional delivery of the material.

I found that the combination of group work and realistic data made for a very lively and enjoyable class for everyone. *Workshop Statistics* offers a wonderful approach to a vital and interesting subject. Even those unsure of adopting this book as a textbook could enhance their class by incorporating a few well-chosen activities from *Workshop Statistics*. My experience is that the students came out of this course with a better grasp of statistics and with a better understanding that statistics can be a very useful and interesting subject. For these reasons alone it is worthwhile giving the *Workshop Statistics* approach a classroom try.

Excerpts from *Activity-Based Statistics*†

Overview to the Student Guide

Their fast-paced world of action movies, rapid-fire TV commercials, and video games does not prepare today's students to sit and absorb a lecture, especially on a supposedly dull subject like statistics. To capture the interest of these students, teaching must move away from a lecture-and-listen approach toward innovative activities that engage students in the learning process. The goal of the Activity-Based Statistics Project (ABSP) is to develop a set of such activities that cover the statistical concepts essential to any introductory course. These activities can be used in a variety of class settings to allow students to "discover" concepts of statistics by working through a set of "laboratory" exercises. Whether the "laboratory" is the classroom, the student's usual place of study, or a more formal statistics laboratory, the traditional lectures in introductory statistics should be supplemented or supplanted by a program that requires the active participation of the students, working individually or in groups. Statistics, then, should be taught more as an experimental science and less as traditional mathematics.

The activities are organized around the major topics covered in most introductory courses. The overarching topic is exploring data. Statistical ideas begin with data, but data should be collected for a purpose. Relating data collection and analysis to the solving of a real problem, much as is done in statistical process improvement, allows exploratory techniques to be used extensively but with a purpose in mind.

Random behavior is fundamental to the decision-making process of statistics but is a difficult topic for students to grasp. Thus, a number of activities concentrate on developing an understanding of randomness, without going into the mathematical formalities of classical probability distributions. Simulation is key to this process. Related material on sampling distributions is included, to be introduced at the instructor's discretion. Since the amount of required probability is highly variable from course to course, the activities throughout the ABSP are designed to be completed with a minimum of probability.

Sampling, such as in the ubiquitous opinion poll, is the most common application of planned data collection in the "real" world and in the classroom. This topic allows the early introduction of the idea of random sampling

† From *Activity-Based Statistics, Student Guide*, by Richard L. Scheaffer, Mrudulla Gnanadesikan, Ann Watkins, and Jeffrey A. Witmer, ©1996 by Springer-Verlag and *Activity-Based Statistics, Instructor Resources*, by Richard L. Scheaffer, Mrudulla Gnanadesikan, Ann Watkins, and Jeffrey A. Witmer, ©1996 by Springer-Verlag. Reprinted with permission of Springer-Verlag.

and its implications for statistical inference. Thus, it serves as an excellent bridge between probability and inference. The difficulty and importance of collecting data that fairly represents a population are emphasized.

Estimation and hypothesis testing frame the basic approach to inference in most courses, and numerous activities deal with the conceptual understanding of the reasoning process used here. Again, simulation plays a key role as concepts of sampling error, confidence interval, and p-value are introduced without appeal to formulas.

Experiments are the second major technique for planned data collection. By appealing to activities that focus on optimization of factors, the ABSP emphasizes that experiments are designed to compare "treatments" rather than to estimate population parameters.

Modeling the relationship between two variables, especially through the use of least-squares regression, is widely used throughout statistics and should be part of an introductory course. Technology is required here in order to use time efficiently. Correlation, a topic much confused by students, is singled out for special study.

The ABSP contains far more activities than can be used efficiently in one course. It is hoped that instructors will choose a few activities from each of the topics so that students will be exposed to a range of concepts through hands-on learning.

Each activity has student pages and notes for the instructor. This allows the flexibility to use the activities as class demonstration, group work in class, or take-home assignments. In whatever setting they may be used, the activities should engage the students so that they become true participants in the teaching-learning process.

Overview to Instructor Resources

Incorporating Activities into a Statistics Course

The ABS collection of activities are many and varied. Some instructors will want to build their introductory course around these activities while others will incorporate selected ones within an existing course. The following outline provides the instructor with examples of activities with which to teach a typical introductory statistics course. Activities shown in italics were used by one of the authors in such a course.

Exploring Data-One Variable

Getting to Know the Class and *The Shape of the Data* can be used on the first or second day of the course. *Measurement Bias* fits with a discussion of measurement and variation. After discussing box plots the *Living Box Plot* activity is a natural choice. *Matching Graphs to Variables* is a good activity for the student who needs to review reading a histogram and encourages the student to think about how the shape of a histogram is related to features in the data. Likewise, *Matching Statistics to Graphs* fits with early work on distributions.

Exploring Data-Two Variables

Getting Rid of the Jitters can be used when students learn about scatter plots and scatter plot smoothing. *Is Your Shirt Size Related to Your Shoe Size?* and *Models, Models, Models* fit with a discussion of regression. *Matching Descriptions to Scatter Plots* helps students develop an understanding of how regression and correlation results can depend on influential points. *The Regression Effect* presents an important lesson about regression. *Predictable Pairs* should be given with an exploration of categorical data.

Data Production

Gummy Bears in Space and *Jumping Frogs* give students a chance to work with designed experiments; they can be used when discussing data production or when discussing ANOVA. *Funnel Swirling* is a more complex activity that might work best as a review lesson late in the course. *How to Ask Questions* goes naturally with a discussion of survey design. *Random Rectangles* or *Stringing Students Along* provide good ways to introduce bias in sampling. *Spinning Pennies* gives an introduction to sampling distributions, *Capture/Recapture* fits in well when discussing how data are collected, and *Flick the Nick* can be used when discussing control charts.

Probability

Any of the random behavior activities (*What's the Chance?*, *What is Random Behavior?*, etc.) can be used when studying probability. The *Dueling Dice* activity can be presented as a way to review sampling distributions under the guise of wanting to study the sampling distribution of the larger of two rolls of a die. In fact, the activity shows that statistical analysis can reveal trends that are otherwise missed by most observers.

Distributions

Estimating Proportions: How Accurate Are the Polls? and *Streaky Behavior: Runs in Binomial Trials* fit with a discussion of the binomial distribution. *Cents and the Central Limit Theorem, Let Us Count,* and *The Central Limit Theorem and the Law of Large Numbers* should be paired with a discussion of sample means and the central limit theorem. *Sampling Error and Estimation* can be used here as well.

Introduction to Inference

What Is a Confidence Interval Anyway?, fits with an introduction to interval estimation. *Introduction to Hypothesis Testing* can be used to introduce the idea of examining evidence against a null hypothesis.

Inference for Means and for Proportions

The Bootstrap can be used to show an alternative to the t-test. *Confidence Intervals for the Percentage of Even Digits* fits with a discussion of proportion data and *Coins on Edge* with hypothesis testing for a single proportion, although it could also be used when introducing hypothesis testing. *Statistical Evidence of Discrimination* aligns with a discussion of equality of two proportions. *Estimating the Difference Between Two Proportions* can be used when discussing the difference between proportions.

Other Topics

Is Your Class Differently Aged?, uses the Chi-square goodness-of-fit test. *Relating to Correlation* correlates with the topic of inference in regression. Either *Gummy Bears in Space* or *Jumping Frogs* can be used as a one-way ANOVA example but they are really designed as two-way ANOVA examples with interactions.

Contents

Cents and the Central Limit Theorem

Scenario.   Many of the variables that you have studied so far in your statistics class have had a normal distribution. You may have used a table of the normal distribution to answer questions about a randomly selected individual or a random sample taken from a normal distribution. Many distributions, however are not normal or any other standard shape.

Question

If the shape of a distribution isn't normal, can we make any inferences about the mean of a random sample from that distribution?

Objective

In this activity you will discover the central limit theorem by observing the shape, mean, and standard deviation of the sampling distribution of the mean for samples taken from a distribution that is decidedly not normal.

Activity

1. You should have a list of the dates on a random sample of 25 pennies. Next to each date, write the age of the penny by subtracting the date from the current year. What do you think the shape of the distribution of all the ages of the pennies from students in your class will look like?

2. Make a histogram of the ages of all the pennies in the class.

3. Estimate the mean and the standard deviation of the distribution. Confirm these estimates by actual computation.

4. Take a random sample of size 5 from the ages of your pennies, and compute the mean age of your sample. Three or four students in your class should place their sample means on a number line.

5. Do you think the mean of the values in this histogram (once it is completed) will be larger than, smaller than, or the same size as the one for the population of all pennies? Regardless of which you choose, try to make an argument to support each choice. Estimate what the standard deviation of this distribution will be.

6. Complete the histogram, and determine its mean and standard deviation. Which of the three choices in part 5 appears to be correct?

7. Repeat this experiment for samples of size 10 and size 25.

8. Look at the four histograms that your class has constructed. What can you say about the shape of the histogram as n increases? What can you say about the center of the histogram as n increases? What can you say about the spread of the histogram as n increases?

Wrap-Up

1. The three characteristics you examined in Activity question 8 (shape, center, and spread of the sampling distribution) make up the **central limit theorem.** Without looking in a textbook, write a statement of what you think the central limit theorem says.

2. The distributions you constructed for samples of size 1, 5, 10, and 25 are called sampling distributions of the sample mean. Sketch the sampling distribution of the sample mean for samples of size 36.

Extensions

1. Get a copy of the current Handbook of *United States Coins: Official Blue Book of United States Coins,* and graph the distribution of the number of pennies minted in each year. What are the interesting features of this distribution? Compare this distribution with the distribution of the population of ages of the pennies in the class. How are they different? Why? How can you estimate the percentage of coins from year x that are out of circulation?

2. In a geometric distribution, the height of each bar of the histogram is a fixed fraction r of the height of the bar to the left of it. Except for the first bar, is the distribution of the ages of the pennies approximately geometric? Estimate the value of r for this distribution. What does r tell you about how pennies go out of circulation? Why is the height of the first bar shorter than one would expect in a geometric distribution?

3. To cut the standard deviation of the sampling distribution of the sample mean in half, what sample size would you need?

Waiting for Reggie Jackson: The Geometric Distribution

Scenario.   Children's cereals sometimes contain small prizes. For example, not too long ago, boxes of Kellogg's Frosted Flakes contained one of three posters: Ken Griffey Jr., Nolan Ryan, or Reggie Jackson. Reggie wanted to get a Reggie Jackson poster and had to buy eight boxes until getting his poster. Reggie feels especially unlucky.

Question

Should Reggie consider himself especially unlucky? On the average, how many boxes would a person have to buy to get the Reggie Jackson poster? What assumptions would you have to make to answer this question?

Objective

In this activity you will become familiar with the geometric, or waiting time, distribution, including the shape of the distribution and how to find its mean.

Activity

1. You will need a die or another method of simulating an event with a probability of 1/3. Roll your die. If the side with one or two spots lands on top, this will represent the event of buying a box of Frosted Flakes and getting a Reggie Jackson poster. If one of the other sides lands on top, roll again. Count the number of rolls until you get a one or a two.

   a. Make a histogram of the number of rolls the students in your class require to get their first Reggie Jackson poster.

   b. Describe the shape of this distribution.

   c. What was the average number of "boxes" purchased to get a Reggie Jackson poster?

   d. Estimate the chance that Reggie would have to buy eight or more boxes to get his poster.

   e. What assumptions are made in this simulation about the distribution of the prizes? Do you think they are reasonable ones?

2. In some games, such as Monopoly, a player must roll doubles before continuing. Use a pair of dice or use random digits to simulate rolling a pair of dice. Count the number of rolls until you get doubles.

   a. Make a histogram of the number of rolls the students in your class required to roll doubles.

   b. Describe the shape of this distribution.

   c. What was the average number of rolls required?

3. In questions 1 and 2, you constructed a waiting time distribution using simulation. In this question, you will construct a theoretical waiting time distribution. Boxes of Post's Cocoa Pebbles recently contained one of four endangered animal stickers: a parrot, an African elephant, a tiger, or a crocodile. Suppose 4,096 children want a sticker of a parrot.

   a. How many of them would you expect to get a parrot in the first box of Cocoa Pebbles they buy? What assumptions are you making?

   b. How many children do you expect will have to buy a second box?

   c. How many of them do you expect will get a parrot in the second box?

   d. Fill in the following table.

Number of Boxes Purchased to Get First Parrot Sticker	Number of Children
1	
2	
3	
.	
.	
.	
20	

e. Make a histogram of your theoretical waiting time distribution.

f. The height of each bar of the histogram is what proportion of the height of the bar to its left?

g. What is the average number of boxes purchased?

Wrap-Up

1. Describe the shape of a waiting time (geometric) distribution for a given probability p of a success on each trial. Will the first bar in a waiting time distribution always be the highest? Why or why not? The height of each bar is what proportion of the height of the bar to its left?

2. Find an example of another real-world situation that would be modeled by a geometric distribution.

Extensions

1. There is some evidence that prizes are not put randomly into boxes of cereal. Design an experiment and determine how this would affect the average number of boxes that must be purchased to get a specific prize.

2. Look at the average waiting times in Activity questions 1, 2, and 3. Can you find the simple formula that gives this average in terms of the probability p of getting the desired event on each trial?

3. Find a formula that gives the probability that the first five occurs on the nth roll of a die.

Reference.
Frederick Mosteller, Robert E. K. Rourke, and George B. Thomas, Jr. (1970), *Probability with Statistical Applications,* second ed., Reading, MA: Addison-Wesley, pp. 176, 189, and 219

Capture/Recapture

Scenario.   Naturalists often want estimates of population sizes that are difficult to measure directly. The capture/recapture method allows one to estimate, for example, the number of fish in a lake. This idea is also the basis of methods that the Census Bureau has developed that can be used in adjusting population figures obtained in the decennial census (although using sampling techniques to adjust the census is controversial).

Question

What is the population of the United States, including those who are not counted in the official census?

Objectives

The purpose of this activity is to introduce the use of statistical models and to learn how assumptions affect statistical analyses. You will also learn about the capture/recapture method and how it is used.

Activity

1. How would you estimate the number of fish in a lake or the number of bald eagles in the United States? Just going out and counting the animals that you see will not work.
2. We will demonstrate how the capture/recapture method works by trying to determine the number of goldfish in a bag of Pepperidge Farm Goldfish crackers. Open one of the bags of goldfish, and pour the goldfish into the "lake."
3. A volunteer should take a large sample from the lake. It is a good idea to get at least 40 or so goldfish in this sample, which often requires taking two handfuls. Then someone needs to count the number, M, of goldfish in the sample; these are the "captured" goldfish.
4. The next step is to put tags on the goldfish. If these were real fish they could be marked with the use of physical tags, but with cracker goldfish we mark them by making them change color. Set aside the captured goldfish and open the second bag. For each goldfish in the captured set, put a goldfish of the other (second) flavor in the lake. (The new goldfish replace the old ones; don't put the old ones back into the lake.)
5. Shake the lake for a while in order to mix the two flavors of fish. Then a volunteer (it need not be the same person who took the first sample) should take a new sample of goldfish; let n denote this sample size, which should again be reasonably large. Count the number in the second sample that are tagged (call this R) and the number that are not tagged ($n - R$).
6. Now consider the percentage of fish in the second sample that are tagged (R/n). A reasonable idea is to set this percentage equal to the population percentage of tagged fish at the time of the second sample, M/N, where N denotes the unknown population size:

$$\frac{R}{n} = \frac{M}{N}.$$

Solving for N, we see that the estimate of the population size is

$$N = \frac{M*n}{R}.$$

Another way to view this is to think of a 2×2 table that gives a cross classification according to whether or not each member of the population was captured in the first phase and in the second phase.

		In First Capture?		
		Yes	**No**	
		(Tagged)	**(Not Tagged)**	Total
In Second	Yes	R	$n - R$	n
Capture?	No	$M - R$		
	Total	M	$N - M$	N

Discussion.   Solving the equation in step 6 is trivial, but the solution makes sense as an estimate of the population size only if it is reasonable to set the sample percentage of tagged fish equal to the population percentage of tagged fish. This depends on many assumptions—for example, that the tags do not fall off. What might go wrong? How would each problem affect the resulting estimate of N? Make a list of assumptions that might be violated and how the estimate of N would be affected in each case.

Wrap-Up

Suppose you wanted to estimate the number of bald eagles in the United States. Explain how you could use the capture/recapture method to do this. What assumptions might be violated? How would this affect your estimate?

Extensions

1. We have now used capture/recapture once and we have an estimate of N. However, this estimate is subject to the uncertainty that arises from the process of taking random samples (rather than counting the entire population). If we repeat the process several times, we will get different estimates of N each time. Repeat the process at least once to see how the estimate of N varies.

2. We can construct a confidence interval for the population size based on a confidence interval for the population percentage tagged. Let p denote the proportion of tagged animals in the population after the first sample (i.e., after step 4); that is, $p = M/N$. Let $\hat{p} = R/n$, the sample percentage tagged. A 95% confidence interval for p is given by $\hat{p} \pm 1.96 * \sqrt{\hat{p}(1-\hat{p})/n}$. (Here we are assuming that n is small relative to N so that we can ignore the finite population correction factor.) Setting M/N equal to the lower limit of the confidence interval for p and solving for N gives the upper limit of a confidence interval for N. Setting M/N equal to the upper limit of the confidence interval for p and solving for N gives the lower limit of a confidence interval for N.

3. The Census Bureau uses the capture/recapture idea in providing adjustments to the decennial census. The capture phase is the census (persons are "tagged" by being recorded in the Census Bureau computer), and the recapture phase is called the Post Enumerative Survey (P.E.S.) conducted after the census. In this setting the appropriate 2×2 table would be as follows:

Recorded in the Official Census?

		Yes	No	Total
"Captured"	Yes	R	$n - R$	n
in the	No	$M - R$		
P.E.S.?	Total	M	$N - M$	N

Only about 96% of all persons in the United States are "captured" in the official census. The percentage of persons in the P.E.S. who were missed in the census, around 4% or so, can be used to adjust original census figures, although whether or not to use the adjusted figures is a hotly debated political issue. For more discussion, see the series of articles that Stephen Fienberg has written for *Chance* magazine. (*Note*: The actual adjustment procedure proposed for the census is based on the capture/recapture idea but involves smoothing of estimates and becomes rather complicated.)

4. Another option is to sample fish one at a time during the recapture phase, stopping when the number of tagged fish, R, is 15, say. Thus, n, the size of the second sample, is random. This sampling method ensures that R will not be too small; that is, it eliminates the possibility that R will be very small by chance, which would lead to a very large estimate of N in Activity step 6.

Technology Extension

We could use a computer to simulate the capture/recapture process. Suppose there are actually 400 animals in the population and the first sample captures 50 of them. Then we begin the second capture phase with a population of 50 tagged animals and 350 untagged animals. If the sample size for the recapture phase is $n = 40$, then we need to simulate drawing a sample of size 40 without replacement from a population of 50 tagged and 350 untagged animals.

One way to do this is to construct a variable of 50 ones and 350 zeroes, with the ones corresponding to the tagged animals from the first sample. Then we sample without replacement 40 times from this variable and count the number, R, of ones in the group (i.e., we calculate the sum of the 40 zeroes and ones). Next we calculate an estimate of N from the formula in Activity step 6. By repeating this many times, we can see how the estimates of N vary from sample to sample.

Here is a box plot of 100 estimates of N from this type of simulation:

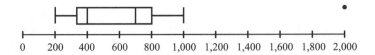

References

1. B. Bailar (1988), "Who counts in America?" *Chance,* 1:9, 17.
2. D.C. Chapman (1989), "The plight of the whales," in J. M. Tanur, et al. (eds.), *Statistics: A Guide to the Unknown,* third ed., Belmont, CA: Wadsworth, pp. 60–67.
3. E.P. Erickson and J.B. Kadane (1985), "Estimating the population in a census year: 1980 and beyond" (with discussion), *J. Amer. Statist. Assoc.,* 80:98–131.
4. Stephen Fienberg (1992), "An adjusted census for 1990? The trial," *Chance,* 5:28–38.
5. Howard Hogan (1992), "The 1990 post-enumerative survey: an overview," *The American Statistician,* 46:261–269.
6. W.E. Ricker (1975), *Computation and Interpretation of Biological Statistics of Fish Populations,* Bulletin of the Fisheries Board of Canada 191, Ottawa, Canada, pp. 83–86.

A Companion Piece to *Activity-Based Statistics*

Bruce King

Over the past quarter-century, I have taught elementary statistics in two-year colleges and at Western Connecticut State University, Danbury, CT. Western is a small comprehensive university that enrolls about 3000 full-time students, most of whom are commuters who work at least part-time to survive. Most recently I taught AP statistics in a distance learning center at Brookfield High School, Brookfield, CT.

At Western, I taught both an introductory biostatistics course to a mixed group of nursing students and medical technology students and an elementary statistics course to more diverse groups of students. Typically these courses meet for a single 2.5-hour evening class each week for 15 weeks. Most of what follows is based upon recent experience in the elementary course.

Since at least the 1960s it has been customary, I believe, for courses in elementary statistics to reflect the organization of a conventional mathematical statistics course, less the proofs (at least the ones that involved calculus). My courses usually included a brief pass at "descriptive statistics," which was followed by the rudiments of probability, including as little combinatorics as possible. Only then did I embark on what I considered the "good stuff": probability distributions—most likely because they are functions and familiar to me from mathematics. Only after drawing my students through a catalog of particular distributions and inferential procedures that rely on them did I embark on regression—more "good stuff" that I recognized from mathematics. The point is that what I did was largely determined by a standard sequence of mathematical theorems (albeit, ones I did not prove), and what I valued most was what I saw as particularly "mathematical." Although I worked hard to make such a course worthwhile, very few of my students shared my enthusiasm for it.

In 1993 I was privileged to participate in the STATS93 workshop at Bowdoin College. For me, the workshop was almost electrifying. I saw a vision of a new kind of elementary statistics course, shorn of its pseudo-mathematical heritage. This is not to say that it involved no mathematics, only that mathematics did not supply the organizing principles for the course. Instead, it sought to present statistics as it is practiced: to incorporate simulations and other activities that students would carry out, thus generating evidence that they "owned" and from which they learned basic principles. It sought also to include material not previously thought to be the province of the statistics teacher, on planning a study, on sources of bias (including non-sampling bias), and on assessing the quality of evidence. This "practice-of-statistics" (POS) course would not rely on fabricated data, but on data culled from real studies and from popular media, and it would emphasize project work in which students would practice what we preached.

This piece is not written because I am one of the more able implementers of the POS-style course. Rather, it is written because I am, like most readers of this volume, a mathematician teaching statistics, and because since 1993 I have tried many things to improve my elementary statistics course—some successful, and some not. My enthusiasm remains high, as does my conviction that the POS course has far greater potential than my previous courses to affect my students' lives—and this includes those students who go on to formal study in, say, engineering or statistics, for they too need their feet firmly planted on the ground.

What follows is a description of my attempts to use in my classes some activities from the Activity-Based Statistics project. I have tried, at least in part, about a dozen of the *ABS* activities. My greatest enemy has been time—time to use the activities and still "cover territory." But this problem is not peculiar to a POS course; it was that way before, also. (This time crunch is one reason why POS courses may take firmer root in the high school AP Statistics course, which has about three times as much instructional time as the corresponding college-level course.) The activities described below are meant to be illustrative, and were more successful than most others I have tried.

Commentary on Three ABS Activities

I. Cents and the Central Limit Theorem. The Central Limit Theorem (CLT) poses significant pedagogical problems, and teachers often revisit the topic several times. *ABS* includes a CLT activity that has demonstrated its usefulness in the classroom. It involves a severely skewed distribution—the distribution of ages of pennies—and samples of several sizes from that distribution.

Many people whose vision is less than perfect will experience some difficulty reading dates on pennies. If you choose to use class time for this, I suggest that you have a few magnifying glasses available. I have a simple one with a plastic lens, which I bought at a local K-Mart for $1.39. Some teacher supply houses also have them, or you might borrow them from your biology storeroom. Consider having students work in pairs: one to read dates, the other to complete a tally sheet of coin dates and ages.

The activity requires that each student take a random sample of size 5 and also one of size 10 from their sample of 25, and to compute the mean of each sample. These are considered as samples from the larger population of all pennies collected by the class. The student is also to

compute the mean of all 25 of their pennies to represent a sample of size 25 from the larger population. Students may use a table of random digits or the random number generator on their calculator to select the samples of size 5 and 10.

While it is useful to have students generate their own data, you may wish to avoid spending class time on reading dates on pennies. The *ABS Instructor Resources* [2, p. 134] offers this good compromise: at the end of some class preceding the one in which the activity will be used, ask each student: (a) to collect 25 consecutive pennies that come into his/her possession; (b) to record the dates and ages of the 25 pennies, and the mean value for that sample and for samples of size 5 and 10; and (c) to bring the completed tally sheet to class.

As an alternative to having students bring in their own pennies, I have a set of pennies that I have prepared in advance. Over a period of a year or so, I dropped into a small box pennies that had accumulated in my pocket. I counted the numbers of pennies by date. (I ignored pennies bearing the current year's date, since their distribution was incomplete at the time of the tabulation.) Figure 1 gives the results, with Year converted to Age (e.g., a 1993 penny was, at the time the results were used, about four years old).

I divided the pennies into 29 samples of size 25, and kept each sample in a labeled Ziploc^{TM} storage bag, which makes it easy to distribute intact samples in class.

Either way, the activity requires that each student or group of students record data, calculate means for their samples, and pool their results with those of others to obtain a single class distribution for each of the three sample sizes.

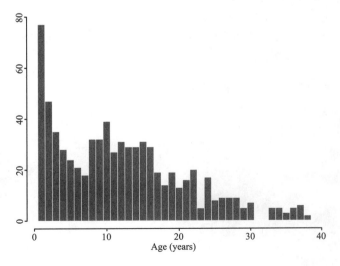

FIGURE 1

Frequency histogram of 725 penny ages in years.

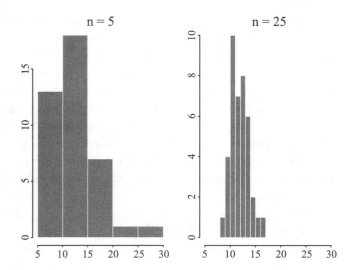

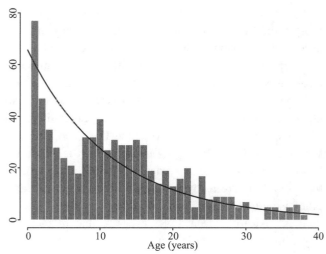

FIGURE 2

Frequency histograms of sample means from the penny ages population. Sample size $n = 5$ is left; sample size $n = 25$ is right. Both histograms contain 40 samples. Sample means are more normal and less variable for larger sample sizes.

FIGURE 3

Frequency histogram of 725 penny ages with a superimposed geometric distribution of frequencies with $\hat{p} = .0829$.

The ABS *Instructor Resources* says that "students love to make" a physical histogram with pennies on a flat surface. An alternative is to build differently colored dotplots on overhead transparencies in class, as students report their penny ages and sample means to you. Overlaying the original dotplot, the dotplot for $n = 5$ or $n = 10$, and the dotplot for $n = 25$ in various combinations makes the point well enough, albeit at the loss of some student involvement. You can further reduce the class time spent on the activity by having students report their penny ages to you via email, between classes, and use the results to prepare the first transparency (the distribution of all penny ages in the class) in advance.

If the classroom is suitably equipped, the student-generated values of $\bar{x}$ may be entered directly into a graphing calculator or statistics program. You may expect results like the following from this activity. Figure 2 shows histograms for the sampling distributions of $\bar{x}$ when $n = 5$ and $n = 25$. Note that the second distribution is more nearly normal than the first, although you are not guaranteed to see this difference with modest class sizes (40, in this case.) Be prepared to run larger simulations to make the point more convincing. Note also that the larger value of n is associated with the smaller variance.

One of the interesting aspects of the *ABS* activities is that, in general, they are quite rich in possibilities. In most cases, "Extensions" to the activities are suggested, and there are many opportunities for the teacher to devise others.

For this activity the second of three suggested activities concerns modeling ages of pennies as a geometric distribution. Recall that in a sequence of Bernoulli trials, if we let X denote the random variable of the number of trials until the first success, then the distribution of X is geometric and

$$P(X = x) = (1 - p)^{x-1}p \quad \text{for} \quad x = 1, 2, 3, \dots$$

where the parameter p is the probability of a "success" in each trial. The ratio of $P(X = x)$ for successive values of x is $1 - p$, the probability of a "failure." Imagine the status of a penny over time as a Bernoulli trials process, with a year that the penny remains in circulation regarded as a "failure"; then "success" refers to the year in which the penny disappears from circulation. So, given a random sample of many such pennies, p measures the "decay rate"—the average annual rate at which such pennies disappear from circulation. Since the mean μ of the geometric distribution is $\frac{1}{p}$, we may expect $\bar{x} \approx \frac{1}{p}$, in which case we can estimate p as $\frac{1}{\bar{x}}$. In the case of the data of Figure 1, $\bar{x} = 12.06$, so $\hat{p} = .0829$, and the graph of $y = 725(1 - \hat{p})^{x-1}\hat{p}$ gives, for $x = 1, 2, 3, \dots$ the "expected" frequencies for the geometric model. Figure 3 shows the graph of this function (extended to the reals) superimposed on top of the histogram. Students can assess the goodness of fit visually or more formally using the χ^2 goodness-of-fit test.

II. Waiting for Reggie Jackson. "Waiting for Reggie Jackson" is another *ABS* activity that involves the geometric distribution. Some time ago, boxes of Kellogg's Frosted

Flakes^{TM} contained one of three posters, one of which was a poster of Reggie Jackson. This activity is primarily an introduction to simulation, and students are asked to use ordinary dice to simulate the distribution of the number of boxes of cereal required to get a Reggie poster.

In general, I use two types of devices for classroom simulations: non-electronic ones (like playing cards, dice, and spinners), and electronic ones (like the TI-83 and computer software like Data Desk). My usual strategy is to use the non-electronic ones until students begin to complain. At that point they are ready for the electronic ones, though I often use a table of random digits as a transitional device.

It is easy to write a TI-83 program that mimics this buy-until-you-get-a-Reggie activity. Looping 100 times, the output from such a program appears in Figure 4.

Such data can be used in a manner similar to the uses of the penny-ages data, described above, but there are additional possibilities. In general, teachers should feel free to modify *ABS* activities to suit their own circumstances. But they also should pay close attention to the suggestions made by the *ABS* authors who, after all, based these volumes on a rich background of classroom experience and formal analysis. An example is the advice in the Instructor Resources for this activity. There one finds the suggestion to have students build a histogram with Post-it^{TM} notes at the front of the room. Although it is not essential to do so for this activity, I would venture that any statistics student could benefit from contributing at least once to such a Post-it histogram. I use marked $2'' \times 3''$ Post-its, turned lengthwise to form the horizontal axis, and distribute $3'' \times 3''$ Post-its that students use to build the histogram. The result is vivid, and

one can readily ask students to estimate probabilities based on the result. For example, the question posed in *ABS* is to estimate the probability that one must purchase at least eight boxes of cereal to get a Reggie card. In the simulated 100 runs given above, 7 times the wait is eight boxes or more, for an estimated probability of .07. The theoretical value is $(2/3)^7 = .0585$ which a larger simulation would be more likely to approximate. Students can gain confidence in the virtues of a well-designed simulation by comparing such a simulation-based estimate to the result of an exact calculation.

Many people seem to accept a "compensation hypothesis"—the so-called "gambler's fallacy"—which assumes that, given a sequence of failures in a Bernoulli trials process (e.g., several consecutive missed free throws in basketball), a success is "overdue," which presumably means that it is more probable than usual. Even when we are satisfied that the trials are independent, no single classroom activity is likely to convince many students to abandon this notion, but it seems to me that we must try. I have used a TI-83 simulation program that mimics purchasing 500 boxes of Frosted Flakes (rather than 100), and have counted the number of times a Reggie card was found within the first four purchases. In one run of this simulation, there were 402 times that a Reggie card was found in the first four purchases; so there were 98 instances in which a Reggie card did *not* appear in the first four purchases. In the 98 four-trial "failures," 31 yielded a "success" (i.e., Reggie card) on the fifth trial—no evidence at all that the probability of a Reggie card is more than the usual one-third.

III. Capture/Recapture. The size N of a wildlife population—say, the number of fish in a lake—sometimes is estimated by using a "capture/recapture" technique. A sample of M fish is captured, marked, and returned to the lake. After a reasonable time period, a second sample of n fish is captured, R of which are <u>re</u>captured (marked) fish.

To simulate this, give a group of students a "lake" (say, a brown paper bag from your grocery store) containing some "fish" (Pepperidge Farm^{TM} Goldfish—say, the Cheddar flavored ones). They take a sample from the lake and "mark" the fish in the sample (by changing their color—say, by replacing them with the Pepperidge Farm Pretzel fish, which look quite different). Shaking the bag gently but thoroughly mixes the tagged and untagged fish, and a second sample is taken.

In the fall semester of 1996, I used this *ABS* capture/recapture activity as the centerpiece of the first class meeting. On that occasion, it worked at least as well as any activity I have tried. Students enjoyed it, and I realized that

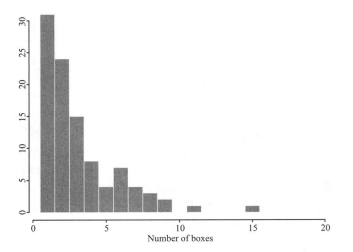

FIGURE 4
One-hundred (100) simulated buy-until-you-get-a-Reggie experiments, generated by a TI-83.

it could serve to foreshadow several statistical and methodological themes that students would encounter later in the course. I describe here how I might use the activity again, based on that experience and on some lessons learned since that time.

Divide the class into several small groups, each of which produces its own estimate for its own population. Even working-adult students enjoy a little competition, so we name the groups ("Tom's Trollers," "Nadine's Netters," etc.), and designate as the "winner" the group that produces the "best" estimate of its N.

Ask the class how to estimate each N, and how to determine the winning group. In my experience, students have little difficulty converging on the common sense notion that $\frac{R}{n} = \frac{M}{N}$, which yields the estimate $\hat{N} = \frac{Mn}{R}$; it takes only a simple diagram and a few appropriate words.

But I did have some difficulty choosing samples of the right size. Here is one way to get useful results. I now use some inexpensive plastic scoops that I purchased in a kitchenware store, each of which holds about 60 fish. With five groups working independently, use two 20-ounce boxes of Pepperidge Farm^{TM}fish, each of which holds about 1000 fish. Pour about one-fifth of the fish into each group's lake. (You might prefer to do this *before* the class meeting. Either way, I handle the Pepperidge Farm^{TM}box because I don't want students to use the serving-size information on the bag to estimate N.) Ask each group to capture *two* full scoops of fish from the lake. That way M tends to be about 120, and $p = \frac{M}{N}$ tends to be about $\frac{120}{400} = .30$. Ask students to recapture by taking a single, full scoop of fish. Then, about 30% of the ≈ 60 fish in the recaptured sample—about 18 of them—will be marked. (The *ABS* authors recommend that the activity be set up so that $R \geq 15$.)

Table 1 displays the results obtained by the fall 1996 class mentioned above. (This was before I was fully aware of the fact that too-small values of R can be a problem: they can easily lead to large overestimates of N.)

Our values of M that evening were too small, which led to values of R that were too small. Nevertheless, it is interesting to note that the estimate obtained by pooling group results (calculated from the data in the last row, not by summing the last column) is almost exactly correct.

These results are unusual in another way. Note that while Group 2 underestimated N, the distribution of $\hat{N}$ is skewed toward higher values, and $\hat{N}$, as a rule, overestimates N. Table 2 shows the results of 10 runs of 1000 simulations using a Minitab macro. We can see in this table that the capture/recapture estimates tend to be biased high. (See [1] for more details.)

Lessons from Capture/Recapture. So, in what ways does this activity "foreshadow several statistical and methodological themes that students would encounter later in the course?" Here are themes I identify in this activity:

(1) *Bias and Variability.* In all ten runs displayed in Table 2, the mean value of $\hat{N}$ overestimates N. Johnson [1, pp. 3–4] discusses the bias in $\hat{N}$ and gives an alternative estimator. Note also the variation exhibited in Table 2. It is usual that, early in the course, the relationship between the mean and median of a skewed distribution arises. Some students may notice this from data like that of Table 2, or such a table may be used to illustrate the point later on.

(2) *Simulation.* Simulations can be an effective way to reveal properties of distributions. But this is not obvious to students until they see it.

Group	N	M	n	R	N-hat
1	371	48	49	6	392
2	335	35	39	5	273
3	476	51	60	6	510
4	503	56	47	5	526
All	1685	190	195	22	1684

TABLE 1
Capture/recapture results from one class, divided into 4 groups.

Five-number Summary for 1000 N-hat's

Run	N	min	Q1	median	Q2	max	Mean of 1000 N-hat's
1	3250	1875	2678	3125	3750	9375	3520
2	3968	2083	3409	4166	5357	37500	4451
3	4947	2205	4166	5357	6250	37500	5736
4	4919	2500	4166	5357	6250	37500	5884
5	3112	1630	2678	3125	3750	18750	3376
6	3371	1704	2884	3409	4166	18750	3711
7	4544	2083	3750	4687	6250	37500	5169
8	4632	2343	3750	4687	6250	37500	5621
9	2548	1293	2205	2500	3125	7500	2709
10	3306	1704	2884	3409	4166	18750	3665

TABLE 2
Ten runs of 1000 simulations of capture/recapture using a Minitab macro that selects a new N with each run. Notice the tendency for $\hat{N}$ to overestimate N.

(3) *Common Sense.* I think it's important to convince students that statistics need not be completely deep, murky, and mysterious; that their common sense can help them to negotiate their way through the course. And I think that point should be made at the first meeting.

(3) *Assumptions.* The *ABS* authors state explicitly that one of the objectives of this activity is "to learn how assumptions affect statistical analyses." So students may be asked here to observe that, "other things being equal," if the assumption that marker tags remain attached to fish indefinitely is violated, then the resulting estimate of N is likely to be an overestimate. And students similarly may be asked to comment on the effect on the estimate if the marked fish tend to be "trap happy." It is important to focus on assumptions early, and to revisit the issue often.

(4) *Inference.* The authors suggest that the results of this activity may be used, later, to construct 95% confidence intervals for N. The confidence interval is not exact, but involves the approximation of one distribution by another. For Group 1, Table 1, a 95% confidence interval for N is given by (225, 1565). Each of the other estimates obtained that evening also cover N, but the wideness of the intervals emphasizes that, when I next use the activity, I need to obtain larger values of R—probably by choosing larger values of M.

(5) *Experimental Design.* The authors point out in the *Instructor Resources* that the variance of the estimator $\hat{N}$ is affected by the sample sizes M and n. They suggest using simulations to complete the cells of a 2x2 design, which makes quite clear that the variation in $\hat{N}$ is large when M and n are both small, and small when M and n are both large.

(6) *Properties of estimators.* We have already mentioned biased estimators. If you want to get into it, $\hat{N}$ is the maximum likelihood estimator of N.

Conclusion

No one would suggest that all of these matters, or that all possible extensions, should be considered, in the context of any single activity, at the time the activity is undertaken. What I do want to suggest is that these are rich activities that can be tapped by teachers willing to think hard about how to adapt them to their own circumstances. Those willing to make that effort may discover anew that statistics, despite its reputation, can be a source of insight and joy. Who would have believed it?

References

[1] Johnson, Roger W., "How Many Fish are in the Pond?," *Teaching Statistics,* **18** (1996), 2–5.

[2] Scheaffer, Richard L., Mrudulla Gnanadesikan, Ann Watkins, and Jeffrey A. Witmer, *Activity-Based Statistics: Instructor Resources,* 1996, Springer-Verlag, NY.

[3] Scheaffer, Richard L., Mrudulla Gnanadesikan, Ann Watkins, and Jeffrey A. Witmer, *Activity-Based Statistics: Student Guide,* 1996, Springer-Verlag, NY.

Excerpts from *Elementary Statistics Laboratory Manual*[†]

PREFACE

Our Observations

Students in beginning statistics courses often view experimentation and data merely as words and numbers in a text. They plug numbers into formulas and then make conclusions about briefly described experiments. At times, students are asked to do some of these routine computations on a computer.

We observe that students generally complete these courses with the false impression that the field of statistics and a career in statistics deal solely with evaluating formulas and that statistical reasoning does not enter an investigation until after the data has been collected. Students generally receive little or no exposure to the important statistical activities of sample selection, data collection, experimental design, searches for sources of variation, the development of statistical models, the selection of factors, and so on. In short, they often leave the first course without understanding the role of statistics and the statistician in scientific investigations. They often leave the course thinking that statistics is dull.

Our Goal

Our primary goal in writing this laboratory manual is to lead students through a series of "hands-on" experiments that illustrate important points of applied statistics. We are attempting to give students examples and experiences that they will remember long after the course is over. We find that students participating in such experiments gain a more accurate impression of the role of statistics and the statistician in scientific investigations and a greater appreciation for science. They also tend to think about statistics at a deeper level than do traditional elementary statistics students. For example, difficult concepts such as outliers, interaction, the need for randomization, and the choice of predictor variables arise naturally and are understood as the students work through the experiments. Students also see that statistics is a fun and exciting field of study.

Our secondary goals are to improve students' technical writing and teamwork skills. These skills, which are highly valued by most employers, are not traditionally emphasized in elementary statistics courses.

[†] From *Elementary Statistics Laboratory Manual*, by John D. Spurrier, Don Edwards, and Lori A. Thombs, ©1995 West Publishing Company. By permission of Brooks/Cole Publishing Company, Pacific Grove, CA, a division of International Thomson Publishing, Inc.

Description of Laboratory Sessions

The experiments are designed such that the data can be collected with reasonably inexpensive measuring equipment. The data is analyzed using Minitab on a Macintosh computer. The sessions were developed using Minitab Release 8.2. All sessions except for Session 9 can be done using the Student Edition of Minitab. No previous experience with Minitab or a Macintosh is required. The level of mathematical maturity required is consistent with that expected for a traditional, noncalculus-based, elementary statistics course. Session I gives an introduction to the Macintosh and to Minitab. Sessions 2 through 17 guide the students through a series of experiments. The experiments do not depend on each other except for Sessions 4 and 12. Complete instructions are given for the use of Minitab in each session. Each session includes a short answer writing assignment and an extended writing assignment. The short answer writing assignment can be completed and graded reasonably quickly. The extended writing assignments, which are more time-consuming, are designed to produce formal reports. The appendixes are particularly helpful for students in the preparation of extended writing assignments. We have found that using extended writing assignments for three sessions and short answer writing assignments for the rest of the sessions is a good mix. Additional instructions for running the session are given in the Instructor's Resource Manual.

Placement of the Lab in the Curriculum

We have run the laboratory as an optional fourth credit hour of our traditional three-semester-hour elementary statistics course. The lab meets weekly for two hours, similar to a biology or chemistry lab. The laboratory also could be used in lieu of some lectures in a three-semester-hour course. Alternatively, the laboratory could be used with upper-division courses in applied statistics, engineering statistics, or mathematical statistics. Some of the experiments have been used as course projects in settings where operation of the entire laboratory was not practical.

CONTENTS

SESSION FIVE: REAL AND PERCEIVED DISTANCES

Introduction

One of the most important aspects of data analysis is the study of relationships between variables. How does a cricket's chirping rate change as temperature decreases? How does the yield of a chemical reaction change when pressure is increased? This session introduces graphical and descriptive tools to help quantify relationships between variables.

Statistical Concepts

Scatter plot, regression, calibration, bias, measurement error, variability within and between individuals.

Materials Needed

For each team, a 50-foot tape measure and a straightedge.

The Setting

Often the measurement we really wish to make on an object is difficult to make (or expensive, toxic, or destructive). If we can find an easily measured variable that is closely linked to the difficult one, we may be able to use the easy one in place of the difficult one. Before doing so, we should do an experiment, called a regression experiment, that involves measuring both variables on each of several objects and then studying the manner in which the easy measurement tends to change with the difficult one. We may then be able to adjust the easy measurement to better approximate the difficult one. This process is called calibration. This session is a regression and calibration experiment to study the manner in which guessed distances between objects (an easy measurement) change in response to true distances (a more difficult measurement).

Background

It is well known that people tend to underestimate the size of faraway objects. Do we also tend to underestimate the distance to faraway objects, or do we tend to overestimate these distances? Or, do we guess right, on average?

The Experiment

STEP 1: DATA COLLECTION.   The class as a group will go to a pre-chosen spot, with lab manuals and pencils. The instructor will identify a fixed reference point, such as a street sign. He or she will then identify a landmark. You should write a brief description of this landmark at the top of column 2 of Table 5.1. The class will then be asked to guess the distance between the reference point and the landmark. Please keep your guess to yourself so as not to influence others. To simplify calculations later, guess in units of feet only. Silently record your guessed distance in column 3 of Table 5.1. Then the instructor will ask you to guess the distance between the reference point and a second landmark, to be recorded in Table 5.1, and then another, and so on, for a total of 13 landmarks. Don't worry that your guesses might be bad. That's variability, and it's what we are studying.

The class will then be split into teams to measure the true distances to the landmarks. Each team will have three members:

1. The Base: This person holds the tape end at the reference point, and at intermediate points along the way if the landmark is too far away to measure in one tape length. He or she also advises the other team members if they are not walking straight toward the landmark and keeps track of the number of full tape lengths that have been used en route to the landmark.
2. The Point: This person takes the tape roll and carefully walks straight toward the landmark, until it is reached or the tape runs out. If the tape runs out, the Point is responsible for keeping track of exactly where the starting point for the next tape length will be while the Base comes forward. Also, the Point verifies the final reading that the Eyes makes.
3. The Eyes: This person walks beside the Point. When the landmark is reached, he or she reads the tape and (in conjunction with the Base and the Point) calculates the final measured distance to the landmark and records it in the appropriate row of Table 5.1, column 4. The Eyes is also the spokesperson for the team in class discussion.

Each of the first 12 landmark distances will be independently measured by at least 3 teams. There are two serious errors that occur with surprising frequency:

1. It is very easy to forget how many tape lengths have been used when measuring distant landmarks. It is the Base's responsibility to remember this, but the other team members should help, too.
2. If the end of the tape is reached, the Point should be very careful where the start of the next tape length is marked. For example, if you are using 50-foot tape measures, the tape is actually longer than 50 feet, but *the new start point should be at the 50-foot mark, not the tape end*. The Eyes should back up the Point to help prevent this error.

Do not measure the 13th landmark distance. It will be a test case. Its true distance has been measured in advance by your instructor, and we discuss it later.

STEP 2: INDIVIDUAL DATA ANALYSIS.   First, the instructor will lead the class in resolving team-to-team differences in measured distances. The median of all the measured distances for each landmark will be used as the *true* distance. Fill in column 5 of Table 5.1 with these medians as the discussion proceeds. Notice that, by using the median of at least three measurements, if one of the teams messed up in a big way, its mistake will not have much effect on the final number.

Landmark Number	Landmark Description	Guessed Distance (feet)	Measured Distance (feet)	Median Measured Distance
1				
2				
3				
4				
5				
6				
7				
8				
9				
10				
11				
12				
13				

TABLE 5.1
Distances Between a Fixed Point and Several Landmarks

Turn on your Mac and launch Minitab. In the new worksheet, give columns Cl, C2, and C3 the variable names **Landmark**, **Guess**, and **True**. Figure 5.1 illustrates the variable names in the Untitled worksheet. Carefully enter your data for the first 12 landmarks from Table 5.1 (columns 1, 3, and 5) for these variables. *Do not enter data for the 13th landmark.* After checking your data carefully, save the worksheet onto your diskette by selecting **Save Worksheet As** from the **File** menu. Name the worksheet distances(mine).

We are now ready to examine the relationship between the true distances and your guessed distances. The most useful graphical tool for examining the relationship between two variables is the **scatter plot**. A scatter plot of guessed distances versus true distances locates a point on the Cartesian plane for each landmark, with the point's coordinates given by (horizontal coordinate, vertical coordinate) (true distance, guessed distance). Note that when we say "guessed distance versus true distance" we mean that guessed distances are to be on the vertical axis. We can make a scatter plot, with an added 45° line to help you judge whether you are an accurate guesser, as follows:

1. Under the **Graph** menu, select **Scatter Plot**. A Scatter Plot dialog box similar to Figure 5.2 will appear.
2. Click in the box to the right of **Vertical axis** and type **Guess**.
3. Click in the box to the right of **Horizontal axis** and type **True**.

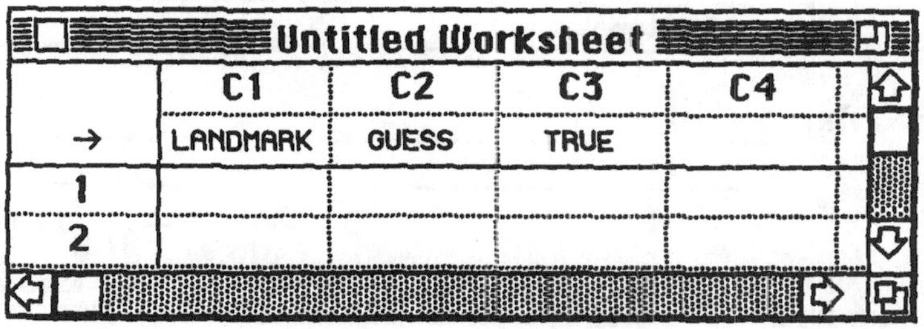

FIGURE 5.1
Variable Names in Untitled Worksheet

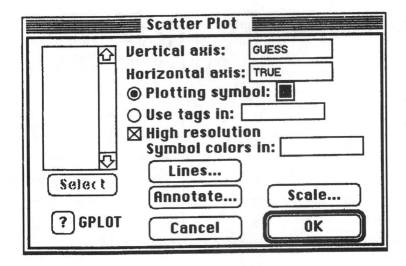

FIGURE 5.2
Scatter Plot Dialog Box

4. Click **Annotate**. An Annotate Scatter Plot dialog box similar to Figure 5.3 will appear.

5. Click in the first **Title** box, and type **My Guesses of Distances to 12 Landmarks**.

6. Click in the first **Footnotes** box and type your name.

7. Click in the **Horizontal Axis Label** box and type **True Distance (ft.)**.

8. Click in the **Vertical Axis Label** box and type **Guess (ft.)**.

9. Click **OK** to end the Annotate command.

10. To add a 45° line to the plot, click **Lines**. A Lines dialog box similar to Figure 5.4 will appear.

11. Click in the first box under **Y column** and type **True**.

12. Click in the first box under **X column** and type **True** again.

13. Click **OK** to end the Lines command.

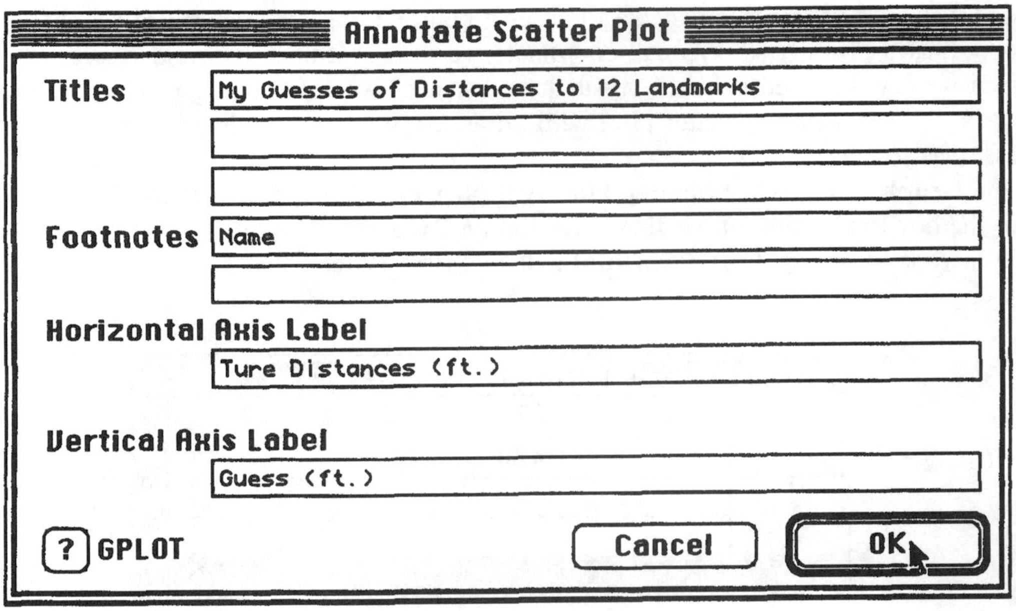

```
┌────────────────────────────────────────────────────────┐
│ ▓▓▓▓▓▓▓      Annotate Scatter Plot      ▓▓▓▓▓▓▓          │
│ ┌──────────────────────────────────────────────────┐   │
│ │ Titles    ┌──────────────────────────────────────┐│   │
│ │           │ My Guesses of Distances to 12 Landmarks ││   │
│ │           └──────────────────────────────────────┘│   │
│ │           ┌──────────────────────────────────────┐│   │
│ │           └──────────────────────────────────────┘│   │
│ │           ┌──────────────────────────────────────┐│   │
│ │           └──────────────────────────────────────┘│   │
│ │                                                   │   │
│ │ Footnotes ┌──────────────────────────────────────┐│   │
│ │           │ Name                                 ││   │
│ │           └──────────────────────────────────────┘│   │
│ │           ┌──────────────────────────────────────┐│   │
│ │           └──────────────────────────────────────┘│   │
│ │                                                   │   │
│ │ Horizontal Axis Label                             │   │
│ │           ┌──────────────────────────────────────┐│   │
│ │           │ Ture Distances (ft.)                 ││   │
│ │           └──────────────────────────────────────┘│   │
│ │                                                   │   │
│ │ Vertical Axis Label                               │   │
│ │           ┌──────────────────────────────────────┐│   │
│ │           │ Guess (ft.)                          ││   │
│ │           └──────────────────────────────────────┘│   │
│ │                                                   │   │
│ │ [?] GPLOT              [ Cancel ]   (( OK ))       │   │
│ └──────────────────────────────────────────────────┘   │
└────────────────────────────────────────────────────────┘
```

FIGURE 5.3
Annotate Scatter Plot Dialog Box

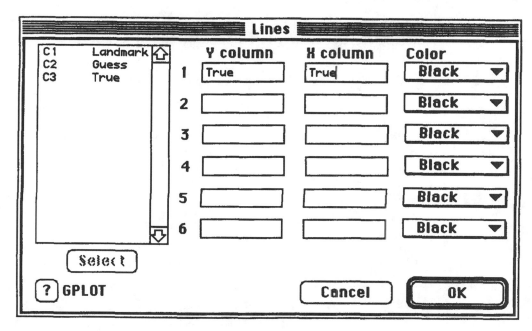

FIGURE 5.4
Lines Dialog Box

14. Click **OK** to end the Scatter Plot command.

The choices in the Lines dialog box are admittedly mysterious, but they tell Minitab to draw a 45° line on the plot. This is because the 45° line is defined by points (x, y) having $y = x$, so we can plot the line simply by using the same variable (any variable) for both X and Y in the Lines command. In this case we used the variable True, but any numeric variable could have been used.

After a short delay, the Gplot 'Guess' 'True' window should open, and you should see your scatter plot with annotations as suggested and the 45° line, analogous to Figure 5.5. Print your scatter plot at this time by selecting **Print Window** under the **File** menu. After you get your printout, quit Minitab by selecting **Quit** under the **File** menu.

STEP 3: CALIBRATION.   Do the points on your own scatter plot lie approximately on a straight line? If so, the relationship between your guessed distances and the true distances is said to be approximately **linear**. Do the points seem to describe a curve? If there seems to be a U-shaped curve, the relationship is said to be **convex**. If it is an inverted U-shape, it is said to be **concave**. How would you describe the relationship shown by the points on your plot?

Ignoring the 45° line, draw the best straight line, smooth convex curve, or smooth concave curve that you can through the center of the point cloud in your scatter plot. Use the straightedge if you decide to draw a straight line. If you draw a curve, make it a smooth curve through the center of the point cloud—don't just connect the dots. What you have just done is sketched an approximate regression line or curve, a line or curve that helps to summarize the relationship between the two variables.

If this sketched line or curve lies below the 45° line, your guesses tend to underestimate the true distances to landmarks. We would then say that as a guesser you are **negatively biased**. This is the case for the majority of guessers, including the one whose data is shown in Figure 5.5. Some guessers are fairly accurate on the average with their guesses. That is, the points on their scatter plot tend to fall along the 45° line. We say they are **unbiased** guessers. A rare few individuals tend to overestimate; the points on their scatter plot tend to lie above the 45° line. We say they are **positively biased** guessers. Of course, one's ability as a guesser may vary from situation to situation.

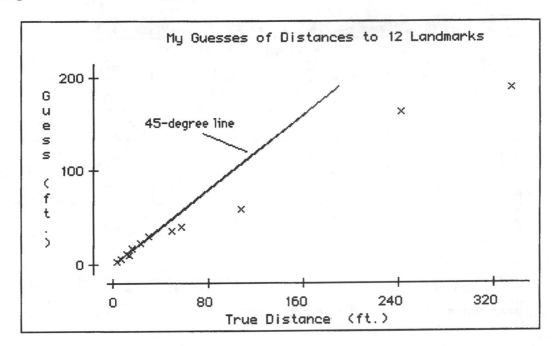

FIGURE 5.5
Scatter Plot with 45° Line for Example Data

If we consider you, as a distance guesser, to be a new sort of measuring instrument, we can use the sketched regression line or curve on your plot to **calibrate** you. Calibration is an activity or operation for correcting bias in a measuring device and is an example of one very important use for regression experiments. We will say you are calibrated as a distance guesser if you always adjust your initial guess in the following way:

1. Locate the point on the vertical axis of your plot that corresponds to your initial guess.
2. With a straightedge, draw a horizontal line from that point across the plot until the line touches the sketched regression line or curve.
3. From that point, drop a vertical line to the horizontal axis.
4. The adjusted guess is the reading on the horizontal axis found at the end of this vertical line.

Figure 5.6 shows the result of using the calibration to adjust an initial guess of 100 feet, using the example data from Figure 5.5. The calibration leads to an adjusted guessed distance of 160 feet in this case, an increase of 60 feet from the initial guess. This makes a lot of sense under the observation that this guesser was negatively biased; if the initial guess is 100 feet, it should be adjusted upward.

Now, you try it. For the mystery 13th landmark, the one whose true distance was not measured, use your guessed distance and your sketched regression line or curve to arrive at an adjusted guessed distance. Your instructor will tell you the true distance. Did the calibration adjustment improve your guess?

STEP 4: GROUP DATA ANALYSIS.   Write your name on your Table 5.1 and give it to the instructor. While he or she is getting organized, choose a Macintosh, launch Minitab, and name the first three columns of a new worksheet **Landmark**, **Guess**, and **True** as you did in Step 2 for your own data. Save the empty worksheet on a diskette as you did in Step 2, except name it **Distances(class)**.

The instructor will then read data to you in groups of three values. The values read will be the landmark number, guessed distance, and true distance for several randomly chosen guessers for each landmark. Type these carefully in rows in your data set as the instructor reads them to you. When all the data has been entered and double-checked, you must again save the complete data set by pushing <**Command**>+**S**.

Make a scatter plot of guessed distances versus true distances for the class's data as you did in Step 2, but modify the title to be **Class's Guesses of Distances to 12 Landmarks.** You'll be asked to comment on this graph in the writing assignment for this session.

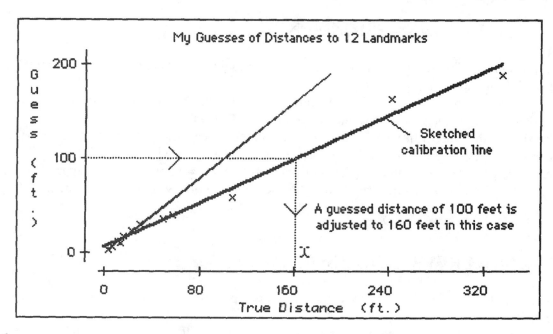

FIGURE 5.6
Calibration with Example Data

Print your scatter plot by selecting **Print Window** under the **File** menu. Then quit Minitab by selecting **Quit** under the **File** menu and, if necessary, copy the data set **Distances(class)** to each computer partner's diskette, as described near the end of Session 1.

Parting Glances

In this experiment, we used an informal regression line or curve to calibrate a "measuring instrument," in this case, a human being guessing distances between objects. A more important calibration exercise was performed to improve verification of nuclear weapons tests under the Threshold Test Ban Treaty between the United States and Russia (Picard and Bryson, 1992). After the cold war, the two countries embarked on an effort to make on site yield measurements of each other's nuclear tests, for the purpose of calibrating a monitoring system based on seismic measurements. That is, there are two measurements of a nuclear explosion's force:
1. The onsite measurement
2. The seismic disturbance as measured by a seismograph halfway around the world

Once a reliable calibration method is constructed, each country should be able to monitor the other's nuclear tests using at-home seismic measurements, instead of traveling overseas to make onsite measurements. Note that this difficult onsite measurement will become impossible if relations between the United States and Russia return to cold war levels. Also, as more is learned about the relationships between the two measuring methods, nuclear testing in countries other than Russia may be more reliably monitored in the United States by seismologists.

Reference

Picard, Richard, and Bryson, Maurice (1992), "Calibrated Seismic Verification of the Threshold Test Ban Treaty," *Journal of the American Statistical Association* 87, 293–299.

EXTENDED WRITING ASSIGNMENT

Refer to Appendix 1, "Technical Report Writing," and Appendix 2, "Technical Report Writing Checklist," for guidance on format and style for your report.

Write a report describing the measuring and calibration experiment. The report should include:
1. A clear description of the experiment, including how the data was collected
2. A discussion of the pattern in your own guesses, including at least one calibration calculation
3. A discussion of the patterns you see in the guesses of the class as a whole

Use the terms provided under the "Statistical Concepts" section wherever they are appropriate. Incorporate your scatter plots into your report. Use answers to the short-answer writing assignment to help guide your discussion.

SHORT ANSWER WRITING ASSIGNMENT

All answers should be complete sentences. Include scatter plots of your data and the class's data with this assignment.
1. What factors might cause your ability as a guesser to vary from situation to situation?
2. Do the points on your own scatter plot lie approximately on a straight line, a convex curve, a concave curve, or in some other pattern?
3. Do your own distance guesses tend to be negatively biased, positively biased, or approximately unbiased?
4. What was your initial guess for the mystery 13th landmark? What was your adjusted guess after calibration? Did the adjustment lead to a more accurate guess in this case?
5. Is the relationship between guessed distances and true distances for the class as a whole approximately linear, convex, concave, or something else?
6. If we obtained guessed distances by randomly picking a class member and then asking him or her to guess a distance, the class's scatter plot is appropriate for calibrating this measurement. Is this measurement negatively biased, positively biased, or something else?
7. What notable differences do you see between the scatter plot of your guesses and the plot for the group as a whole?

A Companion Piece for the *Elementary Statistics Laboratory Manual*

Sneh Gulati
Florida International University

Introduction

A part of the Florida State University System, Florida International University (FIU) was established in 1965, and began classes here in 1972 with about 6,000 students enrolled in various programs. Since then, the University has grown rapidly; it now offers more than 220 degrees to about 30,000 students. When the University was founded, statistics, computer science, and mathematics were all housed together as the Department of Mathematical Sciences. The Department split in 1987 and now statistics is a separate department with ten tenured and tenure-track faculty and two instructors/lecturers. While most of the courses offered in Statistics at FIU are service courses, the department does offer a baccalaureate degree in statistics, graduating an average of five students per year.

The Elementary Statistics Laboratory has been offered twice at FIU: once in Fall 1993 and then again in Fall 1997. The Lab is offered as an optional fourth hour with STA 3163, the first semester of a two semester sequence in Statistical Methods. The Lab was first offered as an experimental course in Fall 1993 with an enrollment of eight students. The majority of the students who registered for the lab in 1993 were statistics majors. In 1997, six students registered for the lab; two of these were statistics majors and the rest math education majors.

The class uses the *Elementary Statistics Laboratory Manual* (Macintosh Version) by John D. Spurrier, Don Edwards, and Lori A. Thombs as the course textbook. The class meets for two hours once a week, and during each meeting the students perform a preassigned experiment from the manual. Of the seventeen experiments in the manual, we have used approximately twelve each time, and in all but the first experiment, the student has to collect data and then analyze it on the Macintosh computer using Minitab. In most of the sessions the students work in teams. The class meets at a central Macintosh lab in the University.

Conducting Lab Sessions

Most of the sessions are easy to conduct. The manual gives students clear instructions on data collection and analysis, but we still advise instructors teaching the course for the first time to consult the accompanying "Instructor's Resource Manual" for additional pointers. In general, sessions begin with a short lecture about the concepts emphasized by that day's experiment. Even though students should have read the session before coming to class, the instructor should remind them how the data will be collected, discuss any problems that they may encounter during the experiment, and tell them how to avoid the problems. At the conclusion of the data analysis, the instructor should lead a class discussion concerning the results of the experiment and the problems encountered during the course of the session. This gives students an opportunity to voice their opinions about the lab, and gives the instructor an indication of how much the students have learned. After each session, we assign students one of two types of assignments: a short answer assignment or an extended writing assignment. The short answer assignments test the students' understanding of what they learned in the session. While the extended writing assignments do this as well, they also help students to improve their technical writing skills. In the extended writing assignments, the students write reports on the session, complete with an abstract, materials and methods used, and the accompanying statistical analysis. Appendices 1 and 2 in the manual give detailed instructions on how to write such reports. Even with these instructions, most students have difficulty writing a good report the first time. It normally takes about three extended writing assignments for students to completely grasp the art of technical writing.

Success of the Labs

The Lab has proved to be a great success and is certainly the way of the future. The basic purpose of statistics is to make inferences about a population from sample data. This involves designing experiments to collect and analyze data. In other words, statistics is a field science and should be taught as such. Traditionally, we have taught introductory statistics courses in a classroom, with chalk and a blackboard being our teaching tools. As a result, we have denied students practical training and the opportunity to appreciate the significance of the inferential techniques they have learned. Lab courses, such as the ones offered at FIU, open up new opportunities by which students learn how to apply the concepts discussed in a classroom. Students come to realize that statistics is not a "scary monster" that has no use in the real world, but rather an invaluable tool, which they will use in every walk of life. A number of times, when we offered a new topic in STA 3163, the students enrolled in the Lab had already performed an experiment based on that topic! Their excitement on seeing a topic on the blackboard that they had already explored in lab was recognized by everyone else in the class. Lab students also appeared to have a better rapport with the teacher and certainly had good ideas whenever there were class discussions in STA 3163. Since most sessions in the manual require students

to work in teams, the Lab students also learned the skills of working in groups and communicating with others.

"Do's" and "Don'ts" of Individual Experiments

We now give some specific pointers about the individual sessions. We start with the "do's" and "don'ts" for the excerpted session—"Real and Perceived Distances"—based on our experiences at FIU. In this session, the student uses simple linear regression to predict the true distance to certain landmarks. The predictor variable is the guessed distance to each of the landmarks.

As mentioned earlier, we start the lab with a lecture on the concepts of predicting the value of a dependent variable on the basis of one or more independent variables. The students have read the session before coming to lab, so the lecture can be short. We next take the students outside to guess the distances to the thirteen landmarks. We have chosen the landmarks well in advance with an assortment of close and distant landmarks. When choosing the landmarks, make sure that there are no obstacles on the way to the landmarks, so that students can measure the distances to the landmarks by walking in straight lines.

Once the students have guessed the distances, we break them into groups of three to measure the true distances to the landmarks. The Instructor's Manual suggests that students learn interpersonal skills best when they face oft-changing team assignments. Hence, we choose groups comprising students who have not worked together previously. We also designate the role that each member should play in the team; otherwise each team member will want to be "the eyes," which is the easiest role. While students are measuring the distances, watch them very carefully and make sure that they are playing out their role responsibly, otherwise they will make many measurement errors. The manual describes two of the common errors; another common error is that students do not always walk a straight line towards distant landmarks. It is the responsibility of the "base" to make sure that this error does not occur, but the instructor should keep an eye on the students as well. Despite the possibility of these errors, students instead of the instructor should take the measurements since this experiment is one of the first ones that establishes the need for precision and interactive teamwork. Depending on the distances of the landmarks from the reference points, the entire data-collection process can take between 45 and 60 minutes.

The data analysis usually proceeds very smoothly and the results of the experiment are as expected. The regression lines have always been linear, and students find that they can predict the distance to the 13th landmark quite accurately using the calibrated line. Although the amount of bias varies, most of our students have tended to be negatively biased.

We conclude the session by sharing everyone's results with the class. Even though the results of the experiment turn out to be as predicted in the manual, students are constantly amazed at how well the guessed distances can predict true distances. Without a doubt, this has been one of the most interesting and successful sessions at FIU. Everyone enjoys working outdoors and as stated earlier, this is the first experiment to truly emphasize the importance of interactive group work.

Below is a commentary on selected sessions, which have produced varying degrees of success.

Session 7: "A Question of Taste."

Students perform a single blind experiment to test whether less than 50% of consumers prefer a bargain cola to a highly advertised cola. The session introduces several important topics: how to design an experiment, randomization, and most importantly, the concept of hypothesis testing and *p*-values.

Hypothesis testing is perhaps the most important topic in any introductory statistics course and can also be the most difficult to teach. When teaching the topic in a classroom, instructors often find it difficult to relate the normal distribution to test statistics, rejection regions, and *p*-values. The student invariably finds the first lecture too abstract. This lab experiment takes away the mystery from hypothesis testing. Since students are actually conducting the experiment, they have no trouble stating the null and the alternative hypotheses. They also see clearly what values the test statistic should take in order to support the alternative hypothesis. Finally, students understand that the test statistic has a binomial distribution under the null hypothesis and, by looking at a graph of the distribution, they can easily understand that a small *p*-value should imply rejection of the null hypothesis.

This experiment should definitely conclude with a class discussion. A discussion can reinforce the concepts of hypothesis testing and can also lead to the raising of other important statistical issues. For example, students notice that some participants do not have a preference but still have to pick one cola over the other. Usually when this happens, participants tend to pick the last cola they tasted and students are apt to notice this. If students bring this issue up in the class discussion, then the instructor has the

perfect introduction to the "multinomial random variable," where the third category becomes "no preference."

Session 8: "Sampling and Variation in Manufactured Products."

Here each team draws a random sample of 36 tacks from a box of 1/2 inch carpet tacks, and measures the length of the tacks in the sample. The experiment illustrates the fact that each tack is slightly different from the others and that none of the carpet tacks actually measures 1/2 inch in length. By calculating the mean length of the tacks, students notice that this quantity is closer to 1/2 inch, pointing to the fact that the box is actually advertising the average length of the tacks. The experiment is very useful for engineering students since it demonstrates that every manufacturing process exhibits random variation. Therefore, at the end of the session, the instructor can give the students a short lecture on random processes and talk about the various probability distributions that are used to model product lifetimes. When conducting the experiment, make sure that the members in the team know that only one of them will be taking the measurements. The manual does not clearly spell this out so that students tend to divide up the task of making measurements, which increases the variability in the sample.

Session 9: "Exploring Statistical Theory through Computer Simulation."

This session is extremely important because it illustrates the Central Limit Theorem and its role in statistical inference. Here the students simulate 600 samples of 20 observations from the standard normal distribution, the standard exponential distribution, the *t*-distribution, and the uniform distribution. They then calculate the sample median and the sample mean of each sample and plot them in a histogram to study their distributions. Using both the sample median and sample mean demonstrates how the mean is less variable than the median. They also see that for a sample size of 20, the histograms of the statistics are symmetric when the samples come from a symmetric distribution, whereas for samples from the exponential distribution, the histogram is slightly skewed, suggesting the need for a larger sample for normality of the test statistic. One might also want to use the session to point out to the students that a lot of present-day statistical research is done using computer simulations.

Session 10: "Improving Product Performance with Planned Experiments."

In this session, we give each team two balsa wood airplanes, a paper clip, and scissors. Students pick two factors at two levels each using the materials provided (e.g., presence and absence of paper clips on the wings, the length of the wings, the angle of take-off, etc.) that could affect the mean flight distance of the planes. After choosing the factors, they conduct a planned experiment to find out which level of each factor maximizes the flight distance. Overall, this is a very useful session that makes students think about the concept of designing experiments. One serious problem with this experiment, however, is the wind. If it is windy outside, the results of the experiment will not be reliable. Hence, with this experiment, the instructor should always have an alternative plan in case of bad weather. Also, since the concept of interaction can be difficult for students, we recommend that the instructor give a brief lecture on interaction before starting the session. The instructor should clearly explain how in the presence of interaction, one cannot separate the effects of the two factors and in this situation, one must find the best "treatment combination."

Sessions that have not worked well at FIU have been Session 3 and Session 6. In Session 3, "Author, Author," the students are supplied with the first page of a text written by one of the authors of the text, whose identity is hidden. Students are supposed to count various discriminators (e.g., average sentence length, average number of times words like 'a', 'an', 'the', etc. are used in a page) and then compare these counts to discriminators in the first page of other chapters for which the authors are known. Students use dot plots and polygon plots to help identify the author. Although the data collection and analysis pose no problem for the students, they do not see the usefulness of statistics in this session. The session uses no formal inference, and the results are not always clear cut. Most students leave the lab wondering what, if anything, they have accomplished. The same problem occurs in Session 6, "Collecting Data Over Time." Here, each team is assigned to different intersections around the campus in order to count the number of cars that pass by in 60 consecutive 15-second intervals. Students plot these counts in a time series using Minitab. The students then look for trends and cycles in the time series and also learn how to use lags to smooth the time series. The students really enjoyed collecting the data and learning a little about time series, but the problem was the inability to completely understand time series. Concepts of lags and moving average smoothing are difficult for undergraduates taking their first course in statistics. Moreover, students also had trouble understanding how the line graph could be used for predicting future observations. Hence, this is another session along with Session 3 that may be avoided.

Conclusion

As stated earlier, the Lab has been a tremendous success at FIU. Students enjoy the course, gain valuable practical experience, and start thinking of statistics as "user friendly." The time has come for us to incorporate this or similar lab courses into all our introductory statistics courses.

Section 4
Textbooks

Certainly the most fundamental of resources for teaching statistics is the textbook. We were tempted to use the phrase "old-fashioned textbook" in the previous sentence, but as you shall see when you read the two articles in this section, some texts deserve that appellation more than others, and we should approach the textbook decision with respect and care.

Robert Hayden of Plymouth State gives us a framework for evaluating and selecting a textbook for the introductory course. He writes the article keeping in mind his audience: mathematicians teaching statistics. It should come as no surprise that a driving force behind his definition of a high quality textbook is the book's use of and treatment of real data.

Katherine Halvorsen of Smith College provides a similar service for us regarding the evaluation of textbooks for the probability and mathematical statistics course. Halvorsen asks readers to take a good look at the goals of their probability and mathematical statistics course because these goals will play heavily into the textbook decision, and her article guides us through the process of making that decision.

Advice to Mathematics Teachers on Evaluating Introductory Statistics Textbooks

Robert W. Hayden
Plymouth State College

Introduction

Here's a little quiz for you. There are no right or wrong answers, and I won't even ask you to tally up a score at the end. It won't tell you anything really important, like whether you are compatible with the person you've been living with for 20 years, but your answers may help you to follow this essay.

> How much mathematical training should a person have in order to *teach* a non-remedial, first-year mathematics course?

> How much statistical training should a person have in order to *teach* a first-year statistics course?

Perhaps it's just paranoia, but many statisticians detect a discipline-centric bias in answers to such questions. As evidence, try to find a discipline in which more college students are taught by people with no degrees in the subject than they are in statistics. I do not raise this point to make you feel bad. The fact that you are reading this volume shows that you feel a need to learn more about the subject you are teaching, and statisticians welcome you with open arms. My real point is a corollary:

> How much mathematical training should a person have in order to *write* a textbook for a non-remedial, first-year mathematics course?

> How much statistical training should a person have in order to *write* a textbook for a first-year statistics course?

Why do I need to read an essay on how to choose a textbook?

The following comments were made by "a mathematician who . . . got slung into the statistical pool by way of a swimming lesson" [7].

> While there are good and bad mathematics texts, I've never seen a pure math textbook with actual errors throughout. Maybe the occasional lapse from Bourbakiste rigor, or a folktale about Galois passed off as history—but that's about the worst. (This is not to say that some of them are not very bad indeed as textbooks.) However, in statistics, I have learned to treat the very factuality of textbooks with suspicion. Most of them are fine in this regard, and the good ones are pedagogically better than almost anything in pure mathematics. But in the three years in which I have taught stats, from three textbooks, I have had more occasions to tell students "The book says this

...please cross it out, and write in a correction, because the book is wrong" than in dozens of math courses. I do not do this on matters of taste, but only when there is an actual error.

The author goes on to wonder why this is so. Perhaps the reason is that introductory statistics textbooks are often written by people with little or no training in statistics. This is very different from the situation in mathematics, at least at the college level. You would expect the author of a calculus text to have a Ph.D. in mathematics and errors to be limited to typos. Failure of the author to grasp the content covered in the textbook would be most unusual. (But then, consider what calculus books would be like if most students took calculus outside the Mathematics Department.) Unfortunately, gross errors are not unusual in elementary statistics textbooks. What is even worse, these books sell. Indeed, they are often among the best selling texts! The reason textbooks written by people who do not know much about statistics sell is that many teachers of statistics do not know much about statistics either, and these two groups suffer a fatal attraction for one another. This explains why errors can go undetected for years: real statisticians do not read these books.

For example, consider this problem on the chi-squared goodness of fit test taken from a popular introductory statistics textbook of nearly twenty years ago.

> Jimmy Nut Company advertises that their nut mix contains 40% cashews, 15% brazil nuts, 20% almonds, and only 25% peanuts. The truth in advertising investigators took a random sample (of size 20 lb) of the nut mix and found the distribution to be as follows:

Cashews	Brazil Nuts	Almonds	Peanuts
6 lb	3 lb	5 lb	6 lb

> At the 0.01 level of significance, is the claim made by Jimmy Nuts true?

A student using this textbook observed that the calculated value of chi-squared for this problem, and thus its significance, could be made to take on any value whatever by a suitable choice of units. For example, converting the weights to metric tons makes Jimmy an honest man, while converting them to nanograms produces the largest chi-squared value ever seen by man or beast. The student's teacher posted a query on the internet asking for an explanation of this paradox. The quote you read above about errors in statistics textbooks was a part of the discussion.

The problem here is that the chi-squared goodness of fit test applies only to categorical (discrete) data. It compares the actually observed *counts* in each category to the counts we would expect if the hypothesis being tested were true. Counts are unitless, and the apparent paradox only arises if you misapply the technique to measurement (continuous) data. You might think that such a gross error would be an outlier, but there is another, similar problem in the same section. You might also expect such an error to be quickly spotted and removed, but the same two problems still appeared in subsequent editions of the same text, published years later. And, the existence of further editions suggests that this text has been successful in the marketplace.

Look for an author who knows more than you do

Far from being an isolated error, Jimmy and his nut company is a symptom of a much deeper problem. Statistics is fundamentally and primarily concerned with analyzing real data. Yet many introductory statistics textbooks continue to be algorithmic cookbooks that mainly offer practice in plugging unreal numbers into formulas. Of course, if your goal is to train students to carry out the computations of statistics (without statistical software), then it really does not matter if the numbers you give them are made up or real. And if the context of the data is also a fiction, then it does not matter whether it is realistic, improbable, or absurd. However, if you are trying to teach the *concepts* of statistics and to help students learn to apply those concepts to real-world problems, asking students to apply a technique that works only for categorical data to measurement data is a mortal sin, a special case of the sin of teaching students to mindlessly apply computational algorithms to numbers. (Note the appropriate word is "numbers," not "data"!) Since computers can do this much more cheaply, and since this is not a task worth doing anyway, such training is a negative contribution to the human enterprise. The problem here is not one of isolated errors, but of a profound misunderstanding of the nature of statistics as a discipline.

While not all of the failings of such texts are as simple and clear cut as Jimmy and his nut company, the failings are widespread. The long-term solution to amateur statistics textbooks is adequate training for people (including textbook authors!) teaching statistics. In the meantime, we have to face the fact that many people who do not already have this training will be called upon to teach statistics. The goal of this paper is to help people "slung into the statistics pool" select a textbook that will be more like a life jacket than ballast.

So, let us suppose that your department chair told you that you will be teaching an introductory statistics class next fall. It's often the case that you have been selected not because of your extensive training in statistics, but because you are at the bottom of the pecking order. This assignment algorithm sends a clear message about how your superiors view statistics, so you seek counsel elsewhere. Since you studied statistics long ago or not at all, you may not notice an error such as applying chi-squared to weights. How can you select a textbook that will lead you and your students down the path of truth rather than error? Statistician Paul Velleman [17] has said:

> If I found myself teaching a law course, I would certainly choose a text by the best lawyer I could find, not one by a friend who also was stuck in the same situation.

Although mathematicians tend to gravitate toward texts written by other mathematicians, such textbooks will re-inforce both your strengths and your weaknesses. I suggest that you find a text that is strong in the areas where you are weak—probably in the actual use of statistics with real-world data. You can easily fill in any weaknesses in the mechanics of getting the calculations done. There are no sure ways of finding such a complementary textbook, but here are some pointers. They admit of exceptions, but they are a start.

First, it would be wonderful if a group of qualified statis-ticians, with an interest in good pedagogy, got together and evaluated the current crop of textbooks and offered their recommendations to the world. As a matter of fact, this has already happened. Such a group recommended text-books for the initial offering of the Advanced Placement Test in Statistics [5, 6], and their recommendations are ap-pended to this paper. It is interesting to note how short the list is! Although most "missing" textbooks are missing for good reasons, a few good books may be missing only be-cause they were published after the list went to press, or because they did not match the AP syllabus.

You may also wish to read published textbook reviews. Unfortunately, textbook reviews vary in quality by almost as much as do statistics textbooks. Too many are just a rou-tine recitation of the table of contents. Certainly you would want to look at reviews in *statistics* journals. One of these is George Cobb's classic, "Introductory Textbooks: A Frame-work for Evaluation (A Comparison of 16 Books)" [4]. I asked myself what made Cobb's paper a classic, and why would anyone feel a need to update it? Beyond its style and wit, the paper is a classic because it provides a frame-work for evaluating textbooks, rather than merely carrying out an evaluation. I think it is seen as dated only because it applied that framework to sixteen textbooks, most of which

are now either out of print or survive in much later edi-tions. So, in this paper I will try to concentrate on the evaluation procedure, citing a few textbooks as examples, but not trying to offer thorough reviews of any. I will try not to overlap too much with the content of Cobb's paper, which is still essential reading. Finally, I will aim my com-ments not at Cobb's audience (professional statisticians), but rather at people who usually teach mathematics rather than statistics.

An evaluation of a textbook might start with an eval-uation of the author's statistical expertise. The danger, of course, is that you may feel more of a sense of kinship with the fellow sufferer than with the expert! However, the less you know about statistics, the more essential it is that the textbook you choose be a reliable guide. The textbook (or its advertisements) may give an author profile. Does it concentrate on how qualified the author is, or on what a great person he or she is? Does it mention any degrees or training in statistics? Lacking that, the text may at least give an affiliation for the author. On the whole, a member of a Statistics Department at a large university is very likely to have solid credentials in statistics. Another indicator is whether the author is a member of the American Statistical Association. If you are an ASA member (and you should be), you can access the member list at www.amstat.org.

In addition to questions of how much training authors have, there is a question of the *quality* of the training. Did they study statistics recently in a leading statistics depart-ment? Or did they take such a course 20 years ago and keep up to date ever since? Or did they take a course 20 years ago that was itself already 20 years out of date, and learn nothing new since? The ASA membership list *sometimes* gives degrees and dates. The *Current Index to Statistics* can tell you if an author has published beyond the introductory statistics level. Again, many fine teachers do not publish much, but publication does suggest that the statistics com-munity thinks the author's ideas are worthwhile.

Look for data in the exposition

After evaluating the expertise of a textbook's author, turn to the text itself. A statistics textbook written by a work-ing statistician is likely to reflect familiarity with current practice in statistics. Certainly your course should do so. For that reason, it may be helpful to have some bench-mark items to look for. Fortunately, we have a landmark to guide us here: the revolution brought about in statistics during the 1960's by John Tukey and others. One part of this revolution was the development of what came to be known as exploratory data analysis (or EDA) [See 15 or

16 for background on EDA]. Often you can get an idea of up-to-dateness by seeing how a text handles EDA.

Some people characterize modern data-analytic statistics in terms of the four R's:

- residuals,
- robustness,
- resistance,
- re-expression.

Checking for these (or synonyms such as "transformations" for "re-expression") in the index can give an idea of the presence and pervasiveness of modern views in a text. To illustrate, Table 1 gives results for some textbooks on hand that show that even this simple technique decisively discriminates between different classes of textbooks. The books included are *not* a random sample of those available! The first four are the books used by the author in the past decade. However, the choice is not entirely idiosyncratic, as these are also (independently) on the recommended list [6] for the Advanced Placement Test in Statistics. Though they are not the only good textbooks available, they represent the kind of textbook I think you should be seeking. In contrast, the last row of Table 1 represents a composite of several textbooks I would *not* recommend. These lesser texts are here because they have sold well and been through many editions, and often end up on 'short lists' when mathematics teachers choose textbooks for statistics.

In constructing the table, I used the editions available to me at the time; questions of how these books have changed over the years will be discussed later. In the meantime, I will use these textbooks to illustrate a variety of points. After the reference number, the table gives the number of pages in each book's index. The next three numbers give the numbers of pages cited in the index for the EDA topics listed at the top of the table—robustness/resistance, transformations (or re-expressions), and residuals. Note that a book with a relatively short index might be expected to have fewer references to *any* topic.

I also counted index references to "outliers," since "resistance" means resistance to outliers. I also counted the

number of sets of parallel boxplots in each book's chapter on Analysis of Variance to see if boxplots were actually used in the context where they are most appropriate. (This also indicates whether the book encourages the reader to LOOK AT THE DATA!) The last column gives the Euclidean norm for the vector whose components are the entries in the previous five columns, which provides a crude "modernity" index for statistics textbooks. The four exemplary texts are fairly similar—certainly in comparison with the texts in the final row. The apparent outlier [13] has an unusually long index and 92 references on transformations.

The counts in the table give a "quick and dirty" rating system meant for rapid screening. Still, you must use it with care. In the "new math" era, many college mathematics textbooks sprouted a "Chapter 0" on sets. This was supposed to integrate the material in the rest of the book, but as sets were never mentioned in the rest of the book, it is not clear how this could happen. Similarly, some of the weaker statistics textbooks have an early section on "current" topics, such as stem-and-leaf displays and boxplots, but then fail to use the tools developed there when they are needed later. For example, a chapter on analysis of variance should certainly include many examples of parallel boxplots, the most appropriate tool for visually comparing the centers of several groups. (This is why these were counted in the table above.) The newer exploratory techniques may also be used to check assumptions underlying an inferential technique. For example, parallel boxplots can also be used to check the ANOVA assumption of equal variances.

In general, make sure a textbook *mentions* assumptions and teaches students to *check* them rather than to *make* them. Cobb [6, p. 329] says he finds "it useful to distinguish *exploratory techniques*, such as stem-and-leaf diagrams and boxplots, from *exploratory attitudes*" such as looking at the data (or residuals), checking for outliers or violations of assumptions, or considering the possibility of transforming the data. "The techniques are relatively unimportant but the attitudes are essential [6, p. 329]."

To illustrate Cobb's distinction, let us take a stroll through specific sections of some of these texts. I will use the sections comparing the means of two groups as an example. This is elementary enough to be in virtually every textbook or course syllabus, but complicated enough that just about everything you would want to take into account in evaluating a text comes up. I strongly suggest that you grab copies of Moore and McCabe [12] and Siegel and Morgan [14], plus any other texts you wish to evaluate, and follow along.

Before undertaking any inferential procedures, an investigator should *look at the data*. Siegel and Morgan get the

Ref.	Pages	Rob/Res	Trans.	Resids.	Outliers	Par.BP	Norm
[11]	6	6	2	13	24	6	28.7
[12]	6	21	12	>19	16	4	34.9
[13]	13	13	92	15	19	6	96.2
[14]	7	6	18	7	13	11	26.4
[??]	3-5	0-1	0	0	0-1	0	0-1.4

TABLE 1
A comparison of textbooks on coverage of EDA topics.

prize for doing this. Their chapter on comparing two groups opens with an extensive analysis of several data sets. They point out that comparing the centers of two sets of numbers is much easier if they differ *only* in center. In particular, it is easier if the two data distributions have the same shape and the same variability. They give examples of a variety of situations with similar or dissimilar shapes and variability, and they show how transformations may be used to achieve similar shapes and/or variabilities. An even more extensive discussion of these issues opens their chapter on comparing several groups. These discussions are worth reading no matter what textbook you adopt.

After description comes inference. Older texts introduce "large sample" (based on the normal distribution) and "small sample" (based on the t distribution) techniques. This terminology is a confusing anachronism. Historically, techniques for large samples based on the Central Limit Theorem and the normal distribution were developed first, while the t distribution was developed later (1908) to correct for errors made when the sample standard deviation is used to estimate the population standard deviation. Although such estimation is usual, the errors introduced are greatest for small samples, and so statisticians trained before 1908 tended to see the t methods as "corrections" to familiar techniques rather than a more exact replacement. Among the books discussed here, Moore and McCabe mention, but then dismiss, the "large sample" technique (without using that confusing name) while Siegel and Morgan discuss *only* the "small sample" procedure.

In carrying out inference comparing the means of two independent groups, the computations will be somewhat simpler if we assume that the two samples come from populations with the same variance, and pool data from the two samples to estimate this common variance. This was relevant in the days of hand calculations, but now most statisticians prefer *not* to make this assumption. From our list, only the Moore books [15,16] agree. (If the computations are too arduous, use statistical software. The preferred method has been the default in Minitab for many, many years.)

Whatever procedure you use, it will have been derived under certain hypotheses or "assumptions". Moore and Mc-Cabe [15, p. 509] are wonderfully direct about this:

The results of t procedures are exactly correct only when the population is normally distributed. Real populations are never exactly normal. The usefulness of the t procedures in practice therefore depends on how strongly they are affected by nonnormality.

Because of this, we need to do two things when we make an inference. We need to assess possible violations of the assumptions, and we need to know how much we can get away with. Moore and McCabe probably do best at the latter [see 16, pp. 509–510, 538, 561–563].

The other three exemplary books in Table 1 also do well at assessing violations. The others gathered in the final row have not a single data display among them. They all use the hypothesis test technique that assumes equal variances in the two groups, and two recommend a preliminary F-test on the two variances. Moore and McCabe explain [16, pp. 557–558] why the F-test is *not* a good idea, and provide a wonderful quote on the subject from George Box.

Now that we have an idea of what should appear in these sections, we can look at how some of the weaker texts get updated. Later editions of weak texts usually tack on some exploratory techniques or terminology but refrain from adopting exploratory attitudes.

For example, a new edition of one text in the last row now has Euclidean norm of 3.3 as a result of some passing references in the index. However, it *still* recommends the preliminary F-test when comparing two independent means. The new edition contains a single set of parallel boxplots in the chapter on comparing two groups. The boxplots are of a simplified kind that does not explicitly flag outliers. However, it is quite clear that there is one—a point that falls eight standard deviations above the mean! The author effectively deletes this from the boxplots before analyzing them, but retains it in the data when doing the hypothesis test! (In addition, proper boxplots would have revealed that both groups have more modest low outliers as well, and a histogram of the data for one group that appears hundreds of pages earlier suggests the group is strongly skewed toward low values.) What purpose the displays serve is not made clear to the reader. As used here, they serve no purpose whatever. The many ways in which the data seem to fail to match the underlying assumptions are simply ignored.

A recent edition of another text included in the last row also adds a few passing references in the index and so now has a norm of 3.0. There is virtually no change in the sections on comparing two or more groups of measurements: variances are pooled (with no F-test), no data are plotted, and instead of checking the ANOVA assumptions they declare by fiat at the top of the problem set: "In each problem assume that the distributions are normal and have approximately the same population standard deviation." In doing a hypothesis test comparing two groups, the authors refer back to earlier discussions of the roles of t and z in testing hypotheses about the mean of a sample drawn from a normal distribution. The earlier edition has a reasonable discussion of the fact that the test statistic has a normal distribution when calculated using the population standard deviation, but that replacing it with the sample standard deviation will give different numerical values with a different t distribution. In the later edition, this is replaced with the incredible claim that it is the sampling distribution *of the mean* (or difference in means) that changes shape depending on whether we know the population standard deviation. I view this as an error comparable in seriousness to a calculus textbook that confuses function multiplication with function composition. (On a good note, I heard as this article went to press that an even more recent edition of this text has given Jimmy a well-deserved retirement from his nut company.)

The new edition of another last row text has exactly the same "length" as the old, though there are some improvements in details. The preliminary F-test is no longer recommended, and the preferred t-test is presented, but there are no data displays. The sections on Analysis of Variance include some displays to illustrate the concepts, but no parallel boxplots, no displays using real data, and no displays to check assumptions.

The need to present attitudes as well as techniques is one of many reasons that a good statistics text will include far more words than a typical mathematics textbook. It will give good advice on *when* to use a t-test as well as information on *how* to do a t-test. The sections on robustness cited in Moore and McCabe or the sections on visually comparing two sets of data from Siegel and Morgan are good examples of the type of discussions you should look for. Generally speaking, books that are not really teaching statistics are teaching arithmetic. You can scan a text quickly looking for a balance between concepts and calculation. An exposition that consists of little more than worked examples for the student to emulate is a bad sign. While this approach might be appropriate in a mechanical skills course such as remedial algebra, it is out of place in statistics because the skills being practiced have no value. In real life these computations are carried out by a computer, so there is no need to practice them until you get good at them. Of course, there are places where "hand" (i.e., calculator rather than computer) calculations help the student understand what is going on, but we must be realistic about our audience, and realize there is little evidence that carrying out a calculation adds to most people's understanding of the *meaning* of what was calculated.

For similar reasons, formulas should be few and far between. For many students, formulas are not a path to understanding, but a source of difficulty. While the formula

for the standard error of the sample mean may make it obvious *to you* that the error decreases with increasing sample size, this may not be obvious to your students, and plugging numbers into the formula is not likely to help them see that unless they do it in a very structured exercise directed specifically at that goal. Concrete examples or computer simulations are more likely to be convincing for many students. In any case, the focus should be on concepts rather than calculations. This can sometimes be a difficult change for mathematics teachers.

Another key feature of a text is its discussion of data production. For example, does the book discuss the difference between observational studies and experiments? Does it discuss randomization and sample selection? Measurement? These are key ideas in statistics that cannot be reduced to formulas. For just that reason, you need to see if the book's exercises (and your own exams) ask for verbal responses on such concepts as well as numerical results [9]. The free response sections of the Advanced Placement Test in Statistics provide some good examples of conceptual questions. Some of these as well as other sample problems are available at the College Board website.

It is worth noting that among the four exemplary books in our sample there is strong agreement between the outcomes of evaluating content and evaluating authors. All of the authors are at major universities. In 1989, about the time these books first appeared, all of the authors were ASA members. CIS cites three of the authors for more than the text at hand: Moore has 42 citations and McCabe and Siegel 25 each. The total for *all* the authors in the last row is zero.

Look at the text at three levels

Once you have eliminated the questionable texts, you will find the stack of candidates has shrunken considerably. Next, you might want to check for any unusual constraints on topical coverage. Most of these texts cover pretty much the same topics, but you may have, for example, a commitment to another department to cover a topic that is missing in some of the candidate texts. After that, you may want to consider the *level* of the textbooks remaining.

For our purposes, there are three levels. The first is the *reading* level. Many introductory textbooks are above— sometimes far above—the reading level of their intended audience. Among our exemplary texts, Moore and McCabe [12] is at the highest reading level. I strongly recommend it as a reference for you, but it will be tough going for many students. Siegel's original text [13] is very simply and clearly written. It has a warm, friendly tone, most unusual in a mathematics or statistics textbook, but not surprising if you have met the author. The second edition [14] is nearly as fine. Clarkson and Williams [3] give an empirical report on the reading level of statistics textbooks. Since the issues are not a great deal different from those for mathematics textbooks, I will not say more about them here.

Another kind of level is the *technical* level. This refers to how deeply the text delves into statistical details. For example, Moore and McCabe [12] goes more deeply into these matters than Moore [11]. Generally, the differences are not great among texts aimed at a first course for a general audience. One exception to be wary of is the cookbook in its umpteenth edition that has added every topic users of earlier editions have ever asked for. Some of these may cover far more topics than Moore and McCabe.

The third kind of level is the *mathematical* level. Here mathematicians are at a disadvantage. First, it is easy to underestimate mathematical level when you yourself are very fluent in mathematics. Second, if you have been previously teaching mathematics majors, you may also underestimate the mathematical skills of a typical statistics student. For a general introductory course, these skills tend to be below the skills one sees in a finite mathematics or precalculus student, and way below what one sees in a calculus student. While mathematics in which a student is fluent can be an aid to precise and rapid communication, mathematics a student has to labor through becomes an obstacle to learning rather than an aid. The good news here is that minimal mathematical skills are sufficient, providing your textbook gives non-algebraic explanations of statistics. The text by Siegel [13] uses little or no algebra. In areas where it cannot be avoided, such as working with straight lines and their equations in regression analysis, it reviews the needed algebra. Siegel and Morgan [14] combine the excellent verbal explanations in [13] with optional formulas.

Look for data in the exercises

Even more important than a textbook's exposition are the problems it sets for students.

> Judge a statistics book by its exercises, and you cannot go far wrong! [6, p. 331]

For one thing, this may be the only part of the book that many students ever read. (One thing that good problems should do is encourage the student to read the rest of the text.)

> In judging the exercises, I think one good way to decide what to look for comes from thinking about

the kind of course that has helped to give our subject a bad name [especially among mathematics majors!]. Because statistics has too often been presented as a bag of specialized computational tools, with a morbid emphasis on calculation, it is no wonder that survivors of such courses regard their statistical tools more as instruments of torture than as diagnostic aids in the art and science of data analysis. All too many textbooks of the past have applied their tools to data sets that have little connection to the body of living knowledge—at worst the numbers have been total fictions, at best they have been dismembered fragments of some old scientific cadaver [6, p. 331].

We look for the same things in the problems that we look for in the body of the text. If the exercises do not ask students to look at the data and check assumptions, then anything we say about those issues will be empty preaching.

> How then do you read the vital signs of the exercises to distinguish the living text from the cold corpse? Look for three things: (a) Are the data sets real or fake? (Real statisticians don't analyze fake data.) (b) Does completing an exercise answer an interesting question, or is the number-crunching a dead end in itself? (Real statisticians don't stop with the arithmetic.) (c) What is the ratio of thinking to mere grinding? (Real statisticians think.) [6, p.331]

While there may be places (such as Anscombe's regression examples [1], succinctly discussed in [2, p.8]) in which a skillfully fabricated batch of numbers illustrates a pedagogical point, most made-up "data" serve only to insulate the student (and the author) from contact with real statistical applications. Be wary of an author who is not familiar with enough real data sets to illustrate a textbook.

Why are real data so important? First, it is the subject matter of statistics. A statistics book without data is like a calculus book without the real numbers. Another reason for using real data is to convince students that statistics is used in the real world.

> At the high end are the books in which you know a data set is authentic, and so do your students, because the author gives its source. There is really no excuse for using a data set without acknowledging the people who did the work, and enough authors are now citing sources that I think we should regard a data set as fake if no source is given. [6, p.331]

Devore and Peck [10, pp. 487-520 and 557-576] give 14 examples and 49 exercises involving real problem situations in their coverage of two-group comparisons, complete with references to the scientific literature where the studies appeared. The many books authored or coauthored by Terry Sincich also have an abundance of examples citing real studies.

> Using real data sets (with sources) is important but only part of the story. A data set should not only be real, it should feel that way. [6, p.331]

At one extreme, consider these flagrantly unreal problem situations:

> Professor Roundhead claims that only 35% of the students at Flora College work while attending school. Dean Bigheart thinks the professor has underestimated the number of students with part-time or full-time jobs.

> The Big Break Moving Company claims a typical family moves every 5.2 yr.

These lead-ins are followed with summary statistics (no data, real or imagined) for which students are asked to test a hypothesis for a single mean or proportion. In the second problem, it would be more instructive to ask students to explain why they should not do the hypothesis test—because times between moves are almost certainly skewed toward high values.

Data that are real can seem unreal to the student if there is not an adequate explanation of the context of the data or the purpose for which it was gathered, or if it is too technical or far from the student's experience. Consider this pair from [8]:

> Here's one to sink your teeth into: The authors of the paper "Analysis of Food Crushing Sounds During Mastication: Total Sound Level Studies," *J. of Texture Studies* (1990): 165–178) studied the nature of sounds generated during eating. Peak loudness (in decibels at 20 cm away) was measured for both open-mouth and closed-mouth chewing of potato chips and tortilla chips. Forty students participated, with ten in each combination of conditions (such as closed-mouth, potato chip, and so on). We are not making this up! [p. 512]

> The effect of plant diversity on beetle density was examined in a series of experiments described in the paper "Effects of Plant Diversity, Host Density, and Host Size on Population Ecology of the Colorado Potato Beetle," *Environ. Entomology* (1987): 1019–1026). Potatoes grown in fallow plots and potatoes grown in plots that also included bean plants and weeds (called *triculture*) were compared on the basis of the number of beetle eggs found on the plant leaves. [p. 517]

While even the authors seem to admit that students might question the authenticity of the chip munching situation, it is certainly a context that students can relate to, and they will know what the researchers were measuring, even if the units (or the motivation) remain unclear. In contrast, the beetle example seems a bit remote and abstruse, even to an author wearing bib overalls. Compare it with the wrenching realism of this example from Siegel and Morgan, which also illustrates the fact that outliers we might think are surely errors may be all too real.

> Display 2.30 shows the age at which a sample of runaway and homeless girls reported first having had sex. Exactly what "having sex" means was left to the individual respondent to decide. The data are part of a database assembled for the study of adolescent pregnancy, and four individuals who reported never having had sex were excluded. *Note:* Some individuals reported having first had sex as toddlers. In some cases, these instances of childhood abuse had been previously reported. [14, p.63]

Another reason for giving students real data is to encourage them to look at their data! In one text, we find fake data for all the exercises on paired data. What would motivate a student to look at fake data? If they found something unexpected in real data, their attention could profitably be focused on real issues, such as searching for influential data points, flaws in the design of the study, or some underlying reason why things might be different than they at first appear. If we find something unexpected in fake data, it merely suggests a sloppy forgery.

Real data also allow students to check to see if the assumptions underlying the techniques they apply have been met. For their exercises on independent samples, the same text gives no data at all, only summary statistics. This makes it impossible to check assumptions, and gives the impression that doing so is superfluous. These examples violate the dictum: "Check assumptions, don't make them." A similar cavalier attitude is shown toward issues of design and sampling, with random sampling decreed by fiat, as in: "a random sample of 10-year-old students with IQ scores below 80" or "a random sample of 15 U.S. adults." It would be much more enlightening to discuss why such samples are unlikely to have been taken. In addition, this text throws a red herring across the path of the unwary student: while no data are given for any independent situation, data (or numbers) are given for *every* paired sample situation. The obvious conclusion: use the paired technique when you have data, the independent samples technique when you don't. In contrast, Devore and Peck [8] give 38 examples of real problem situations involving independent samples. Unfortunately, they give raw data for only four of their problems. Hence, students can see that statistics is used in the real world, and see how it is used, but they cannot look at the data nor check inferential assumptions. In contrast, while Moore and McCabe [16, Ch. 7] give a mixture of real and unreal data and/or summary statistics, they do an outstanding job of asking students probing questions about the data or the design or the sampling procedure. Here are a few instructive examples:

> You should be hesitant to generalize these results to the population of all middle-aged men. Explain why.

> Explain in language that the manager can understand why he cannot be certain that sales rose by 6%, and that in fact sales may even have dropped.

> Examine each sample graphically with special attention to outliers and skewness. Is the use of a t procedure acceptable for these data?

> What assumptions does your statistical procedure in (a) require? Which of these assumptions are justified or not important in this case? Are any of the assumptions doubtful in this case?

> The distribution of earnings is strongly skewed to the right. Nevertheless, use of t procedures is justified. Why?

> Once the sample size was decided, the sample was chosen by taking every k-th name from an alphabetical list of undergraduates. Is it reasonable to consider the samples as [if they were] simple random samples from the male and female undergraduate populations?

> What other information about the study would you request before accepting the results as describing all undergraduates?

In contrast, nearly all the problems in the texts in the last row of Table 1 ask the student to merely grind out the computations and reject or fail to reject the null hypothesis.

I have already mentioned the use of real data to illustrate the type of data for which different statistical techniques are used. While it might seem unbelievable that anyone would present a technique without telling what it is used for, the discussion of boxplots in some books gives no clue as to their primary uses, which are to compare multiple groups and to provide a mechanism for flagging potential outliers. Instead, boxplots for a single batch of numbers

are introduced early in the text, but not used later when multiple groups are compared. One gets a sense of readers of earlier editions asking for boxplots and the authors trying to accommodate their wishes without understanding their reasons.

Contrast this lack of exploratory attitude with the books by Siegel, the master of using data to illustrate what a technique can do for you. In [14] he explains how to make a stem-and-leaf plot and a histogram. Then he looks at specific examples of data, with subsections on symmetric, Gaussian, skewed, long-tailed, rectangular and bimodal distributions as well as outliers. For bimodal distributions, he gives data on prize monies awarded in golf tournaments, and comments:

> When we see a data set with more than one mode, we should immediately consider the possibility that more than one group is being represented. We need to try to identify the groups, which may require creativity, imagination, and detective work. [14, p.42]

This presents a more attractive image of statistics than endless number-crunching exercises! (Note: Siegel finds the cause of the bimodality. What do you think it was?) Next he uses 45 histograms to show what happens when you take samples of various sizes from various theoretical distributions. For boxplots [14, pp. 87–96], he shows how to make one and then immediately uses six sets of parallel boxplots to compare gas mileage for different makes of car.

One objection to using real data is that the data sets are too large and the numbers too inconvenient for hand calculation. Making six boxplots for one data set will take a lot of time. That may be true, but the solution is to abandon hand calculation except for simple examples that help students to understand the ideas. This is but one of many reasons for using statistical software in a first course.

Summary and Conclusion

People with little or no training in statistics often teach statistics. Some of these people write textbooks, which may then be adopted by others with similar backgrounds. A better alternative is to adopt textbooks that are strong in areas where the teachers are weak. Mathematicians are likely to be strong in computation and in stating and interpreting the theorems of mathematical statistics. They are likely to be weak in knowledge and experience in applying statistics to a real world in which the hypotheses of theorems are never met. Find textbooks that are strong in these areas, even if you have to supplement them with formulas and computational algorithms, or clean up occasional imprecise statements. A text that contains little or no real data is not likely to be much help in learning to work with and interpret real data. You can automate the computational aspects of analyzing real data with modern statistical computing software and focus students' attention on learning statistical concepts.

To make that job easier, seek a textbook that

- has a qualified author,
- reflects current statistical practice,
- includes real applications,
- includes real data,
- looks at the (real) data,
- explains how real data are produced,
- provides a context for the data it uses,
- includes more concepts than calculations,
- interprets the results of calculations in the context of the data,
- checks assumptions for every inference, and
- asks probing questions about the data.

This paper opened with a quiz and I'll close it with another.

What word appears most frequently in the list above? Why?

In recent years, statistics has infused much of the K–12 mathematics curriculum. One reason for this is that statistics offers mathematics teachers a much better opportunity than, say, factoring quadratics to convince students that quantitative reasoning is useful in the real world and relevant to the issues of our day. (For endless examples of the latter point, see the Chance website.) Statistics can also offer this advantage to college mathematics teachers, but only if it is taught in connection with real problems and real data.

Note. Parts of this paper were presented at the Conference on Assessment in Statistics Courses sponsored by the Boston Chapter of the American Statistical Association, 19 April 1997. The author wishes to thank Don Burrill, Farid Kianifard and Paul Velleman for helpful comments on earlier drafts of this paper; George Cobb for comments on recent versions, and many wonderful quotes, both cited and stolen; Katherine Halvorsen, Farid Kianifard, and Joan Weinstein for assistance with the references; Chris Olsen for information on AP Statistics; and most of all Tom Moore, who nursed this article through an unexpectedly difficult path from a talk at a meeting to a paper suitable for inclusion in an MAA Notes volume.

A list of resources for teaching statistics

Textbooks Recommended for the Initial Offering of AP Statistics

This list comes from AP publications [5, 6] and the AP listserve. The list shifts slightly, but this is the core, as I see it.

Devore and Peck [8]
Iman [10]
Moore [11]
Moore and McCabe [12]
Siegel and Morgan [14]
Wardrop [18]

Other Resources

The American Statistical Association has a web site at: www.amstat.org.

The *Current Index to Statistics* is published jointly by the American Statistical Association and the Institute of Mathematical Statistics. The paper version covers the preceding year. A CD-ROM version is cumulative over the past 20+ years.

The College Board has a website with information on AP Statistics at: www.collegeboard.org. It provides guidance to all aspects of the first course, and it is geared toward people whose normal assignment is teaching mathematics.

And the Chance Project has one at: www.dartmouth.edu/~chance.

References

1. Anscombe, F. J., "Graphs in Statistical Analysis," *The American Statistician,* **27**(1), 1973, 17–21.
2. Chatterjee, Samprit, and Bertram Price, *Regression Analysis by Example,* 1977, John Wiley and Sons, New York.
3. Clarkson, Sandra, and William Williams, "The Readability of Some Popular Elementary Statistics Texts," *Proceedings of the Section on Statistical Education of the American Statistical Association,* 1996.
4. Cobb, George W., "Introductory Textbooks: A Framework for Evaluation (A Comparison of 16 Books)," *Journal of the American Statistical Association,* **82**(397), 1987, 321–339.
5. College Board, *Advanced Placement Course Description: Statistics,* 1996, The College Board, Princeton, NJ.

6. College Board, *Suggested Resources for Teaching Statistics,* 1996, The College Board, Princeton, NJ.

7. Dawson, Robert, email message, 1994.

8. Devore, Jay, and Roxy Peck, *Statistics: The Exploration and Analysis of Data,* 2nd edition, 1993, Duxbury Press, Belmont, CA.

9. Hayden, Robert W., "Using Writing to Improve Student Learning of Statistics," in *Using Writing to Teach Mathematics,* Andrew Sterrett, ed., 1990, Mathematical Association of America, Washington, DC.

10. Iman, Ronald J., *A Data-Based Approach to Statistics,* 1994, Duxbury Press, Belmont, CA.

11. Moore, David S. *The Basic Practice of Statistics,* 1994, W. H. Freeman, New York.

12. Moore, David S., and George P. McCabe, *Introduction to the Practice of Statistics,* 2nd edition, 1993, W. H. Freeman, New York.

13. Siegel, Andrew F., *Statistics and Data Analysis: An Introduction,* 1988, John Wiley and Sons, New York.

14. Siegel, Andrew F., and Charles J. Morgan, *Statistics and Data Analysis: An Introduction,* 2nd edition, 1996, John Wiley and Sons, New York.

15. Tukey, John W., *Exploratory Data Analysis,* 1977, Addison-Wesley, Reading, MA.

16. Velleman, Paul F., and David C. Hoaglin, *Applications, Basics, and Computing of Exploratory Data Analysis,* 1981. Duxbury Press, Boston.

17. Velleman, Paul F., email message, 1997.

18. Wardrop, Robert L., *Statistics: Learning in the Presence of Variation,* 1995, William C. Brown, Dubuque, IA.

Note. Wardrop's book is no longer published by the publisher listed above, but is available (at a much-reduced price) through the author's home address: 5573 Kupfer Road; Waunakee, WI 53597.

Assessing Mathematical Statistics Textbooks

Katherine Taylor Halvorsen
Smith College

Introduction

The motivation for reviewing mathematical statistics textbooks arose several years ago from my need to choose a textbook for a course I planned to teach. The books I had used in graduate school could not be used with undergraduate mathematics majors, and my colleagues teaching mathematical statistics at other liberal arts colleges were not entirely satisfied with the textbooks they were using. All of us wanted a summary of the textbooks available and some criteria for drawing distinctions between the books.

In general, statistics textbooks for advanced undergraduates or first-year graduate students have been written by professional statisticians, and comparisons among texts focus primarily on criteria that will allow us to match the textbook to the audience and to course goals. The intent of this review is twofold: to provide specific information about the books included in this review and to provide criteria teachers can use to evaluate new books that may become available in the future. This paper follows the comprehensive model provided by Cobb [1] in his review of introductory textbooks. It examines each of fifteen currently available textbooks with respect to the mathematical maturity required of the student using the book, the breadth of statistical topics covered in the text, the proportion of the text devoted to probability theory, and the quality of both the exposition and the exercises. We may think of a book written at a more advanced technical level as requiring more mathematical maturity in the student who uses the book. As Cobb [1] has pointed out "technical level is largely impossible to tease apart from other elements that affect the quality of a book's exposition," and I will follow the precedent of discussing technical level and quality of exposition in the same section.

Selecting Textbooks for Review

This review began by identifying well-known or recently published textbooks in mathematical statistics written for the junior or senior level undergraduate or first-year graduate student in statistics. Sources included: textbooks I have used, textbooks colleagues have recommended, textbooks found at book displays at the Mathematical Association of America or at the American Statistical Association national meetings, textbooks found in publishers' advertising, and textbooks identified by publishers' representatives as mathematical statistics texts for undergraduates at the junior or senior level or for first-year graduate students in their first statistics course. If a textbook had more than one edition, I used the most recently published edition. In all, I found fifteen textbooks published since 1977. These are shown in the following list.

(BE) *Introduction to Probability and Mathematical Statistics, Second Edition.* Lee J. Bain and Max Engelhardt. Belmont, CA: Duxbury Press, An Imprint of Wadsworth Publishing Company, 1992. xii + 644 pp.

(BL) *Statistics: Theory and Methods, Second Edition.* Donald A. Berry and Bernard W. Lindgren. Belmont, CA: Duxbury Press at Wadsworth Publishing Company, 1996. xi + 702 pp.

(BD) *Mathematical Statistics: Basic Ideas and Selected Topics.* Peter J. Bickel and Kjell A. Doksum. Englewood Cliffs, NJ: Prentice Hall, Inc., A Simon & Schuster Company, 1977. ix + 493 pp.

(CB) *Statistical Inference.* George Cassella and Roger L. Berger. Belmont, CA: Duxbury Press at Wadsworth Publishing Company, 1990. ix + 650 pp.

(D) *Probability and Statistics, Second Edition.* Morris H. DeGroot. Reading, MA: Addison-Wesley Publishing Company, 1989. v + 723 pp.

(DM) *Modern Mathematical Statistics.* Edward J. Dudewicz and Satya N. Mishra. New York, NY: John Wiley & Sons, Inc., 1988. xix + 838 pp.

(H) *Probability and Statistics.* Kevin J. Hastings. Reading, MA: Addison-Wesley Publishing Company, 1997. xii + 670 pp.

(HC) *Introduction to Mathematical Statistics, Fifth Edition.* Robert V. Hogg and Allen T. Craig. Upper Saddle River, NJ: Prentice Hall, Inc., Simon & Schuster/ A Viacom Company, 1997. xi + 564 pp.

(HT) *Probability and Statistical Inference, Fifth Edition.* Robert V. Hogg and Elliot A. Tanis. Upper Saddle River, NJ: Prentice Hall, Inc., Simon & Schuster/ A Viacom Company, 1997. xiii + 722 pp.

(L) *Statistical Theory, Fourth Edition.* Bernard W. Lindgren. New York, NY: Chapman & Hall, An International Thomson Publishing Company, 1993. xii + 633 pp.

(LM) *An Introduction to Mathematical Statistics and Its Applications, Second Edition.* Richard J. Larsen and Morris L. Marx. Englewood Cliffs, NJ: Prentice Hall, A Division of Simon & Schuster, Inc., 1986. x + 630 pp.

(MM) *John E. Freund's Mathematical Statistics, Sixth Edition.* Irwin Miller and Marylees Miller. Upper Saddle River, NJ: Prentice Hall, Inc., 1999. xii + 624 pp.

(Ri) *Mathematical Statistics and Data Analysis, Second Edition.* John A. Rice. Belmont, CA: Duxbury, An Imprint of Wadsworth Publishing Company, 1995. xx + 602 pp + appendix 50 pp.

(Ro) *A Course in Mathematical Statistics, Second Edition.* George G. Roussas. San Diego, CA: Academic Press, 1997. xx + 572 pp.

(WMS) *Mathematical Statistics with Applications, Fifth Edition.* Dennis D. Wackerly, William Mendenhall, III, and Richard L. Scheaffer. Belmont, CA: Duxbury Press an Imprint of Wadsworth Publishing Company, An International Thomson Publishing Company, 1996. xv + 798 pp.

These books do not all cover exactly the same material and are not all written for the same students. Some are only appropriate for students with one year of calculus while others provide a challenge for first-year graduate students who have an undergraduate degree in mathematics. These books show the range of mathematical statistics textbooks available for this audience, and they give teachers a variety of choices, at several levels of mathematical expertise, from which to select a textbook.

A Textbook's Stated Objectives

Typically authors state their objectives for their book in the preface, and using these statements about the books I sorted the books into two groups: books that use mathematics to develop statistical ideas and books that primarily focus on the mathematical theory of statistics. **WMS** (p. *xiii*) provides an example of a statement from a book that falls into the first group. The preface states that the text is intended to "provide an indication of the relevance and importance of the theory in solving practical problems in the real world." **HC**'s (p. *ix*) statement of the objective for the fifth edition puts this book squarely in the second group. The preface states, "Allen and I wanted to write about the mathematics of statistics, and I have followed that guideline."

I have begun to think of books in the first group as mathematics-based statistics (MBS) books and books in the second group as theoretical statistics (TS) books. Seven of the fifteen books appeared to belong to the MBS category: **BL, DM, H, HT, LM, Ri,** and **WMS.** Their prefaces make statements about the importance of applications (**BL**), data analysis (**H, LM, Ri**), a data-oriented approach (**HT**), or their intention to give a "flavor of the applications" (**DM,** p. *vii*). The prefaces of the remaining eight books (**BE, BD, CB, D, HC, L, MM, Ro**) made statements that suggest the mathematics is of primary importance. Their statements included "intended for a year's course in the theory of statistics" (**L,** p. *xi*), "a calculus based introduction to the mathematics of statistics" (**MM,** p. *xi*), and "The purpose of this book is to build theoretical statistics... from the first principles of probability theory" (**CB**, p. vii). The classification for **D** was difficult to make. The preface states, "Theorems and proofs are presented where appropriate" (p. *iii*) which suggests the book belongs in the second group, but it goes on to say, "illustrative examples are given at almost every step of the way" which may indicate the book belongs in the first group. I put this book in the second group because its stated goal is "to equip the student with the theory and methodology that have proved to be useful in the past and promise to be useful in the future," and because "none of the exercises in this book requires access to a computer" (p. *iv*).

This classification into the MBS and TS groups was a preliminary one based entirely on the objectives stated in the preface. We will check this initial grouping by considering the topics covered in the books, the methods used to present the material, and the types and quantity of examples and exercises.

Mathematical Maturity Required of the Reader

Mathematical maturity in a student means having attained both technical skill and the ability to think mathematically. In considering a textbook for possible use in class, teachers may check the prerequisites recommended in the preface as a guide to the mathematical expertise required of the reader. Unfortunately, the recommended prerequisites sometimes differ from the mathematical skills actually required of readers. Although many textbooks say "one year of calculus" or "a background in differential and integral calculus" is sufficient preparation, all of those I examined contained topics usually taught in a third semester of calculus at my college. To check whether this decrepancy is common, I scanned each book to see which technical tools the reader is asked to use.

All of the textbooks expect the reader to have a working knowledge of differential and integral calculus and multivariable calculus, and they use these tools. Three books do not appear to use matrix algebra in their exposition: **HT**, **LM**, and **MM**. All of the other books include some use of matrix algebra. Most of these use it only in the chapters that cover regression analysis, linear models, or the multivariate normal distribution. Only **HC** and **Ro** discuss the properties and distributions of quadratic forms, and they make extensive use of matrix algebra. All of the authors who recommend a prerequisite of matrix algebra use it in the text. Some of the authors who only recommend one year of calculus also use matrix algebra, but they teach the reader matrix notation and operations as they use them.

Four texts (**BL, H, Ro, WMS**) provide an appendix that teaches readers the matrix algebra that the text uses.

Two texts **BD** and **Ro** recommend prior knowledge of advanced calculus but not measure theory; however, **Ro** introduces the concepts of field and sigma-field and gives the definition of a random variable as a measurable function. **Ro** does this "so that students without a sophisticated mathematical background can assimilate a fairly broad spectrum of the theorems and results from mathematical statistics" (p. *xviii*). **BD** mentions measurable sets and functions, but restricts this to footnotes in the appendix. The need for advanced calculus is most apparent in the material on limit theorems in which modes of convergence are discussed.

Only one text (**BD**) assumes prior knowledge of probability, and it uses the first chapter to review relevant probability concepts. It also provides an appendix summarizing the introductory probability concepts on which the text relies. Each of the other books uses between four and nine chapters to develop the probability theory needed for the statistical inference subsequently presented.

A graph plotting the number of proofs versus the number of examples given in each text may provide some insight into the level of mathematical maturity required of the reader. In general, a larger number of proofs may suggest that more mathematical maturity is required of the reader. For example, **BL** requires only differential and integral calculus and makes a point of saying, "Although statistical theory involves mathematics, this is a statistics text, not a mathematics text. So we do not use the 'definition-theorem-proof' approach." (p. *x*). The book gives heuristic arguments for results that have proofs beyond the scope of first-year calculus, and it gives proofs (including the proof of the Neyman–Pearson Lemma in the continuous case) when the proof does not exceed that scope.

To estimate the number of proofs and examples in each text, I counted the numbers of proofs and examples in the chapters devoted to hypothesis testing. To adjust for differing numbers of pages given to hypothesis testing in the texts, the counts are adjusted to provide an estimate of the count per 100 pages of text. I chose hypothesis testing because I expected most texts would prove the Neyman–Pearson Lemma, but might not prove other propositions. Only proofs and examples so designated in the text were included in the calculations. All proofs were counted regardless of the text's designation of the original proposition as a theorem, lemma, corollary, or proposition.

Figure 1 shows a scatterplot of number of proofs to number of examples. Texts judged from their preface to be mathematics-based statistics texts are indicated by plusses, and those judged to be theoretical statistics texts are indi-

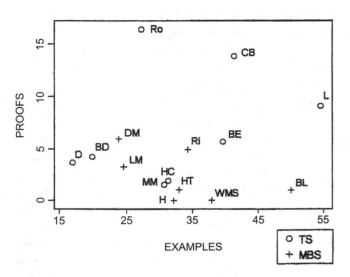

FIGURE 1
Proofs and Examples per 100 Pages, by Group

cated by open circles. Twelve of the fifteen texts cluster in the 0 to 6 range for proofs, while **Ro** with 16, **CB** with 14, and **L** with 9 stand out as high values. All three of these texts are theoretical statistics texts.

The range in the number of examples per 100 pages runs from 17 to 55. It should be noted that a text may have few examples either because it does not present many or because the examples it presents are each quite long, thus not allowing space for many. For example, Case Study 6.2.1 in **LM** covers a page and a half and is typical of the examples and case studies in this book. Also, only text labeled as an example or as a case study was included in the count of examples. Texts sometimes include examples in the explanation of a new concept but these are not included in my counts because they were not labeled as examples in the text. With the exception of **Ro**, **CB**, and **L**, the plot does not show a clear separation between books in the MBS and TS groups.

Technical Level and Quality of Exposition

In judging the technical level of introductory statistics books, Cobb [1, p. 323] suggests that we consider the extent to which a book's use of formulas obscures or focuses attention on the basic concepts and on the book's reliance on algebra to make connections between basic concepts. We can also use these two criteria to examine how more advanced texts focus attention on basic concepts and how they make connections between these concepts.

To compare the books in this collection, I looked at how they treat the concept of sufficiency. The basic idea un-

derlying sufficiency involves data reduction. Any statistic summarizes the data, and some statistics provide more useful summaries than others. A statistic that is sufficient for a parameter θ is one that summarizes all the information in the sample about θ. The Factorization Theorem gives us a simple way to find a sufficient statistic, and the sufficiency principle says that if two different samples give the same value of the sufficient statistic then the statistician should draw the same inference about θ from the two samples. A text, no matter how advanced, needs to explain these basic concepts.

There are several connections that may be made. The likelihood function $L(\theta)$ and the maximum likelihood estimate of θ (if it is unique) are functions of the sufficient statistic. Conditioning any unbiased estimator on a sufficient statistic will improve the estimator in the sense of giving an estimator that has variance no greater than that of the original estimator (the Rao-Blackwell theorem). The exponential family of distributions is a family of distributions that have sufficient statistics of the same dimension as the parameter space regardless of the sample size, and, using the Factorization Theorem, it is easy to find a sufficient statistic for the exponential family of distributions. A sufficient statistic is called minimally sufficient if it achieves the greatest possible reduction of the data and still retains all the information about θ that is in the data.

There are some warning tags that should be attached to the concept of sufficient statistic. We cannot keep only the sufficient statistic and throw out the data. The sufficient statistic may provide all the information the data have about θ, but the data still retain other information. **Ri** (p. 280) says it clearly, "The values of the X_i might indicate that the model did not fit or that something was fishy about the data. What would you think, for example, if you saw 50 ones followed by 50 zeros in a sequence of supposedly independent Bernoulli trials?"

CB provides one of the more comprehensive and readable discussions of sufficiency. It first describes the basic ideas and the connections without reliance on formulas. The descriptions are then made rigorous through definitions, theorems, and proofs, and they are illustrated by examples. The book emphasizes the main idea by grouping sufficiency with likelihood and invariance and giving the chapter the title, "Principles of Data Reduction." **CB** anticipates sufficiency much earlier in the book where it introduces exponential families and tells readers that these families have nice properties, including a data reduction property that they will see again when sufficiency is discussed. Books written for audiences that have less mathematical maturity than **CB** requires can still present the basic concepts clearly, without making them more rigorous through the use of theorems and proofs. **WMS** provides an example of such a book.

In evaluating mathematical statistics books, we have to question what is lost when a definition is made less technical. I would argue that little, if anything, is lost and much may be gained by presenting a simple definition. Most students, having read the earlier parts of the book, can understand **CB**'s definition of sufficiency: "A statistic $T = t(X)$ is a *sufficient statistic for* θ if the conditional distribution of the sample X given the value of $T(X)$ does not depend on θ" (p. 247). I am less certain that this is true for the definition given in **DM**. "A statistic $t(X_1, \ldots, X_n)$ is sufficient (for θ) iff

$$P_\theta[(X_1, \ldots, X_n) \in \mathcal{U}|t(X_1, \ldots, X_n) = c] = l(\mathcal{U}|c)$$

for all θ and all $\mathcal{U} \subseteq \mathcal{R}^n$, that is, iff the left side of (the) equation (above) is a function of $\mathcal{U}$ and c, say $l(\mathcal{U}|c)$, but not a function of θ" (p. 393).

HT uses the factorization theorem to define sufficient statistics, and **BL** uses the likelihood function to define them. "A statistic $T = t(\mathbf{X})$ is sufficient for a family of distributions $\{f(x|\theta)\}$ if and only if the likelihood function depends on $\mathbf{X}$ through the value of t : $L(\theta) = g[t(\mathbf{X}), \theta]$" (**BL**, p. 319). Both these definitions avoid the complexities of finding the conditional distribution of the data given the parameter, but they lose intuitiveness.

Probability and Statistics Topics Included in the Texts

All of the textbooks reviewed here contain material on probability theory, estimation, and testing hypotheses. All of the books also have additional topics, but the content and number of additional topics varied from text to text. I looked for two types of additional topics to help distinguish between the books, what I call traditional and nontraditional topics in a mathematical statistics text. The traditional topics include regression, ANOVA, non-parametric methods, Bayesian estimation and testing, and decision theory. The non-traditional topics I checked for include EDA methods (including stem-and-leaf plots, box plots, residual analysis, and outlier labeling), the bootstrap, permutation tests, and simulation.

To compare the amount of probability in the books, I looked at the proportion of pages each book devoted to teaching probability. The proportion is calculated by dividing the number of pages used for probability topics in the body of the text by the total number of pages of text used for exposition and exercises. The total page count does not

include appendices, statistical tables, indexes, bibliography, references (if these are at the end of the book), or answers to exercises. This means, for example, that the appendix on probability in **BD** is not included in this estimate, either in the pages used for probability or in the total page count.

Which pages should count as probability material was not always clear, and two books put probability material both before and after traditional statistics topics. **LM** locates a chapter on the normal distribution following the chapters on estimation and on hypothesis testing. **BL** puts distributions of order statistics and limit theorems in a chapter with traditional estimation concepts of likelihood and sufficiency and following a chapter on descriptive statistics. I included both of these chapters in the page counts of probability material in their respective books. Two more books contain a chapter on sampling distributions that might be counted as either a probability chapter or a statistics chapter. I counted them as probability chapters because one (**MM**) contains the distribution of order statistics along with the t, F, and chi-square distributions. The other (**BE**) contains the t, F, chi-squared, and Beta distributions and large-sample approximations to these distributions (including the Wilson-Hilferty approximation to the chi-squared distribution).

In reading through the topics in probability in these texts, it became apparent that almost all texts present the central limit theorem (CLT) in the last chapter on probability, typically in a chapter with a title such as Limit Theorems or Sampling Distributions. Two texts stood out as unusual in this regard. **BL** put the CLT in Chapter 8, following the other probability material in Chapters 1 to 6, and following Chapter 7, Organizing and Describing Data, which includes descriptive statistics and graphs. Similarly, **LM** includes the CLT in Chapter 7, The Normal Distribution, which follows four chapters of probability theory, one chapter on estimation, and another on testing hypotheses. Two of the books that include the CLT in the final chapter on probability (**CB, MM**) do not name it in the table of contents, but list it in the index.

All texts define the moment-generating function and give examples of its use. Seven of the fifteen books define the characteristic function (**CB, DM, H, HC, L, Ri** and **Ro**). Only **DM, L,** and **Ro** contain examples, theorems, or exercises that use the characteristic function.

To check the breadth and depth of coverage of estimation theory, I checked to see which properties of estimators each book discussed. In particular, I looked for discussions of efficiency, sufficiency, consistency, completeness, or ancillarity of estimators. I also looked at whether each book discussed exponential families (which have many nice mathematical properties), the Rao-Blackwell Theorem (which shows the usefulness of sufficient statistics), or large-sample properties of MLEs (which help explain the importance of MLEs to statistical theory and practice). To check the breadth of coverage of hypothesis testing, I looked for discussion of likelihood ratio tests, the asymptotic distribution of the likelihood ratio statistic, and uniformly most powerful (UMP) tests.

Table 1 gives the proportion of pages each book devotes to probability, and it provides a summary of the topics found in each book. For each topic, an 'X' in a cell indicates that the textbook listed in the column heading contains some discussion of the topic named on the row heading. A book received credit for inclusion of a topic if it provides at least a definition or some discussion, however brief. It is possible that some of the blanks in the table occur because I could not find a topic in a text. Some of the topics I looked for are not listed in the table of contents or in the index of some of the texts. For example, **DM** does not list UMP tests in the table of contents or the index but gives a definition in Section 9.3, The Neyman–Pearson Lemma: Its Generalization and Uses (p. 450). If I could not find a topic in the table of contents or the index, I tried to find it by reading through the text under topics closely related to the one I was looking for.

Table 1 also shows whether each book provides a bibliography or references and answers to exercises (N = none, O = odd problems, E = even problems, S = selected problems, A = almost all problems). The last line in Table 1 shows the group to which I assigned each text based on the discussion in the preface, mathematics-based statistics (M) or theoretical statistics (T). The texts are listed in order by date of publication starting on the left side with **BD**, published in 1977, and ending on the right side with **Ro**, published in 1997. I looked for, but, with one exception did not find, an index to the examples or data sets used in the texts. **Ri** gives an index to the data sets analyzed in the book along with a subject index and an author index.

Table 1 shows that except for **BD** these books devote between 31 (**Ri**) and 54 (**MM**) percent of their pages to teaching probability. This is generally enough material for a one-quarter or a one-semester course in probability. **BD** uses only 13 percent of pages for probability or 18 percent if we add the section on probability in the appendix to both the pages of probability and to the total pages.

Estimation and hypothesis testing are the core concepts introduced in every text. A glance at Table 1 tells us that all the books define efficiency and sufficiency and all but two define consistency. Only six texts discussed completeness of estimators and only three of those defined an an-

cillary statistic. All but one (**MM**) of the books classified as theoretical contain discussions of exponential families, the Rao-Blackwell theorem, and large-sample properties of MLEs, and three of the books classified as mathematics-based contain all three as well. All texts define likelihood ratio tests, and all except **H** and **LM** define UMP tests. Only **D** omits the asymptotic distribution of the likelihood ratio statistic.

HT stands out as unusual. The book is written for undergraduates who have had "a standard course in calculus," and it responds to recent trends in statistics education by taking a data-oriented approach in the text and by including graphical methods and descriptive statistics. It solves the problem of how to combine theory and practice in one book by writing a separate chapter, Chapter 12, called Theory of Statistical Inference. Chapter 12 is the last chapter in the book, and it contains sufficiency, Bayesian estimation, asymptotic distributions of MLEs, convergence in probability, Chebyshev's inequality, best critical regions, and likelihood ratio tests.

Regression, analysis of variance, and non-parametric methods appear most frequently among the traditional topics texts might include. Only **BE** omits both regression and ANOVA, although the text defines the conditional mean of Y given x to be the regression function when X and Y have a joint bivariate normal distribution. Only **CB** omits non-parametric methods. Three texts omit discussions of Bayesian statistical methods (**H, LM, WMS**), but all of these include Bayes' Rule (called Bayes' Theorem in some texts) in the exposition of probability. Almost half of the texts (seven of the fifteen) omit decision theory.

The table makes apparent that among the non-traditional topics, simulation began to appear regularly in mathematical statistics texts with the publication of **L** in 1993. In most texts the discussion is quite limited. Some of the texts provide only a very brief description or definition, but three texts (**BL, H, Ri**) provide definitions, discussion, and examples. **BL** and **Ri** include simulation in the chapter on sampling; **H** includes it in the chapter on transformations of random variables. Five texts (**BL, H, HT, L, Ri**), all published in 1993 or later, include some exploratory data analysis techniques such as stem-and-leaf plots, boxplots, residual analyses, and the definition of an outlier. All, except **L**, belong to the MBS group. **L**, a member of the TS group, contains Section 7.2, "Describing Samples," that gives both histograms and boxplots. The bootstrap and permutation tests are each found in two texts. **Ri** includes both topics.

Topics	Text														
	BD	LM	DM	D	BE	CB	MM	L	Ri	HC	BL	WMS	H	HT	Ro
Year of publication	77	86	88	89	89	90	92	93	95	95	96	96	97	97	97
Proportion Probability	.13	.49	.45	.46	.49	.41	.54	.34	.31	.48	.49	.43	.49	.34	.52
Estimation															
Efficiency	X	X	X	X	X	X	X	X	X	X	X	X	X	X	X
Sufficiency	X	X	X	X	X	X	X	X	X	X	X	X	X	X	X
Consistency	X	X	X	X	X	X	X	X	X	X	X	X			X
Completeness	X		X			X		X	X	X					X
Ancillarity			X			X				X					
Exponential families	X		X	X	X	X		X	X	X	X		X	X	X
Rao-Blackwell theorem	X	X	X	X	X	X		X	X	X	X	X	X		X
MLE: large sample prop.	X		X	X	X	X		X	X	X	X	X		X	X
Hypothesis tests															
Likelihood ratio tests	X	X	X	X	X	X	X	X	X	X	X	X	X	X	X
Asymptotic Distrib. of LR	X	X	X		X	X	X	X	X	X	X	X	X	X	X
UMP tests	X		X	X	X	X	X	X	X	X	X	X		X	X
Traditional topics															
Regression analysis	X	X	X	X	X	X	X	X	X	X	X	X	X	X	X
Analysis of variance	X	X	X	X		X	X	X	X	X	X	X	X	X	X
Non-parametric methods	X	X	X	X	X		X	X	X	X	X	X	X	X	X
Decision theory	X		X	X		X	X	X	X	X					X
Bayes estimation & tests	X		X	X	X	X	X	X	X	X	X			X	X
Non-traditional topics															
EDA								X	X		X		X	X	
Simulation			X					X	X	X	X	X	X	X	X
Bootstrap			X							X					
Permutation tests								X	X						
Other features															
Bibliography/References	X	X	X	X	X	X	X	X	X	X	X	X	X	X	
Answers to exercises	N	O	S	E	S	N	O	A	S	S	S	S	S	O	S
Group	T	M	M	T	T	T	T	T	M	T	M	M	M	M	T

TABLE 1
Content Of Textbooks

I also looked for two features in the texts that are not related to the statistical material covered by the texts: a bibliography or references section and answers to some or all of the exercises. All but one text (**Ro**) provided references to the probability and statistics literature for further reading. All of the books except **BD** and **CB** provide answers to selected exercises. Only **L** provided answers to almost all the exercises. I also looked for indexes to the examples and data sets used in the texts but did not list these in Table 1 because I found so few. None of the texts provided an index to the examples, and only **Ri** included an index to the data used in examples in the text along with a floppy disc containing the data.

Quantity and Quality of Exercises and Examples Provided in the Texts

Cobb [1] argued strongly that real data are an essential component of examples and exercises in textbooks at the introductory level, and statistics educators appear to have reached a consensus on this point. It is still arguable, however, to what extent authors should have real examples and exercises in their mathematical statistics textbooks.

In considering the examples and exercises provided in these texts, we need to keep in mind the authors' intentions. Some clearly state that they "wanted to write about the mathematics of statistics" (**HC**, p. *ix*), and that is why they have "resisted adding 'real' problems," (**HC**, p. *ix*). Others reflect the view stated by **WMS** (p. *xiii*): "The intent of the text is to present a solid undergraduate foundation in statistical theory and, at the same time, to provide an indication of the relevance and importance of the theory in solving practical problems in the real world." We might use an estimate of the proportion of examples and exercises that use a concrete context as a measure of the degree to which the text emphasizes statistical content over mathematical content. We would expect this measure to agree with our earlier classification of the texts into the MBS and TS groups, based on the objectives stated in the preface.

Having already counted the examples in the chapters on hypothesis testing, I also counted the exercises in these chapters so that I could fairly compare the examples with the exercises. If an example or an exercise used real data or the problem had a realistic setting, I classified it as having a concrete context. For example, a problem that uses an election poll setting would be counted as having a concrete context whether or not the data came from an actual poll. A problem needed only a bare minimum of realism to be counted as concrete. A problem that began with "An urn contains 10 balls,..." (**DM**, p. 443) was counted as con-

crete because the reader can visualize the action of drawing balls from an urn. I did not include in the counts exercises that referred to a concrete exercise or example given previously if the exercise asked a theoretical question or just asked for a recalculation using a different method or another value of a parameter. For example, Exercise 13.64, taken from **MM**, Chapter 13, p. 437, "Use the statistic of Exercise 13.49 to rework Exercise 13.63," asks students to calculate a Z-statistic for a two-sample test of proportions. It does not use the context given in Exercise 13.63, and the point of the exercise appears to be drill in calculating the test statistic. Exercise 13.63 merely provides data for the calculation. The question might have become more meaningful if it had also asked students to compare the results they obtained in 13.63 with those in 13.64. Exercise 13.63 asks students to compute the Chi-square statistic for the same data, and students should recognize the relationship between the results of the two exercises.

Books that use real data in examples and exercises demonstrate the importance of the theory in the real world. Real problems with real data seem to capture student attention far more quickly in my classes than manufactured data. For this reason, I value books that provide a real-world context in their examples and exercises. To see how frequently these more theoretical books include real data, I also estimated the proportions of examples and exercises that use real data. To be included in this count, an exercise or an example needed to cite the study from which the data were taken or cite the newspaper or magazine that reported the study.

Table 2 gives the number of pages used to obtain the counts reported for each book. The table contains the total numbers of exercises and examples found, the number that contain a concrete setting, and the number that contain a citation for the source of the data. The last column gives the group to which I have assigned the book, based on the objectives stated in the preface, M for the MBS and T for the TS books.

We would like to compare the books' use of concrete and real examples and exercises but the counts come from different numbers of pages in each book, because the books devote different numbers of pages to hypothesis testing. Figure 2 plots the proportion of concrete examples against the proportion of concrete exercises in each text. Figure 3 plots the proportion of real examples against the proportion of real exercises in each text.

In each figure, books that lie closer to the upper right corner of the graph have a larger proportion of concrete or real exercises and concrete or real examples. Books in the

Text	Pages Counted	Total Examples	Concrete Examples	Real Examples	Total Exercises	Concrete Exercises	Real Exercises	Group
BD	95	19	6	0	102	10	2	T
LM	61	15	3	9	63	13	19	M
DM	117	28	9	0	139	17	4	M
D	82	14	4	0	111	26	0	T
BE	53	21	2	0	40	7	1	T
CB	58	24	1	0	60	4	0	T
MM	65	20	14	0	130	58	0	T
L	66	36	8	1	91	20	1	T
Ri	102	35	11	10	99	9	24	M
HC	51	16	0	0	55	3	0	T
BL	102	51	24	13	129	31	30	M
WMS	66	25	16	0	110	47	21	M
H	56	18	6	8	81	14	26	M
HT	94	31	19	1	117	87	3	M
Ro	55	15	0	0	47	19	0	T

TABLE 2
Number of Concrete Examples and Exercises in Hypothesis
Testing Sections

lower left corner have a smaller proportion of concrete or real exercises and examples.

The graph provides a line that represents equal proportions of concrete examples and exercises. Both **LM** and **L** are located very close to the line, indicating that each book contains about the same proportion of concrete examples and exercises. About .2 of **LM's** exercises and examples have a concrete context, and **L** has about .22. Four of the TS books, **BE, CB, HC,** and **Ro,** lie close to the line or slightly above it. Books lying above the line have a greater proportion of concrete exercises than concrete examples. All of these books have a proportion of less than .10 of concrete examples, and only **Ro** has a proportion greater than .18 of concrete exercises. The remaining three TS books, **BD, D,** and **MM,** all lie below the line, and books lying below the line have a smaller proportion of concrete exercises than concrete examples. With the exception of **HT,** all of the MBS books lie on or below the line.

We might expect the theoretical statistics (TS) books to use fewer concrete settings in their examples and in their exercises than the MBS books, but the graph does not appear to confirm this belief. **MM,** a book in the TS group, has a proportion of .70 of concrete examples and .45 of con-

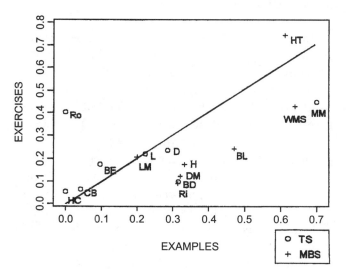

FIGURE 2
Proportion of Exercises and Examples that have a Concrete Context

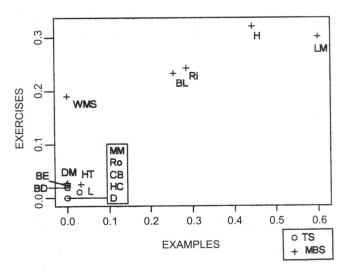

FIGURE 3

Proportion of Examples and Exercises that Cite a Study as the Source of the Data

crete exercises. It sits near **WMS** on the graph and closer to books in the MBS group than to books in the TS group. A glance back at Table 1 provides further evidence that this book may be classified incorrectly. The table shows that **MM** does not discuss any of the more mathematical concepts in estimation: completeness, ancillarity, exponential families, the Rao-Blackwell Theorem, and large sample properties of maximum likelihood estimators. If we change the classification of **MM** to MBS, then the graph will show a slight clustering of MBS books in the upper right corner. Even after this reclassification, however, the evidence that TS books use fewer concrete settings does not appear strong.

The MBS and TS groups are not clearly separated in Figure 3. The proportion of examples and the proportion of exercises that cite the source of the data are each .03 or less in ten books. All eight of the TS books are in this group and so are two of the MBS books (**DM, HT**). Only four books have more than .2 of both their exercises and examples that cite sources (**BL, H, LM, Ri**). Two books stand out as unusual. **LM** has the highest proportion of exercises (.3) and examples (.6) citing sources of data. **WMS** cites sources in .19 of its exercises and in none of its examples.

Note that **MM** and **HT** appear in the upper right corner in Figure 2, and both move to the lower left corner in Figure 3. It is possible that some of the data sets used in the exercises and examples in these books come from real studies, but they do not have citations and were excluded from my counts for that reason. For example, **HT** uses a table in Example 7.6.3 (p. 405) that reports the number of

undergraduates at the University of Iowa by college and by gender. The authors say, "Incidentally, these numbers do actually reflect the composition of the undergraduate colleges at Iowa, but they were modified a little to make the computations easier in this first example." The availability of modern computing equipment and graphing calculators make the argument for ease of computation less plausible. This example would hold more interest for the reader if it cited a report from the registrar and the year in which the data were collected.

Summary and Conclusion

The textbooks examined here represent a diverse group of books that are all sold under the heading "mathematical statistics." They have different goals and different audiences. Although these books cannot be definitively classified into mathematics-based statistics books and theoretical statistics books, the categories are useful. The theoretical statistics books may be more suitable for a lecture-style course, taught to more mathematically mature students. In these courses the students often view the textbook as a supplement to lectures, and they tend to use the textbook as a reference. The mathematics-based statistics books may be more appropriate for a course in which activities and discussions figure prominently, and for the majority of these texts, the students may need less mathematical sophistication.

The classification we made in the beginning needs only slight modification to reflect what we have learned from our comparisons of these books. Table 2 suggests that **DM** should be moved into the TS group because it includes almost all of the topics listed in the table. Analogously, **MM** does not belong in this group because it omits five of the eight estimation topics checked. Possibly, **Ri** could be moved to the TS group, but its extensive use of real data in exercises and examples argues for leaving it in the MBS group. **D** sits between the two groups and perhaps somewhat closer to the MBS group. Its omission of a few of the more advanced topics and its moderate proportions of concrete examples and exercises put it into the MBS class, but its omission of any real data makes it more like the TS books. This omission may be due to its publication in 1989, before most statistics textbooks started to include real data in their exercises and examples. With these changes, the books that appear to belong to the TS group include: **BD, BE, CB, DM, HC, L,** and **Ro.** The MBS books include: **BL, D, H, HT, LM, MM, Ri,** and **WMS.**

These mathematical statistics textbooks give the instructor a wide range of choices from which to select a textbook.

I am convinced that for students in the introductory applied statistics course the use of real data in examples and exercises improves student understanding. I believe it is also true for mathematical statistics students in their first course. The use of real data may be less important for more advanced courses in mathematical statistics where the emphasis is on understanding mathematical principles rather than on using statistical tools for solving real-world problems. Instructors need to choose the position their course will take on the continuum between these two poles and select a text accordingly.

In reviewing future editions of these books or new books, the reader should ask: is the author's objective to teach mathematical theory or to use mathematics to develop statistical concepts; to what extent does the book include real data in its examples and exercises; how does the text focus attention on the basic concepts, and how does it provide connections between these concepts? No text perfectly matches an instructor's ideal syllabus. This review gives the instructor some criteria for selecting a text that will match the students' preparation and support the course goals.

References

Cobb, George W., "Introductory Textbooks: A Framework for Evaluation, A Comparison of 16 Books," *Journal of the American Statistical Association,* **82** (1987), 321–339.

Section 5
Technology

In previous sections several authors have commented on the use of technology in their own programs. Given the number of new technological products that are available, and a growing amount of experience in using them, we can now provide a practical guide to the world of technology-based statistics teaching.

The bread-and-butter technologies for teaching statistics continue to be computer software or the graphing calculator for basic data analysis. The article "Evaluating Statistical Analysis Packages for Introductory Statistics Teaching" (Lock, Moore, and Roberts) gives a framework to help you select the package that best meets your needs.

In "Using Graphing Calculators for Data Analysis in Teaching," Pat Hopfensperger tells about the benefits of using modern graphing calculators in an introductory statistics course. He avoids button-pushing discussions, because they are model-specific, and concentrates on describing how teachers can use calculators to teach concepts and statistical thinking.

Next we describe a quartet of new software packages that teach statistical concepts without putting heavy computing demands on the student. Roxy Peck's companion piece describes her teaching with three of these: *An Electronic Companion to Statistics*, *Visual Statistics*, and *StatConcepts*. Maria Ripol's companion piece describes teaching with *ExplorStat*.

ActivStats, developed by Paul F. Velleman, is a multimedia packaging of elementary statistics that encompasses simulations, interactive text, videos, activities, and a data analysis package. Amy Fisher's companion piece describes what it is like to teach with *ActivStats*.

The video series "Against All Odds: Inside Statistics" has become a classic in educational film-making with its 26 half-hour presentation of introductory statistics. Indeed, many of the newer computer-based statistical teaching products incorporate video clips from this series. This series provides a relatively inexpensive tool for self-instruction, but it is also handy to be able to show short clips from the videos in class. Edd Mansfield's "Time-Subject Index" makes this practical. (The long version is available at the volume's web site.)

Finally, Robin Lock shares with us his extensive knowledge about using the internet to find resources for teaching statistics. Moreover, he will keep us up to date through the web site (either go directly to the address he gives in his article or link to it from the volume's web site).

Note: The volume's web address is: `http://www.math.grinnell.edu/~mooret/maa-notes/`.

Evaluating Statistical Analysis Packages for Introductory Statistics Teaching

Robin H. Lock
St. Lawrence University

Thomas L. Moore
Grinnell College

Rosemary A. Roberts
Bowdoin College

ABSTRACT. This paper outlines a series of tasks designed to allow the reader to evaluate and compare statistical analysis packages for use in teaching statistics. Tasks include basic data entry and analysis, importing datasets, performing simulations, doing two-group comparisons, fitting linear regression with diagnostics, and producing a final report.

Each term, instructors of introductory statistics face a constantly changing universe of statistical packages they might use in their courses. Instructors' needs are individual and change from time to time. A comprehensive review of packages available today will be dated before it is printed. Thus, we here suggest a framework of computer-related tasks commonly included in introductory statistics courses that you can use to assess and compare the functionality of possible software packages.

We have divided each task into some "basic" objectives and a few "challenges." We view the basic objectives as typical of minimal functionality that most reasonable candidate packages should provide. The challenge tasks allow you to stretch the capabilities of these packages in more demanding directions, which might not be essential for your particular teaching situation but provide a means for differentiating between packages that satisfy the basic requirements. In no way do we intend for these tasks to cover the complete gamut of ways one might use statistical software in teaching statistics. They are designed to provide a representative sample of the sorts of activities that are common to many courses. We would hope that a package that performs satisfactorily on these tasks would also be likely to handle most of the other statistical analysis chores in a typical introductory statistics course.

TASK A: Data Entry & Basic Analysis

Table 1 contains the lengths of reign (rounded to the nearest year) of forty British rulers since William the Conqueror in 1066. The dataset is from Activity 2-2 in [3].

Basic.

A-1   Use the information in Table 1 to create a dataset in the statistics package. Including the names of the rulers is optional.

A-2   Calculate basic summary statistics (mean, standard deviation, median, and quartiles) for the lengths of reign.

A-3   Produce a histogram of the reign lengths.

Challenge.

A-4   Adjust the histogram to have four classes of equal width with a minimum boundary at 0 and a maximum at 80. Note: These are not the best settings for displaying

Ruler	Reign	Ruler	Reign
William I	21	Edward IV	6
William II	13	Mary I	5
Henry I	35	Elizabeth I	44
Stephen	19	James I	22
Henry II	35	Charles I	24
Richard I	10	Charles II	25
John	17	James II	3
Henry II	56	William III	13
Edward I	35	Mary II	6
Edward II	20	Anne	12
Edward III	50	George I	13
Richard II	22	George II	33
Henry IV	13	George III	59
Henry V	9	George IV	10
Henry VI	39	William IV	7
Edward IV	22	Victoria	63
Edward V	0	Edward VII	9
Richard III	2	George V	25
Henry VII	24	Edward VIII	1
Henry VIII	38	George VI	15

TABLE 1
British Ruler's Reigns

a histogram of these data, but serve as a test for the ease with which you may adjust parameters in the plot beyond the default settings.

A-5 Superimpose a normal distribution over the histogram from A-3, with mean and standard deviation matching the summary statistics.

TASK B: Importing a Dataset

Statistical software allows instructors and students to work with rich datasets containing many variables and cases, but creating such datasets can be very time consuming and tedious. Fortunately, electronic venues, such as the World Wide Web, provide excellent means for obtaining and sharing interesting data. However, with varying data formats, one must often do a bit of work to import the data into a package. Data files in ASCII format can be downloaded from the WWW, produced with a word processor, generated with a scanner, embedded in e-mail messages, or found on a diskette accompanying a textbook. How much effort does your package require to convert such data into a useable form?

Basic.

B-1 A dataset on human body temperatures is part of the Journal of Statistics Education (JSE) dataset archive at: `amstat.org/publications/jse/datasets/normtemp.dat`. There are data on three variables, body temperature (in °F), gender (1 = Male, 2 = Female), and pulse rate (beats per minute). An article [4] describing some pedagogical uses for these data is at `amstat.org/publications/jse/v4n2/datasets.shoemaker.html`.

Download a copy of the body temperature data from the JSE dataset archive and import them to form a dataset in your statistics package with appropriately named variables.

B-2 A dataset giving average household spending on alcohol and tobacco products for eleven regions of Great Britain can be found at the Data and Story Library (DASL) with URL `lib.stat.cmu.edu/DASL/Datafiles/AlcoholandTobacco.html`. Here the data appear at the bottom of a web page that describes them. Again, your task is to import the data into your statistics package. You might try to use a cut-and-paste operation, but watch out for the blanks embedded in the region names. You may need to do some editing in a word processor before importing the data.

Challenge.

B-3 Another JSE dataset gives information on automobiles from the 1993 model year [2]. Due to the constraints of some e-mail systems, the data for the 26 variables occupy two rows for each car in the sample. In addition, a few missing values (like the cylinders variable for the rotary engine Mazda) are denoted with an asterisk. Successful importation may require some tedious editing through all 93 cases or careful use of a format statement. Links to the raw data, documentation, and a JSE article on using the data can be found near the top of the JSE Dataset Archive web page at `amstat.org/publications/jse/archive.htm`.

TASK C: Simulation

A common method for illustrating a sampling distribution or the central limit theorem, either by instructor demonstration or student activity, is through some sort of simulation exercise. Typically, one simulates many small samples from some parent distribution, calculates a statistic for each sample, and then displays a plot of the empirical distribution of these sample statistics.

Basic.

C-1   Simulate 500 samples of size $n = 5$ from a uniform distribution.

C-2   Compute the sample mean for each of these 500 samples.

C-3   Display a histogram of the 500 sample means and compute the mean and standard deviation of the sample means.

C-4   Repeat the process with a sample size of $n = 25$.

Challenge.

C-5   Display the histograms for samples of size $n = 5$ and $n = 25$ on the same scale.

C-6   Automate the process in C-1 through C-3 so that students may easily adjust the sample sizes.

C-7   Allow students to specify an arbitrary discrete or continuous distribution from which to select the samples. Display both the distribution of the sample means and the original population distribution using plots with identical horizontal scales.

TASK D: Two Group Comparisons

We refer back to the body temperature data that was imported in task B-1. Is there a significant difference in average body temperature between males and females? Note: If you had difficulty getting the data from the web, a few sample cases are given in Table 2 and you may enter them directly to attempt this task.

Basic.

D-1   Compute the mean, median, interquartile range, and standard deviation for the body temperatures in each group (males and females). Also calculate these statistics for the combined sample.

D-2   Produce side-by-side boxplots or back-to-back stemplots to compare graphically the distributions of body temperatures of the two groups.

Males	97.2	97.8	97.1	98.2	98.2	98.8
	98.4	97.4	97.6	98.8	99.0	98.5
	98.6	96.3	98.8	97.3	97.9	
Females	98.8	98.3	98.2	98.0	98.0	
	98.8	98.5	99.3	98.2	97.2	
	99.9	97.8	98.2			

TABLE 2
Body Temperatures in °F

D-3   Calculate a confidence interval for the difference between the mean pulse rates of the two genders.

D-4   Perform a two-sample t-test for a difference in means. Compare the results for using pooled vs. unpooled variances.

Challenge.

D-5   Use resampling procedures to demonstrate how a permutation test could be used to investigate the difference in average body temperature between the two groups.

TASK E: Linear Regression and Diagnostics

Table 3 contains information on the average gestation period (in days) and average adult body weight (in kgs.) for 60 species of mammals. The purpose of this task is to use linear regression techniques to build a model to predict body weight based on gestation time. The data were originally part of a paper on the sleep patterns in mammals [1] made available through the Statlib dataset archive by Roger Johnson at the URL lib.stat.cmu.edu/datasets/sleep. That dataset also contains information on the amount of sleep, predation danger, brain weight, and lifespan for these animals. The data from Table 3 may be obtained at it.stlawu.edu/~rlock/math113/mammals.dat.

Basic.

E-1   Produce a scatterplot with body weight on the vertical axis and gestation on the horizontal axis.

E-2   Run a simple linear regression to obtain the coefficients of the least squares line to predict body weight based on gestation.

E-3   Show the least squares line on the scatterplot.

E-4   The plot in E-3 should show two serious outlier points. Can you identify these animals using just the plot?

E-5   Re-run steps E-2 and E-3 without the two extreme points (i.e., no elephants).

E-6   The results should look a bit better, but still not very linear. Produce a normal probability plot of the residuals from the model in E-5.

E-7   Produce a plot of the residuals vs. fitted values from this same model.

E-8   Will a transformation help? Use ln(body weight) as the response variable and redo steps E-5 through E-7.

Mammal	Gestation	Body Weight	Mammal	Gestation	Body Weight
African Elephant	645	6654.00	Little brown bat	50	0.01
African giant pouched rat	42	1.00	Man	267	62.00
Arctic fox	60	3.39	Mole rat	30	0.12
Arctic ground squirrel	25	0.92	Mountain beaver	45	1.35
Asian elephant	624	2547.00	Mouse	19	0.02
Baboon	180	10.55	Musk shrew	30	0.05
Big brown bat	35	0.02	N. American opossum	12	1.70
Brazilian tapir	392	160.00	Nine-banded armadillo	120	3.50
Cat	63	3.30	Okapi	440	250.00
Chimpanzee	230	52.16	Owl monkey	140	0.48
Chinchilla	112	0.43	Patas monkey	170	10.00
Cow	281	465.00	Phanlanger	17	1.62
Donkey	365	187.10	Pig	115	192.00
Eastern American mole	42	0.08	Rabbit	31	2.50
Echidna	28	3.00	Raccoon	63	4.29
European hedgehog	42	0.79	Rat	21	0.28
Galago	120	0.20	Red fox	52	4.24
Giraffe	400	529.00	Rhesus monkey	164	6.80
Goat	148	27.66	Rock hyrax (Hetero. b)	225	0.75
Golden hamster	16	0.12	Rock hyrax (Procavia hab)	225	3.60
Gorilla	252	207.00	Roe deer	150	14.83
Gray seal	310	85.00	Sheep	151	55.50
Gray wolf	63	36.33	Slow loris	90	1.40
Ground squirrel	28	0.10	Tenrec	60	0.90
Guinea pig	68	1.04	Tree hyrax	200	2.00
Horse	336	521.00	Tree shrew	46	0.10
Jaguar	100	100.00	Vervet	210	4.19
Kangaroo	33	35.00	Water opossum	14	3.50
Lesser short-tailed shrew	21	0.01	Yellow-bellied marmot	38	4.05

TABLE 3
Gestation Time (days) and Adult Body Weight (kgs.) for Species of Mammals

Does this help? Can you suggest a more appropriate transformation?

Challenge.

E-9 Show the fit from the transformed model on the original body weight vs. gestation scatterplot (with elephants omitted). Include some sort of 95% confidence bounds—either for $E(Y|x)$ or prediction intervals.

E-10 Refer back to the temperature data of Task B. Produce a scatterplot showing body temperature vs. pulse rate, with separate symbols (or colors) to distinguish males from females and superimpose two regression lines showing the least squares fit to predict body temperature from pulse rate for each gender.

TASK F: Producing a Report

Your final task is to incorporate some statistical results into a written report. We assume that you will produce the report in your favorite word processor with results, tables, and graphs from your statistical package. Referring to the two-group comparison task (Task D), compile a report that includes the following features:

Basic.

F-1 A paragraph that explains the source of the data.

F-2 A table with the summary statistics for the two groups (as found in D-1). Format this table clearly, and align numbers using reasonable choices for numerical precision.

F-3 A copy of the side-by-side boxplot (or other graphic) with an appropriate title, followed by some text that explains what the plot shows.

F-4 The results of the two-sample confidence intervals and tests with textual interpretations.

F-5 A compact table of the raw data.

Challenge.

F-6 How much of the formatting of the report can be accomplished within the statistical package without using a separate word processor?

Conclusion

One must weigh many factors when choosing statistical software to support teaching. These factors include: costs, availability of computing equipment, lab facilities, instructional support, textbook support, and the level of sophistication of the students, the course, and the instructor! This article has focused on general statistical analysis packages, although software now exists to support instruction through multimedia textbooks and web-based materials. Two good sources of reviews for current statistical packages are the Statistical Computing Software Reviews section of *The American Statistician* and the CTI Statistics web site of reviews at `stats.gla.ac.uk/cti`. An excellent list of links to the web sites of many statistical package vendors is maintained by the Stata Corporation at `stata.com/support/links/stat_software.html`.

References

[1] Allison, T. and D. Cicchetti, "Sleep in Mammals: Ecological and Constitutional Correlates," *Science*, **194**, 1976, 732–734.

[2] Lock, Robin H., "1993 New Car Data," *Journal of Statistics Education*, `amstat.org/publications/jse/v1n1/datasets.lock.html` (on line), **1**(1), 1993.

[3] Rossman, Allan J., *Workshop Statistics: Discovery with Data*, 1996, Springer-Verlag, New York.

[4] Shoemaker, Allen J., "What's Normal? Temperature, Gender, and Heartrate," *Journal of Statistics Education*, `amstat.org/publications/jse/v4n2/datasets.shoemaker.html` (on line), **4**(2), 1996.

Summary of Web Links Used

1. Alcohol & Tobacco Dataset, `lib.stat.cmu.edu/DASL/Datafiles/AlcoholandTobacco.html`
2. Body Temperature Dataset, `amstat.org/publications/jse/datasets/normtemp.dat`
3. 1993 Cars Dataset, `amstat.org/publications/jse/datasets/93cars.dat`
4. CTI Statistics Web Site, `stats.gla.ac.uk/cti`
5. Dataset and Story Library (DASL), `lib.stat.cmu.edu/DASL/`
6. Journal of Statistics Education, `amstat.org/publications/jse/index.html`
7. Journal of Statistics Education Data Archive, `amstat.org/publications/jse/archive.htm`
8. Sleep & Mammals—full dataset, `lib.stat.cmu.edu/datasets/sleep`
9. Sleep & Mammals—Table 3, `it.stlawu.edu/~rlock/math113/mammals.dat`
10. Stata Corportation's List of Statistical Software Vendors, `stata.com/support/links/stat_software.html`
11. Statlib Dataset Archive, `lib.stat.cmu.edu/datasets/`

Using Graphing Calculators for Data Analysis in Teaching

Patrick W. Hopfensperger
Homestead High School
Mequon, WI

Introduction

As a project, a group of students in a statistics class wanted to determine if there was a relationship between a student's GPA and their ACT score. After the students collected data, they began their analysis. As the statistics teacher walked around the room observing and helping students with their analysis, Cory, trying to find the best model to fit the set of data, asked, "Because the linear regression model has a high r value, does that mean it is the best model that would fit the data?" The other students in Cory's group reminded him that he should also look at a plot of the residuals to help make a decision. Cory, using a graphing calculator, quickly made a residual plot and concluded that since the plot indicated there was somewhat of a pattern, he would need to study other models.

This brief classroom scenario demonstrates how the teaching and learning of statistics is changing, due in part to the development of graphing calculators with advanced statistical capabilities. With the graphing calculator, students can display plots and quickly do sophisticated statistical calculations, allowing the students time to interpret the results and draw proper conclusions. The graphing calculator has become a valuable tool for teaching students introductory statistics.

Rationale for Using the Graphing Calculator

The focus of teaching statistics should be to foster student belief about the positive use of statistics in making decisions. Classroom activities should engage students in constructing their own knowledge. Student assignments should emphasize analysis of data and the communication of this analysis. As much as possible, we should use real data in all our examples and activities. Before teaching formal algorithms and formulas, we should introduce students to explorations and simulations. The graphing calculator meshes well with this approach to teaching statistics. Access to graphing calculators gives students the opportunity to work with data and allows them to focus on interpreting calculations rather than on doing calculations.

The *Advanced Placement Course Description: Statistics* [2], states that the "AP Statistics course depends heavily on the availability of technology suitable for the interactive, investigative aspects of data analysis." The Course Description also states that the computer is the fundamental tool of data analysis. It is not possible at this time for students taking the AP Statistics exam in our program to have access to a computer during the exam, therefore students are expected to bring to the exam a graphing calculator with statistical capabilities. The graphing calculator cannot re-place the computer as the tool of choice for analyzing large data sets or conducting large simulations, but students need to have a computing tool available at all times, in the class-room and at home, to aid in their analysis of data.

I have been teaching a statistics course to high school seniors for twelve years and an AP Statistics course for the past three years. During this time, I have used both the computer and the graphing calculator as tools for students to use during the course. When deciding which tool to use, there are these issues to consider:

- How much data has been collected? For large data sets, the computer is the choice because of it's ability to han-dle large data sets and the speed of its calculations.
- How accessible are computers? Many students have lim-ited access to computers at school and at home. Even though most schools have computer labs, many depart-ments share these labs and they are usually closed be-yond the school day. Classroom demonstrations require expensive display devices and one station does not allow for all students to be actively involved in the analysis of the data.
- How much money can be spent on statistical comput-ing? The cost of equipment is an issue for many school districts. The cost of one computer can pay for approx-imately 25 graphing calculators. Instead of having 25 students view one computer screen, each student can use a calculator that allows him or her to take an active part in analyzing data.

Statistical Capabilities of the Graphing Calculator

The *Curriculum and Evaluation Standards for School Mathematics* [3] suggests classroom practices that are cen-tered on discussion and investigation and that make math-ematical ideas accessible to a wide range of students. This vision of mathematics eduation assumes the availability of graphing calculators with statistical capabilities. Graphing calculators can help with the analysis of data entered into lists as single variables, as ordered pairs, or entered into matrices as arrays. Students can edit, sort, store, graph, and calculate with any data they enter into the calculator. They can also generate data using various random num-ber generators on the calculator. The statistical capabilities of graphing calculators differ slightly from one model to another; the following are some of the capabilities of the TI-83Plus:

- plotting histograms, box plots, normal probability plots, and scatter plots;

- calculating means, medians, quartiles, and standard de-viations;
- calculating correlation coefficients;
- calculating equations of least squares regression lines;
- calculating residuals;
- calculating normal probabilities;
- calculating binomial probabilities;
- calculating z-statistics and p-values for 1-sample z-tests, 1-sample proportion z-tests, 2-sample z-tests, and 2-proportion z-tests;
- calculating t-statistics and p-values for the 1 sample t test and 2 sample t test (with and without using a pooled SD);
- calculating confidence intervals for means and propor-tions;
- calculating the Chi-Square statistic.

Advantages of Using the Graphing Calculator

There are several advantages of using graphing calculators to teach and learn statistics. They are very easy for students to learn how to use and are portable, which allows *all* stu-dents access to the statistical functions—instead of only those students with computers. They allow students to vi-sualize relationships in the data and do calculations quickly and accurately. They perform essentially all the tests and functions that are found in a first course in statistics. They allow students to manipulate lists of data and matrices, which helps students develop an understanding of statisti-cal concepts such as variance and correlation. They allow students to examine the implications of an analysis without actually doing all the calculations. They allow students to easily add to or delete from lists, which permits them to determine if there are outliers or influential points in the data set and thus to reach correct conclusions.

For classroom demonstrations, larger data sets can be stored, retrieved, and linked to student calculators, which lessens the time of entering larger sets of data. The calcu-lators can also be linked to a computer, which allows the transfer of data from various internet sites or from devices such as the CBL (calculator-based laboratory). Finally, a big advantage of using the graphing calculator is that the teaching of statistics, with students actively involved in the analysis of real data sets, is easier to implement, making statistics a more exciting and interesting course for both students and teachers.

Examples of Graphing Calculator Use

The following examples demonstrate how the calculator can be used to meet the challenges of teaching an introductory statistics course.

Analysis of univariate data.   A telephone survey of randomly selected dog kennels and dog breeders in Southeastern Wisconsin produced the list of prices, in dollars, of a Labrador puppy. The sample was taken in October 1997 by a group of AP Statistics students.

275, 500, 200, 200, 300, 350, 35, 275, 375, 290,
350, 500, 400, 500, 600, 350, 300, 500, 350, 500,
475, 460, 490, 425, 450, 475, 500, 500

To begin the analysis of the data, students enter the prices into a list on their calculators. The list feature of the calculator is similar to a spreadsheet: students can enter data into columns, label the columns, and perform calculations on the columns. Figure 1, generated by a TI-83Plus, shows the data entered into a list that has been labeled PRICE.

Now the students can plot the data. Suppose they want a histogram of these data. Figure 2 shows the window nec-

essary for choosing the type of plot; they choose histogram. Figure 3 shows the window used for choosing the histogram settings, and Figure 4 shows a histogram of the data.

A useful feature, to help in the analysis of the data, is the Trace button. After pressing the Trace button, the calculator displays a cursor at the top and midpoint of a bar. A window at the bottom displays the class limits and the number of observations in the class. Since the calculator does not print a scale on the screen, the trace feature helps

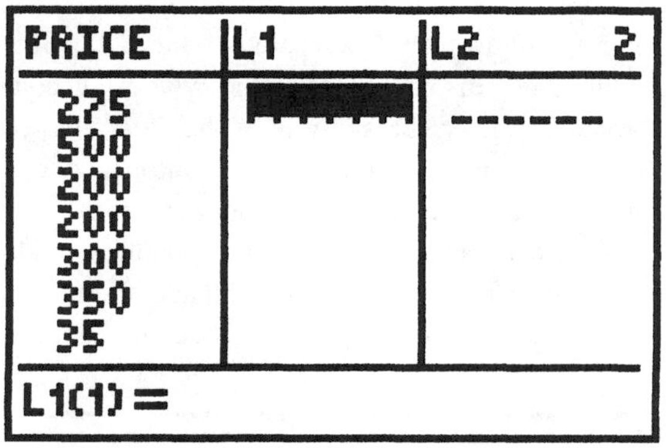

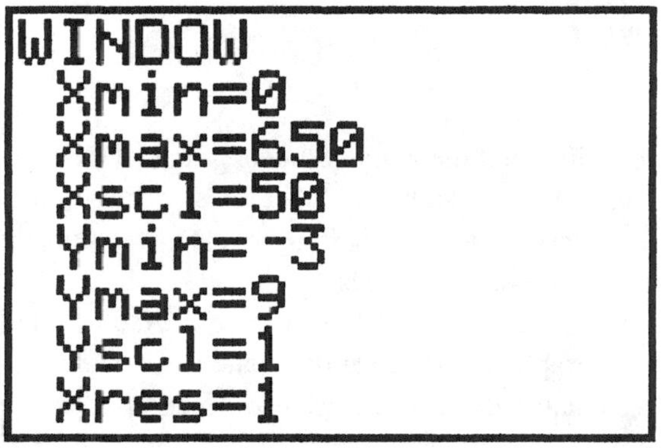

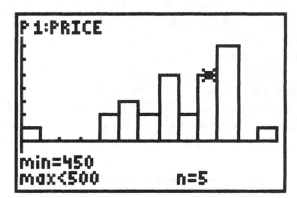

FIGURE 3

FIGURE 4

FIGURE 1

FIGURE 2

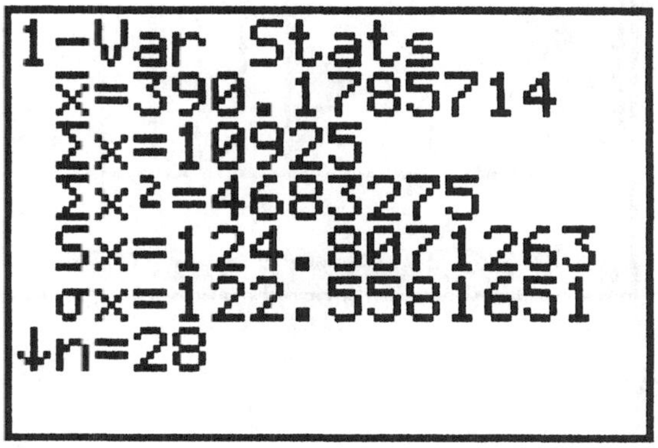

FIGURE 5

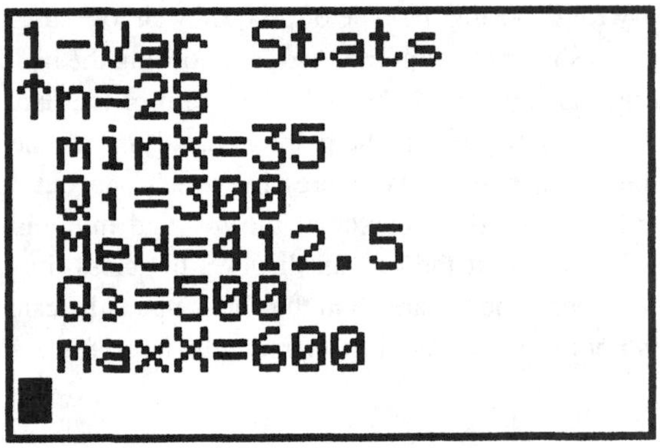

FIGURE 6

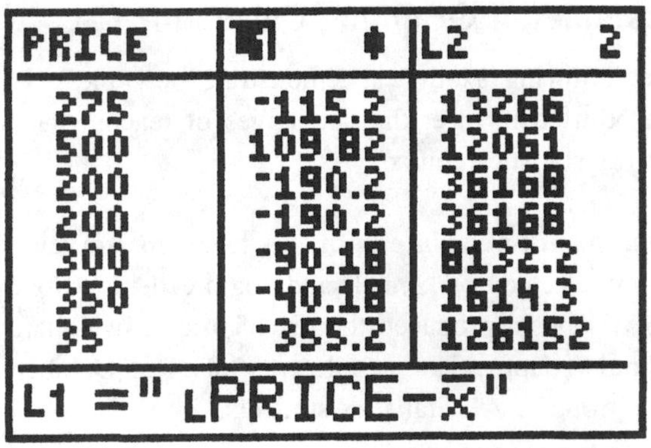

FIGURE 8

students interpret the graph. Students can then make a hand sketch of the histogram and label the sketch with the scale clearly marked. After plotting the data, the students can compute summary statistics.

Another feature available to trace a graph is the free-moving graph cursor. Once this cursor has been activated, the calculator displays the screen location of the cursor as x and y coordinates. If students want to estimate the location of the mean on the histogram, they can use this free-moving cursor. Figure 7 shows one such estimate of the mean of this distribution of Labrador puppy prices. This visual reinforcement can help a student's understanding of the mean as a balance point.

The list feature of the calculator can also be used to develop an understanding of the standard deviation. Figure 8 shows (1) the data in list PRICE, (2) the deviations from the mean, and (3) list L2 as the square of L1. The students can then find the sum of L2, divide this sum by $(n-1)$, and then take the square root of this value to find the standard deviation. Using the list frees the student from tedious calculations and helps develop conceptual understanding of the standard deviation.

Analysis of Bivariate Data. Below is a sample taken from the Milwaukee Journal-Sentinel (12/14/97), of 19 Ford Escorts listing their age in years and the asking price for the car in dollars. Suppose students want to use age to predict cost.

Figure 9 shows the scatterplot of the data. Since the graph does not display a scale, the window becomes an important feature in the analysis of the data. Students can again make good use of the Trace button and the free-moving cursor in the analysis of the scatterplot.

First we can have students use the calculator to develop the concepts of least squares and residuals. Using the Draw feature and the free-moving cursor, students "draw" a line

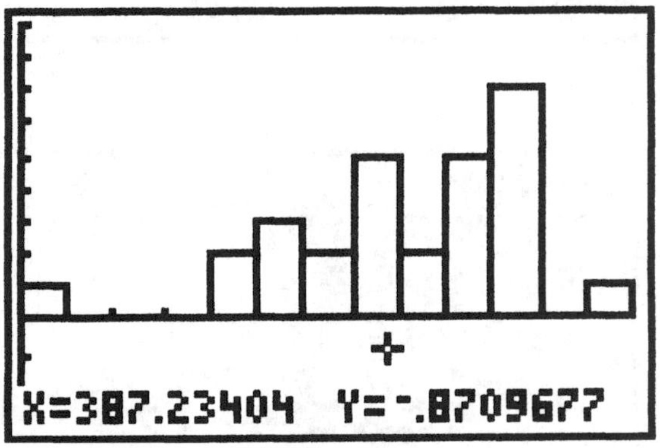

FIGURE 7

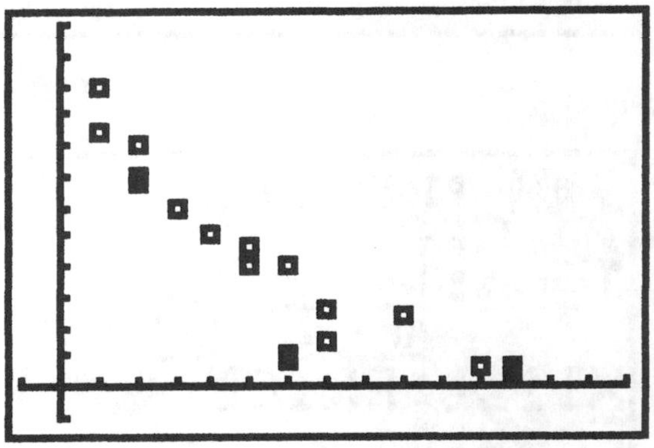

FIGURE 9

Age(yrs)	12	12	11	9	7	7	6	6	6	5	5	4	3	2	2	2	1	1	1
Cost ($)	500	595	775	2300	1475	2650	3995	795	1000	3990	4677	4977	5990	6995	7995	6688	8495	9995	9990

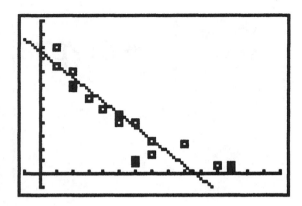

FIGURE 10

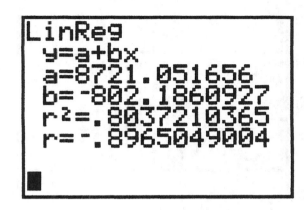

FIGURE 12

AGE	COST	◼	◆ 3
12	500	2712.5
12	595	2807.5
11	775	2004.5
9	2300	1563.5
7	1475	-1220
7	2650	-52.5
6	3995	309.5

L1 = " LCOST−Y₁(LA...

FIGURE 11

that they feel best represents the data; an example is shown in Figure 10. Each student finds the equation of the line ($y = 9583.5 - 983x$ for the example of Figure 10) and enters it into the calculator. The students then find the sum of the squared residuals for their lines (46,485,688 for Figure 10) to determine who has the best line. Figure 11 shows the data in lists labeled Age and Cost; L1 contains the residuals. Students can then compare their results to the least squares regression line. Figure 12 shows the results of the linear regression calculations.

A quick look at a residual plot shows a pattern in the residuals, indicating that students might want to investigate a quadratic model.

Simulation and Sampling Distributions. An important part of the AP Statistics curriculum is simulating a sampling distribution. The ability to design and conduct a simulation helps students truly understand the concept of a sampling distribution, which leads to the development of hypothesis testing. The following example demonstrates how the graphing calculator can be used to conduct a simulation.

According to the Census Bureau, about 12% of American families have three or more children. The Gallup organization randomly selects 90 American families. Estimate the probability that at least 15 families will have three or more children.

Students can use the calculator to generate a list of 90 random integers between 1 and 100 and then have the calculator count the number of values between 1 and 12. After repeating this procedure numerous times, students can enter the results of each trial in a list and have the calculator draw the sampling distribution and calculate the summary statistics. Figures 13, 14, and 15 show the results of 85 trials.

Inferences for Two-Way Tables. The graphing calculator can also be used to perform some of the standard hypothesis tests found in many introductory statistics courses.

A poll taken by the Gallup Organization in March 1995 for *U.S. News and World Report* found that 34% of men and 44% of women said that they have been accused of

```
WINDOW
 Xmin=.5
 Xmax=18.5
 Xscl=1
 Ymin=-2
 Ymax=15
 Yscl=1
 Xres=1
```

FIGURE 13

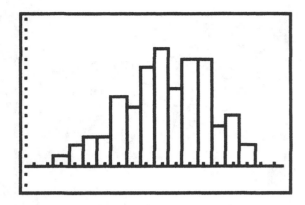

FIGURE 14

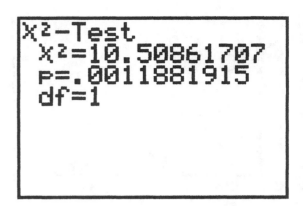

FIGURE 16

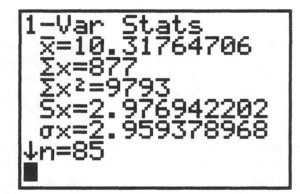

FIGURE 15

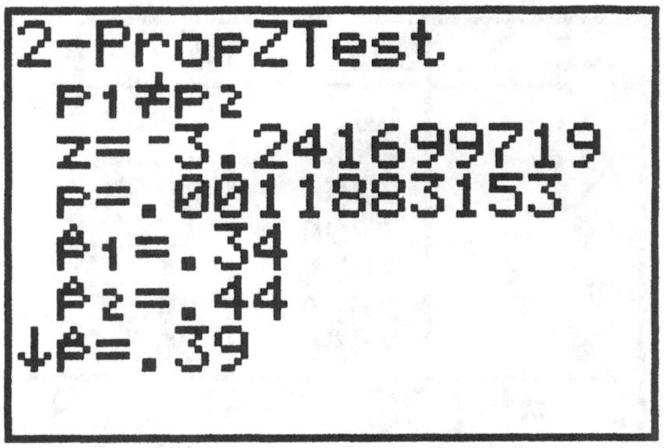

FIGURE 17

being a "back-seat" driver. Assume there were 500 men and 500 women in the survey. Is there a difference between how men and women answered the question?

Students can use the calculator to perform a Chi-Square test and a 2-proportions z-test. The results are shown in Figures 16 and 17. Since the calculator can perform these statistical tests quickly, it is important that instructors maintain a balance between appropriate calculator use and non-calculator experiences. They should stress that students clearly state the reasons they chose a particular statistical test prior to using the calculator's statistical functions to perform the chosen test. Based on the results of the calculations, students should then clearly state the conclusions that can or cannot be drawn.

Concluding Remarks

The examples illustrate how the graphing calculator makes advanced statistical ideas accessible for a broad range of students. These calculators provide a personal, portable tool that students can use in class and at home. They minimize the amount of time required to do tedious calculations, thus

allowing more time for the development of concepts and the interpretation of results. Finally and most importantly, the graphing calculator opens opportunities for discovery learning. Even though the calculator cannot replace the computer for certain tasks, the lines between the two are becoming blurred. In the future the computing and visual power of calculators will be greatly increased.

No matter which tool is used, it is important that teachers provide classroom experiences that pave the way for students to make sense of the results the calculator produces. Students need to be able to interpret calculator or computer output and reach proper conclusions. As these challenges are met, the graphing calculator and the computer will continue to grow in their importance as tools in the teaching and learning of statistics.

References Cited

1. Burrill, Gail, "The Graphing Calculator: A Tool for Change," in *Calculators in Mathematics Education*, edited by James Fey and Christian Hirsch, 1992, National Council of Teachers of Mathematics, Reston, VA.

2. The College Board, *Advanced Placement Course Description: Statistics*, 1997, New York, NY.

3. National Council of Teachers of Mathematics, *Curriculum and Evaluation Standards for School Mathematics*, 1989, Reston, VA.

4. Texas Instruments, *TI-83 Graphing Calculator Guidebook*, 1996, Dallas, TX.

5. Watkins, Ann, *Teacher's Guide—AP Statistics*, 1997, The College Board, New York.

Bibliography of Calculator Resources for Statistics

Statistics Textbooks

These textbooks use the TI-83 Graphing Calculator throughout the book.

Rossman, Alan and J. von Oehsen, *Workshop Statistics: Discovery with Data and the Graphing Calculator*, 1997, Springer.

Yates, Daniel, David Moore, and George McCabe, *The Practice of Statistics TI-83 Graphing Calculator Enhanced*, 1999, W. H. Freeman.

Resource Books

These books provide examples and the calculator key strokes.

Barrett, Gloria, *Statistics with the TI-83*, 1998, Meridan Creative Group.

Barton, Ray and John Diehl, *TI-83 Enhanced Statistics*, 1997, Venture Publishing.

Kelly, Brendan, *Exploring Statistics with TI-83 Graphics Calculator*, 1987, Brendan Kelly Publishing.

Morgan, Larry, *Statistics Handbook for the TI-83*, 1997, Texas Instruments.

Schneider, Robert and George Best, *Introductory Statistics with the TI-83*, 1998, Venture Publishing.

Replacement Units

These books provide modules that can be used to replace or supplement certain units in an introductory statistics course.

Brueningsen, Chris, Bill Bower, Linda Antinone, and Elisa Brueningsen-Kerner, *Real-World Math with the CBL System: Activities for the TI-83 and TI-83 Plus*, 1999, Texas Instruments.

Burrill, Gail, Jack Burrill, Patrick Hopfensperger, and James Landwehr, *Exploring Regression*, 1999, Dale Seymour Publications.

Burrill, Gail, Jack Burrill, James Landwehr, and Jeff Witmer, *Advanced Modeling and Matrices*, 1999, Dale Seymour Publications.

Burrill, Jack, Miriam Clifford, and James Landwehr, *Modeling with Logarithms*, 1999, Dale Seymour Publications.

Hopfensperger, Patrick, Henry Kranendonk, and Richard Scheaffer, *Probability Models*, 1999, Dale Seymour Publications.

Hopfensperger, Patrick, Henry Kranendonk, and Richard Scheaffer, *Probability Through Data*, 1999, Dale Seymour Publications.

Articles

These articles give specific examples of using the graphing calculator to teach such topics as correlation, least squares, and simulations.

Coons, Al and Bob Cornell, "Random Selection without Replacement by Calculator," *Mathematics Teacher* 91(8), November 1998, pp. 736, 739.

Dessart, Don, "The Correlation Coefficient and Influential Data Points," *Mathematics Teacher* 90(3), March 1997, pp. 242–246.

Vonder Embse, Charles, "Visualizing Least Squares Lines of Best Fit," *Mathematics Teacher* 90 (5), May 1997, pp. 404–408.

Excerpts from *An Electronic Companion to Statistics*[†]

Preface

Four Kinds of Understanding

To gain a thorough understanding of statistics, you will need to combine several different kinds of thinking:

1. Computational/numerical;
2. Visual/graphical;
3. Verbal/interpretive;
4. Structural/deductive.

Computational/numerical. This is what many people think of when they think of statistics: memorizing rules and formulas, then plugging in numbers and doing a lot of calculating. Although statistical work does rely on a lot of computing, there is almost no value in just memorizing rules. If you find yourself doing that, you are probably not using your time efficiently. Learning the rules can be a useful step toward understanding, however, *provided you relate them to their visual, verbal, and structural meanings*.

Visual/graphical. Learning how to use graphs to represent numbers and how to read patterns in graphs is essential to understanding statistics. The mechanical part—constructing the graph—is just the beginning. The more important part is learning to *think* visually about numbers.

[†] From *An Electronic Companion to Statistics,* by George W. Cobb with the cooperation of Jonathan D. Cryer, ©1997 Cogito Learning Media, Inc.

Verbal/interpretive.   "Data are not just numbers, but numbers with a context."[1] In statistics, any calculating you do, and any graphs you construct, ought to be part of a search for meaningful patterns in real data. (Exception: When you're *first* learning a new skill, it is sometimes useful to practice with lists of numbers that have no context, but only at first.) Try to make it a habit to ask, "What does this tell me about the data (in relation to its context)?" The search for meaning is what makes statistics worthwhile.

Structural/deductive.   The methods and concepts of statistics are related to each other by a logical structure. This structure is part of the "big picture" that should gradually come into focus for you as you work at understanding statistics.

Four Key Themes

One approach to the big picture is to relate what you learn to four basic themes:
1. Production;
2. Exploration;
3. Repetition;
4. Inference.

Production   How and why were the data produced? This may seem like an obvious question to ask, but as a rule, it doesn't get enough attention. Bad planning and careless data collection can ruin an experiment or survey. Principles of good planning and careful collection can't be put into mathematical formulas, but the principles are important all the same.

Exploration   Data = Pattern + Deviation. Data analysis is intended to be a search for meaningful patterns. No one pattern is likely to tell the whole story, though. A useful pattern must be simpler than the actual data, which means that the data deviate from the pattern, at least a little. Exploring a data set means trying out a variety of patterns to see how well they fit: What's the balance between pattern and deviation?

Repetition   What will happen if I repeat this a large number of times? Statistics is sometimes defined as the science of learning in the presence of *variation*. If I do an experiment today and repeat the same experiment next week, the two sets of results will most likely be somewhat different. Statistics has value because it gives us a way to learn from the results of a single experiment or survey, even though we would get somewhat different results from a second one. Imagine repeating the experiment a large number of times and looking at all the results together. Part of what we see will be pattern—those aspects of the results that we expect to be the same from one repetition to the next. The rest will be deviation—the part that varies from one repetition to the next. We can sometimes use statistical logic (inference) to decide, from the results of just one experiment or survey, what patterns to expect from a large number of repetitions.

Inference   Be suspicious of any theory that makes your data into an unlikely outcome. One major branch of statistics deals with production: how to plan experiments and surveys. Another deals with exploration: finding and describing patterns in data. Yet another deals with inference: drawing conclusions about the long-run patterns we think would emerge if we were to repeat the data-production process a large number of times. For any set of results, we can try out a variety of theories (usually called models and hypotheses) about the process that created our data. We can then ask what sort of data our theoretical process (model, hypothesis) would be likely to generate. The basic logic of inference is that we should not ordinarily trust any model that would be unlikely to give results like our actual data.

---

[1] Moore, David S. (1992). "Teaching Statistics as a Respectable Subject," in Florence Gordon and Sheldon Gordon, eds., *Statistics for the Twenty-First Century,* MAA Notes no.26, Washington: The Mathematical Association of America.

This logic takes some getting used to, not because it is unfamiliar, but because in everyday life it is so automatic we don't think about it. (For example, you automatically rule out rain when the sky is cloudless.) Statistics uses the same logic in a more formal way.

This introduction is necessarily somewhat abstract. The four kinds of understanding and four basic themes will take on more meaning as you have the chance to relate them to the methods and concepts of statistical thinking.

Many Kinds of Problems

This workbook has problems of various kinds.

Simple drills for basic skills. These problems use simple, made-up data, to be easy and quick. Their purpose is to help you learn the mechanical skills. Just as a piano player practices scales and a beginning language student learns rules of grammar, you may find it useful, at first, to practice the mechanics in a simple setting with no "story" to take your mind away from learning the skills.

Skills in context. Just as pianists practice scales in order to build skills for playing real music, and language students learn grammar in order to read literature or have real conversations, your goal in learning statistical skills should be to use them to find meaning in real data. Many of the problems in the workbook could be labeled "skills in context"; they ask you to apply your skills in real-world settings with authentic data. At this stage in your learning, you may find it helps to have some coaching about what to look for. The problems are designed with that in mind.

Simple drills on basic concepts. Along with the numerical skills, you also need to practice the basic concepts you need for statistical thinking. We've included a number of problems that ask you about these ideas in a "clean" setting with no "story."

Concepts in context. Once you have the basic ideas clearly in mind, you'll be ready to go on to the harder but more rewarding problems that ask you to use the ideas of statistics in a real-world setting.

Contents

Excerpts from *Visual Statistics*[†]

Preface to Instructor's Edition

Visual Statistics is specifically designed to help you, the instructor, teach statistics. It doesn't try to replace you. That task is well beyond the best artificial intelligence software, and is a dubious goal in any case. Instead, *Visual Statistics* is a tool that increases your effectiveness in the classroom and lets students work independently to explore statistical ideas. Its 15 modules, each with software and a chapter in this worktext, cover many challenging topics in a one-semester undergraduate statistics class. The software uses data visualization methods, animation, scenarios, and sample data sets to help students *see* statistical ideas in action. The modules are independent and give you different options to match your style. Use the modules in any order you want, in the way you find most effective. *Visual Statistics* was designed to increase your instructional options, not to be a technological straight jacket.

Visual Statistics gives you new ways to teach by removing traditional classroom limitations. For example, suppose you prepare an overhead transparency showing a scatter plot of a data set with a correlation of 0.8. A student asks, "But what would it look like if the variances were different?" You can explain that the plot would look more or less the same, but the axes would change. Their range would grow or shrink, depending on the change in variance. Would the students in your class understand? Those who can imagine the change, building the right pictures in their heads, would follow your explanation. But what about the students who are less skilled at abstract reasoning? For them, you might want to create a new transparency showing the new axes. But do you have the time to create transparencies for every question that inventive students ask?

That's where *Visual Statistics* comes in. With a few clicks of a mouse button, you can generate and plot a new data set with new variances right in the classroom. It only takes moments to illustrate the effects of changes in means, sample sizes, correlation, and even the distributions from which the samples are drawn (after all, not everything in the world is normally distributed, is it?). You could use a traditional statistical analysis package to create data sets for plotting, perhaps generating 10 new displays per hour, if you plan well. But *Visual Statistics* will let you create these displays in a few minutes and the displays are *live* in the classroom,

---

[†] *From Visual Statistics - Part I,* Instructor's Edition, by David P. Doane, Kieran Mathieson, and Ronald L. Tracy, ©1997 Irwin/McGraw-Hill.

able to be changed at will. You don't have to predict every question ahead of time. You can create the display you want in the classroom, quickly and easily.

Why does *Visual Statistics* have the advantage in the classroom? The reason is simple. Data analysis packages like SAS, SPSS, and Minitab are designed to do just what you expect them to do: analyze data. *Visual Statistics,* on the other hand, is designed to help you *teach statistics.* Although some of the modules do let you analyze data, that is not their main purpose. Their goal is to give you, the instructor, more powerful tools for explaining statistical ideas.

Visual Statistics can also help students working outside of class. Each chapter in this text has learning exercises that students can complete in about an hour. There are also advanced learning exercises for more motivated students. The exercises promote inductive learning. That is, they encourage students to explore statistical concepts and discover new ideas themselves. *Visual Statistics'* emphasis on graphics and easy experimentation can help them achieve those sudden flashes of insight that make a class rewarding and memorable.

Answers to exercises are included in this Instructor's Edition. Although the exercises can be turned in and graded, they can also just be examined for completeness and returned to the student. Students will learn by completing the exercises. After students complete the exercises you may wish to put the answers on reserve in your school's library.

Each chapter of the worktext has a self-evaluation quiz that students can use to test their own knowledge, plus a glossary of terms. There are also individual and team projects that are open-ended exercises requiring the student to investigate a problem using *Visual Statistics.* Individual projects generally take an hour or two of computer work and about two hours to write. The team projects are designed for two to four students. Our experience suggests that students should complete the learning exercises before doing any of the projects. Notes on a possible approach to each project are given in Appendix B of this Instructor's Edition.

To use *Visual Statistics* to augment your lecture, you will need a computer with *Visual Statistics* preloaded and a projection system (LCD panel and overhead projector, or a video projector). If the room is very dark, our experience suggests that student attention will wane quickly if your demonstration takes more than 15 minutes. For each module we have provided an outline of a computer demonstration (Appendix A). Use this as a guide. The demonstration can be completed in as little as 10 minutes or can form the basis of an entire lecture. You can also use a module of *Visual Statistics* to illustrate a concept without using all of the module's features.

It is important that every *Visual Statistics* module be easy to use. This is addressed in several ways. First, *Visual Statistics'* modular design limits the complexity of each program. The Visualizing Analysis of Variance module covers only one-factor ANOVA. Students can use it without being distracted by program features that are not relevant to the problem at hand. Second, the interfaces use familiar Windows controls like buttons, drop down lists, and scroll bars. Anyone who has used applications like Word or Excel will be comfortable with *Visual Statistics.* Third, each module's interface has been customized to improve its "fit" with the concepts it explores. For example, the interface of the Visualizing Two-Sample Hypothesis Tests module was specifically designed to help students with that particular task. Fourth, each module has its own context-sensitive help file. It explains how to use the program, discusses the concepts being illustrated, defines terms, gives formulas where appropriate, and so on. It can also be searched for keywords.

Each module should not only be easy to use, it should be easy to *learn.* After all, time spent learning a program is time that could be better spent learning statistics. A key part of each chapter in the text is the Orientation. Each one is essentially a script that introduces a module. It takes students about 15 minutes to run through an Orientation. Classroom testing has shown that students who use a module's orientation have little trouble with the program.

We hope you and your students will find *Visual Statistics* useful. If you have teaching ideas or questions you wish to share with other *Visual Statistics* instructors, use our Web page at `http://www.mhhe.com/sciencemath/statistics/doane/`. The page will also be used to disseminate information about *Visual Statistics* updates, licensing, and technical support.

Preface

This textbook began in 1992 when Tracy walked into Doane's office to see if he would be interested in writing a National Science Foundation (NSF) grant proposal to develop software to teach statistical concepts. The collaboration was natural. Each had been teaching for many years, and had evolved definite approaches to teaching statistics. Both had experience writing computer software.

During that fall semester our ideas began to take shape. We believed it was time to bring the computer into the *classroom*. Although students had been doing computer lab projects for decades, the classroom had remained basically unaffected by the computer. We wanted to use computers to teach *concepts* rather than just analyze data. We wanted to stress visual displays rather than numbers, equations, and calculations. While an equation is an explanation to some students, it is a barrier to others. Understanding the full implications of an equation is not a trivial matter for most people, but a series of pictures or a simple animation can illustrate fairly complex ideas in a few minutes. Our proposal asked the NSF to support our efforts to bring the power of computers into the statistics classroom.

In the spring of 1993 we were awarded the NSF grant. Since neither of us had experience in writing programs for the Windows environment, we went looking for an expert. Luckily for us, Oakland University had recently hired such a person. We approached Mathieson who agreed to help us as a consultant. By July it was clear that Mathieson had become an integral part of the project. This marked the beginning of our collaborative efforts.

Our approach is based on four assumptions: (1) For many students visualization is a key to learning; (2) existing statistical packages were designed for data analysis, not visualizing concepts; (3) today's computers have enough power to support visualization; and (4) individual instructors lack the time and resources to design their own software. Our goal was to create learning modules which illustrate concepts that cannot easily be shown mathematically or with packages such as Minitab or Excel. We sought to minimize duplication of capabilities already available in data analysis software.

We wanted to promote learning through active self-discovery (inductive learning) as well as to support the instructor in the traditional lecture/lab setting (deductive learning). A student using a software module with the Learning Exercises in this worktext will be led through experiments that promote self-discovery. Team and Individual Learning Projects pose less-structured problems that continue this process. The software is designed to encourage experimentation. A student can use replication to simulate the "experimental" side of statistics.

These same features can be used effectively by the instructor in the classroom or the computer laboratory. The instructor can use a software module to illustrate a concept (e.g., the relationship between a confidence interval and a test statistic). The concept can then be reinforced with a simulation experiment.

We wanted flexible software. Instructors can omit topics or vary their order. No module requires knowledge of another module. Students can learn in different ways and at different rates. Although each module is aimed at the average learner, each was designed to offer options for those who desire more analytical depth (or who are just adventuresome). We designed modules that allow you to set parameters in several ways. For example, you can manipulate the parameters of some demonstrations using scroll bars (simple level), by typing parameter values (intermediate level), or by choosing a known distribution and its parameters (advanced level).

Every *Visual Statistics* module opens with a virtual Notebook (a familiar ring binder with pages you can turn). The Notebook organizes the options and provides a link with the *Visual Statistics* worktext and your textbook. The Notebook contains tabs that you can click. These tabs divide the Notebook into different sections. Notebook tabs include **Introduction** (general idea of what is in the module), **Concepts** (main topics covered), and **More Information** tab (references to chapters or other textbooks). Other tabs vary from module to module, such as **Examples** (real data on a variety of topics), **Scenarios** (context for realistic sampling simulations), **Databases** (real data sets), **Templates** (icons to choose specified distributions or trends), **Do-It-Yourself** (control panels to manipulate parameters of an experiment), and **Data Editor** (to enter data or paste data from a spreadsheet to create your own example). You may return to the Notebook while running the program. This allows you to change scenarios, pick a different example, or choose a different set of options.

Every module has its own Help system, similar to that in other Windows programs. It includes definitions, examples, equations, graphics, and hints. You can use the table of contents and use the hypertext capabilities to jump to topics you want to learn more about. You can also do keyword searches using each Help file's extensive index. You will get more from *Visual Statistics* if you learn to use the Help system.

Our software uses familiar Windows visual controls (command buttons, scroll bars, list boxes, option buttons, and so on). Input is mostly from a mouse rather than from the keyboard. This interface will seem quite natural to most people. If you have used other Windows programs such as Word, Excel, or even Solitaire, you already know how to use *Visual Statistics* controls.

Visual Statistics is to be used with a textbook or other course materials. It complements these traditional sources, it does not replace them. However, you'll find topics in these sources easier to understand after you *see* them in *Visual Statistics*.

Visual Statistics consists of 15 software modules and a worktext. Each chapter of the worktext begins with a list of the key concepts the chapter will cover and a short list of learning objectives. Each concept is reviewed and illustrated. A short (about 15 minute) orientation to each module is provided. Past users have told us that this orientation is invaluable. Learning Exercises and Advanced Learning Exercises are provided for each module. These exercises guide you in self-discovery learning. Team and Individual Learning Projects continue this process with open-ended questions. A Self-Evaluation Quiz allows you to test your understanding of the material. Solutions and a guide to answering each question are provided. A Glossary at the end of each chapter provides definitions of terms used in the chapter. Although we take responsibility for all remaining errors, our project has benefited greatly from field testing, advice, and comments of faculty colleagues and their students at other universities. We thank these individuals for their dedication and interest in our project.

Contents

Excerpts from *StatConcepts*[†]

Preface

Introduction

Most introductory statistics courses have three parts: (1) *descriptive statistics,* which uses numbers and graphs to summarize the information about a data set, (2) *inferential statistics,* which draws conclusions about numerical characteristics of entire populations of objects from those of samples from the populations, and (3) *statistical concepts,* which are the basic logical and mathematical ideas underpinning descriptive and inferential statistics.

A wide variety of computer programs make it easy for students to accomplish what is required for the first two of these parts, but very little software has been developed for illustrating statistical concepts. That's why we wrote StatConcepts—as a set of "laboratories" for illustrating these concepts.

StatConcepts is actually a collection of programs written in the language of StataQuest, a student version of a program called Stata that is designed to do descriptive and inferential statistics.

StatConcepts is not intended as a text, but as a supplement to introductory statistics texts. Its main focus is on correct intrepretation and understanding of statistical concepts, terminology, and results, not on computation for a given problem. However, StatConcepts does contain some labs that allow students to compute results.

In many ways, the computer is the laboratory for the science of statistics. Most statistical investigations have their roots in a statement along these lines: "If we did this procedure over and over again, then this is what we would see." The only way realistically to do things over and over again is on a computer. In these labs, we have tried to use graphics to show what, in fact, we would see if we did various things over and over again.

We assume that instructors will not incorporate all of the labs in the StatConcepts collection (there are 28 of them!) into their courses, but rather pick and choose those they feel would be most useful in the course (and have time to cover in their already cramped schedule).

We hope that instructors can show the labs to students using some kind of projection, but each chapter of this book contains a "guided tour" through each lab that a student could read while at a computer. These guided

---

[†] From *StatConcepts: A Visual Tour of Statistical Ideas (w/disk for Windows), 1st edition,* by H. J. Newton and J. L. Harvill. ©1997. Reprinted with permission of Brooks/Cole Publishing, a division of Thomson Learning.

tours cannot totally replace an instructor, but they can certainly help instructors use the labs as a supplement to their courses.

Although the labs and this book are intended primarily for introductory courses, we have found them very valuable in courses at all levels. We have kept the material as nontechnical as possible, but more advanced students will be able to relate to the graphs and descriptions at a more mathematical level.

Computer Requirements for Using StatConcepts

From a software point of view, StatConcepts is totally self-contained and requires only a computer running Microsoft Windows.

The Structure of the Chapters

Except for the introductory lab and the *Calculating Confidence Intervals, Calculating Tests of Hypotheses,* and *Calculating One-way ANOVA* Labs (which are more calculation than concepts oriented), each chapter in this book is structured in the same way:

1. *Introduction:* The first section provides background information needed for the lab or labs in the chapter.
2. *Objectives:* This section briefly summarizes the concepts the lab or labs illustrate.
3. *Description:* This section briefly describes how the lab or labs work and what the items in the dialog box are.
4. *Guided Tour of the Lab:* This section is the heart of each chapter. Although the labs are best used while in front of the computer, we have included enough graphs from the labs to communicate the basic ideas by simply reading the tour. Some of the tours have many stops. Again, we have tried to design them so that readers can visit as many of the stops on a tour as they have the time or interest for.
5. *Summary:* This section summarizes what the guided tour has illustrated.
6. *Lab Exercises:* This section contains a set of exercises that can be used to further illustrate the key ideas.

Brief Contents

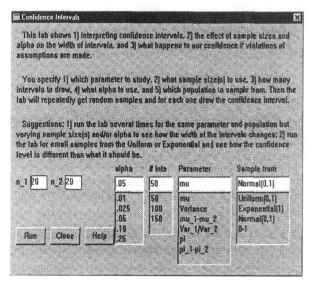

FIGURE 11.1
Dialog box for the *Interpreting Confidence Intervals* Lab

11.3 Description

To start the lab, choose `Interpreting Confidence Intervals` from the `Labs` menu. The dialog box shown in Figure 11.1 will open. This dialog box contains a host of information, including a brief narrative on how to use the lab. Below that narrative are six boxes in which you will supply information.

1 `n_1`: To the immediate right of `n_1` is a box where the value of a sample size is to be entered. The initial value of `n_1` is 20. If you are using a one-sample procedure, type the value of the sample size here. If you are using a two-sample procedure, type the value for the size of the sample from the first population. The values of `n_1` are restricted to numbers between 5 and 500.

2 `n_2`: To the immediate right of `n_2` is a box where you enter the value. The initial value of `n_2` is 20. If you are using a one-sample procedure, this value is ignored. If you are using a two-sample procedure, type in the value for the size of the sample from the second population. The values of `n_2` are restricted to numbers between 5 and 500.

3 `alpha`: Directly beneath the label `alpha` are values that may be chosen so that the level of confidence for the intervals calculated is $1-$ `alpha`. For example, the initial value is 0.05, so the initial level of confidence for the intervals calculated is 95%. The value of `alpha` is not restricted to those shown. To calculate confidence intervals for a value of `alpha` not supplied, simply type in the desired value.

4 `# Ints`: Directly beneath this label are values that indicate the number of samples to be drawn. The initial value is 50. For each sample drawn, a $100(1-$ `alpha`$)$ confidence interval is calculated. The value of `# Ints` is not restricted to those shown. To have a number of samples drawn for a value that is not supplied, simply type in the desired value for `# Ints`.

5 `Parameter`: Below this label are six different cases that correspond to the six confidence intervals outlined under item 4 in Subsection 11.1.1. The initial value is `mu`. This will calculate confidence intervals for the population mean μ. To calculate confidence intervals for the ratio of two variances σ_1^2/σ_2^2, choose `Var_1/Var_2`. The values for parameter are restricted to those shown.

6 `Sample from`: Below this label are the names of four different distributions. The distribution chosen specifies the distribution of the population from which the samples are being taken. The initial distribution is the `Normal(0, 1)` distribution. The distributions for `Sample from` are restricted to those shown:

  (a) A Uniform(0,1) distribution with mean $\mu = 0.50$ and variance $\sigma^2 = 1/12$.

  (b) An Exponential(1) distribution with mean $\mu = 1$ and variance $\sigma^2 = 1$.

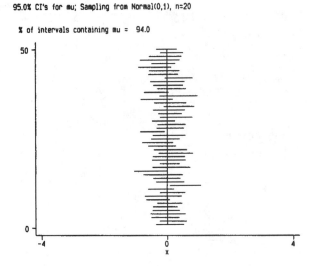

FIGURE 11.2

Fifty 95% confidence intervals for the mean μ of a N(0,1) population with $n = 20$ for each interval.

(c) A Normal(0,1) distribution with mean $\mu = 0$ and variance $\sigma^2 = 1$.

(d) A 0–1 population with proportion of 1's $\pi = 0.50$ and variance $\pi(1 - \pi) = 0.25$.

In the bottom left-hand corner of the dialog box are three buttons.

1 Run: Before you click on Run, be sure a value has been specified for all of the boxes just described. When you click on this button, a graphics window opens (see Figure 11.2). The caption includes information on the confidence level, the population from which samples are being drawn, and the sample size(s). A red vertical line representing the value of the population parameter appears on the graph. The computer randomly generates # Ints sets of n numbers from the specified population in Sample from and for each set of numbers calculates the 100(1− alpha) confidence interval for the parameter specified in the Parameter box. As each interval is calculated, a horizontal line beginning at the lower confidence limit and ending at the upper confidence limit is drawn. If the confidence interval contains the value of the parameter, the horizontal line will intersect the vertical line and will be drawn in red. If the confidence interval does not contain the value of the parameter, the horizontal line will not intersect the vertical line and will be drawn in yellow. After all # Ints samples are chosen and all confidence intervals are calculated, a second heading appears at the top of the graphics window giving the percentage of intervals that contained the value of the parameter for this run of the lab. You may click on Run as many times as you wish.

2 Close: Clicking on this button closes the lab and returns you to the StatConcepts menus.

3 Help: Clicking on this button opens a help window containing information about the lab.

11.4 Guided Tour of the Lab

We start our tour with the simplest case, namely calculating confidence intervals for the mean of a population whose distribution belongs to the family of normal distributions. Note that, when the lab first begins, the mean mu is already specified in the Parameter box. We will use the initial values in all the boxes. Thus we will be calculating fifty 95% confidence intervals using samples of size 20 from a Normal (0,1) population. Finally, since the population we are sampling from is Normal (0,1), the mean of that population is $\mu = 0$. This is represented by a red vertical line above 0.

Before we proceed, one final note is in order. In practice, we do not know the value of the mean (the parameter) of the population, and a single confidence interval is used to estimate the population mean (or parameter) with a specific degree of "confidence." One objective of this lab is to examine the behavior of all confidence intervals. To do this, many random samples are generated, and a confidence interval for each sample is calculated. This allows us to observe their performance in a controlled situation. By doing so, we will learn what to expect when we actually use these confidence intervals and will develop an understanding of what is truly meant by "95% confident."

To begin, click on Run. This causes the lab to randomly select the 50 samples, each containing 20 observations. For each sample, the lab calculates the sample mean $\overline{X}$ and the sample standard deviation s, and then finds the lower and upper limits of the confidence interval using

$$\overline{X} \pm t_{0.025,19} \frac{s}{\sqrt{20}}.$$

For each sample, a horizontal line is drawn above the horizontal axis from the lower confidence limit to the upper confidence limit.

One possible result was shown in Figure 11.2. You will probably get a slightly different graph because the lab selects a different set of 50 samples every time it is run. In this figure, 47 of the 50 samples (or 94%) have confidence intervals containing the true mean value of 0. Can you find the three intervals in the figure that don't "capture" the true mean? When you run the lab, how many of your 50 samples have intervals containing 0?

You can rerun the lab under these same conditions by clicking on Run. Each time you do, 50 new samples are selected, and the corresponding confidence intervals are calculated and drawn. For each set of intervals, you should notice that the percentage containing the population mean will be close to 95%. You should also pay close attention to the width of the intervals.

11.4.1 The Effect of Sample Size.

To see the effect of sample size on the width of a confidence interval, change the sample size in n_1 from 20 to 5 and click on Run. The confidence intervals calculated are now of the form

$$\overline{X} \pm t_{0.025,4} \frac{s}{\sqrt{4}}.$$

The result is shown in Figure 11.3 (again, your result should be similar but probably will not be the same). Notice that this figure is on the same scale (−4 to 4 on the horizontal axis) so that we can easily compare the widths of the intervals from the two sample sizes. For the smaller sample size, the widths of the confidence intervals are larger. We would hope this is the case, because it means that having more data (a larger sample size) will let us estimate the parameter more precisely.

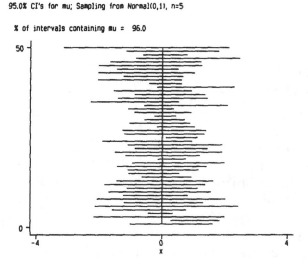

FIGURE 11.3
Fifty 95% confidence intervals for the mean μ of a N(0,1) population with $n = 5$ for each interval.

Note that the probability of capturing the true value of the parameter is the same in both figures because we used $\alpha = 0.05$ in both. Stated another way, a larger sample size has no effect on the probability of capturing the value of the parameter in the confidence interval! The sample size affects only the precision of our estimator.

11.4.2 The Effect of Confidence Level.

To see the effect of α on the behavior of confidence intervals, change n_1 back to 20, select `alpha = 0.25`, and run the lab again. The confidence intervals are now of the form

$$\overline{X} \pm t_{0.125,19} \frac{s}{\sqrt{20}}.$$

The result is shown in Figure 11.4. Notice that the intervals are narrower than in the $n = 20$ and $\alpha = 0.05$ case, but a much larger percentage of intervals do not contain the population mean. This is what being only 75% confident means: The chance that any one sample will result in a confidence interval containing the population mean is now only 75%. In other words, now that $\alpha = 0.25$, of all the possible samples we could choose, only 75% of them will result in a confidence interval containing the true value of the mean.

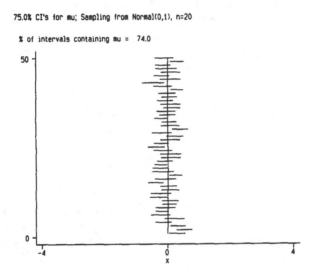

FIGURE 11.4
Fifty 75% confidence intervals for the mean μ of a N(0,1) population with $n = 20$ for each interval.

11.4.3 Violation of Assumptions.

As noted previously, the confidence interval formula for μ is only valid under two conditions:

1. For any sample size when the distribution of the population from which the sample is being taken belongs to the family of normal distributions.
2. For a continuous population with any distribution when the sample size is "large." We will now examine the effect of violating these assumptions. Change the value of n_1 to 5 and the distribution in Sample from to Exponential(1). (For this distribution, the population mean $\mu = 1$.) Graphs of the exponential curves are given in the *How Are Populations Distributed?* Lab. The exponential distribution with $\mu = 1$ is not shown, but by observing the trend in those graphs, you can see that the Exponential(1) distribution is even more skewed than those shown in that lab. From these graphs, you can see that such populations are not bell shaped at all, but rather are heavily skewed to the right.

The result of running the lab for $\alpha = 0.05$ is shown in Figure 11.5. Notice that instead of capturing the true mean approximately 95% of the time, the true mean was in only 42 of the 50 intervals, or 84% of the time.

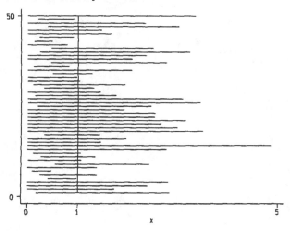

FIGURE 11.5
Fifty confidence intervals for the mean μ of an Exponential(1) population.

This shows how important such a violation of assumptions can be. Instead of being 95% confident, we can, in fact, be only around 84% confident.

Using *An Electronic Companion to Statistics, Visual Statistics,* and *StatConcepts* to Teach Introductory Statistics

Roxy Peck
California Polytechnic State University, San Luis Obispo

Introduction

Cal Poly is a four-year comprehensive state university of approximately 15,000 students. The primary focus is on undergraduate education. In addition to the traditional academic disciplines in the arts and sciences, we also have programs in engineering, architecture, and agriculture. All introductory statistics courses at Cal Poly are taught by the Statistics Department, although a number of disciplines teach applied research methods courses that follow the one or two quarter course taught by the Statistics Department.

At Cal Poly, we are very fortunate to have received funding for a studio classroom for statistics instruction. This classroom is equipped with computers and work areas for group and individual activities, and has fancy audio-visual equipment and computer projection capabilities. This room has enabled instructors to experiment with different pedagogies that are made possible by this type of non-traditional teaching space. All of the workstations in the room are equipped with Minitab, *An Electronic Companion to Statistics, Visual Statistics,* and *StatConcepts*. Minitab is used as the primary data analysis tool for in-class activities and labs. The other three packages are used for classroom demonstrations. A typical class meeting consists of a short quiz based on a reading assignment from the textbook, a brief mini-lecture that focuses on concepts and interpretations rather than computations, and then some sort of activity or lab that requires application of the topic covered. I use *An Electronic Companion to Statistics, Visual Statistics,* and *StatConcepts* primarily to enhance the mini-lecture portion of the course. Each of these packages does things that the others don't, and having access to all three allows me to incorporate the best of each. I realize that the facilities that I describe here are not common, but you can use these computer visualization and simulation tools in essentially the same way in any classroom that can accommodate a computer and an overhead projection device.

An Electronic Companion to Statistics

An Electronic Companion to Statistics by George W. Cobb with the cooperation of Jonathan D. Cryer is an interactive multimedia package that is designed to complement, rather than replace, introductory statistics texts. The package consists of an interactive CD (Windows or Mac) and a 356-page workbook. The *Electronic Companion* includes most topics in a traditional introductory statistics course, as well as some that are not as common, such as statistical process control. Institutional agreements for in-classroom use and for student computer lab use are available through the publisher.

Although the workbook and CD include some information on the "how to" aspects of statistical methods (the easy part), the primary focus is on developing conceptual understanding (the hard part). By using video, animation, clever analogies, and interesting real data as the basis for examples and interactive exercises, the *Electronic Companion* challenges students, creates interest, and enhances their understanding of difficult abstract concepts.

Key Features of the *Electronic Companion*

The *Electronic Companion* has many features that make it useful for students as a tool to enhance understanding of statistical concepts or for instructors as a demonstration tool to enliven and broaden classroom presentations. In what follows, I describe the features that have led me to incorporate the *Electronic Companion* into my courses.

Animations and Visual Metaphors. The interactive CD has wonderful animations to illustrate some of the key concepts in statistics. Some of them are a bit hokey in places, but students remember them. In fact, a number of students surprised me by answering questions on a midterm exam by referring back to some of these animations. For example, one student wrote "Yes it would surprise me to see this kind of sample result if the statement is true. The dog is just too far away from the fire hydrant." The student then went on to correctly explain in statistical terms what she meant by that last sentence. Now if you haven't yet looked at the *Electronic Companion*, you are probably wondering what in the world this student meant by "The dog is just too far away from the fire hydrant." In explaining the Empirical Rule, the *Electronic Companion* introduces the visual metaphor of a dog (called Data) for a sample statistic, a fire hydrant for the corresponding population parameter, and the length of the dog's leash for the standard error of the statistic. The Empirical Rule is then illustrated visually by showing that the dog tends to stay close to his fire hydrant. About 68% of the time, Data stays within one leash length of his fire hydrant, and so on. This visual metaphor is carried through to other topics, including confidence intervals and significance testing. The basis for confidence intervals and the rationale for significance tests become Data (dog) tends to stay within two standard errors (leash lengths) of its parameter (fire hydrant). If Data is at 100 and his standard error is 10, it is not believable that his parameter is at 60. And, of course, all this is done visually with clever animations.

I know that this sounds silly when you try to say it in words (I wouldn't recommend this explanation if you rely solely on talking—students will think you have lost it!), *but, when combined with the animation, the explanation works. Students see it, understand it, and remember it.* I was a bit wary when I first showed these animations in class. Students giggled in some places and groaned at some of the jokes and puns. But in the end, they related it to the fundamental ideas of confidence intervals (What are plausible values for the parameter when Data is at 100?) and significance tests (How far is Data from the hypothesized value, and is it believable that he would be this far away?). Students also gained a common visual format for all of the confidence intervals and significance tests introduced, helping them to see clearly the common structure.

Video Clips. Most of the topics included on the CD begin with a brief video clip from the *Against All Odds* programs (which are discussed elsewhere in this volume). While I am a fan of the *Against All Odds* series, I rarely show an entire program in class, preferring to show just enough to set the stage for an example or discussion. The segments chosen for inclusion in the *Electronic Companion* are perfect for this. They are short, to the point, and effective in introducing a practical and interesting application of the topic. I show a number of them in class. They require very little class time, and they are well worth the time spent.

Concept Maps. The *Electronic Companion* uses concept maps to show visually how the individual concepts and methods of a topic fit together, as well as to show how the topic fits into the larger framework of the entire course. These maps help students organize the course material and understand the *process* of data analysis. Too often, students leave their first statistics course with the impression that they have just seen a series of unrelated mechanical techniques. They fail to see the common structure of many of the techniques (even though the instructor has described this common structure both verbally and algebraically). Nor do most students appreciate that data analysis is an iterative process that requires thoughtful application of several tools. The *Electronic Companion*'s concept maps show these things visually, and, like a road map, students can refer back to the concept maps whenever they are lost.

Figure 1 shows a sample concept map for the unit on inference for relationships. Each button in the concept map represents a key step in the process, and each button expands to provide a guide to the corresponding step. For example, the "Choose a Model" button in the map expands as shown in Figure 2.

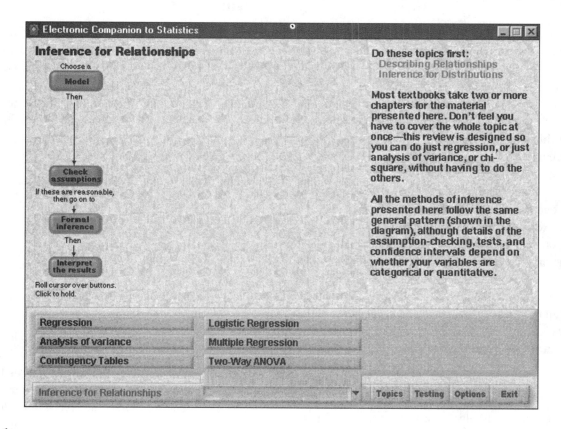

FIGURE 1

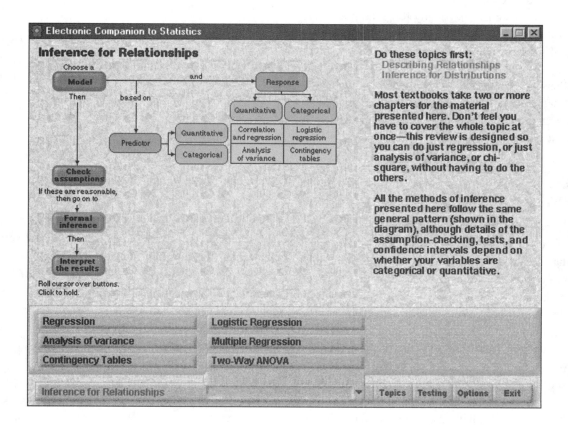

FIGURE 2

When the topic is first introduced in class, it is helpful for students to see the skeleton map, which gives an overview of the process. As each step in the process is covered, the map can be augmented, which helps students see how each new idea introduced fits into the "big picture." This is especially important in a topic like inference for relationships because it takes several weeks to develop all of the components essential to complete the picture.

Exercises. Although the exercises in the companion workbook tend to be somewhat mechanical in nature, the interactive exercises included in the testing part of the CD are based on real data and many are quite challenging. Most of the exercises have a hint button, which allows students to request help if they are unable to get started with a problem. Working through these exercises gives students the opportunity to test their understanding of the material (and before I do it!). Two sample questions from the unit on regression are shown in Figures 3 and 4. Figure 4 shows the hint provided when an incorrect response is chosen.

I am particularly impressed with the way in which the authors have been able to construct questions that really do get at the concepts, but which are in an objective format that can be scored by the computer. Looking at the CD exercises has prompted me to try writing more of this type of question on my exams. They really force the students to think about the concepts, and a side benefit is that they are quite easy to grade.

Linked Glossary. The *Electronic Companion* includes a linked glossary for statistical terms. Students can click on any of these highlighted terms, and a definition window is shown on the screen.

How I Use the *Electronic Companion* in the Classes I Teach

I use the *Electronic Companion* in two ways. I show many of the video clips to set the stage for an example or lab exercise that is part of my classroom presentation. I also incorporate many of the animations. With several of them, I show the animation, we discuss the main concepts illustrated in the animation, and then I show the animation a second time. I have found that the animations are effective. Students remember them—and not just the "silly dog and the fire hydrant," but the statistical ideas they represent. In addition to using the *Electronic Companion* as a presentation tool, several times during the quarter I distribute the CD's to the students and have them work through the exercise sections of several topics. They then use the CD to

review any topic for which they have difficulty in providing correct answers, which may be different for each student. Since sound is an integral part of the videos and animations, I quickly learned that headphones were one piece of equipment that we had neglected to purchase for the studio, and we now have headphones available for any student who does not happen to have a set in their backpack (I was surprised at how many do!).

How My Students Use the *Electronic Companion*

My students also use the *Electronic Companion* in two ways. First, they see it as part of the classroom presentations and use it on the occasions that I incorporate exercises from the CD into the classroom activities. The second way that my students use the *Electronic Companion* is to study and review course material outside of class. This is probably the use that the authors of this package envisioned. Students can come into the studio during open lab times and have access to any of the packages that we use in class. Students check out the CD and can work through the various topics at their own pace, review the animations and videos, and test their understanding using the self-test exercises. The lab monitors tell me that the *Electronic Companion* is the most often-requested resource during the open lab hours, so students must see value in it. A number of students have elected to purchase the package for use at home, even though it is not required for the course. Next year our bookstore will stock it as an optional text for my course, and I anticipate that many students will opt to purchase it when they see what it offers them.

Visual Statistics

Visual Statistics by David Doane, Kieran Mathieson, and Ronald Tracy is a collection of fifteen interactive tools designed to illustrate key statistical concepts of the introductory statistics course. The software is available by site license, and a student version that comes with a 340-page lab manual is also available. *Visual Statistics* is designed to complement a traditional introductory statistics textbook.

Visual Statistics provides the best overall set of interactive conceptual tools that I have come across. The software modules do an outstanding job of illustrating various statistical concepts visually. The modules are well-designed, have been programmed effectively, and each tool allows for a number of different possible explorations.

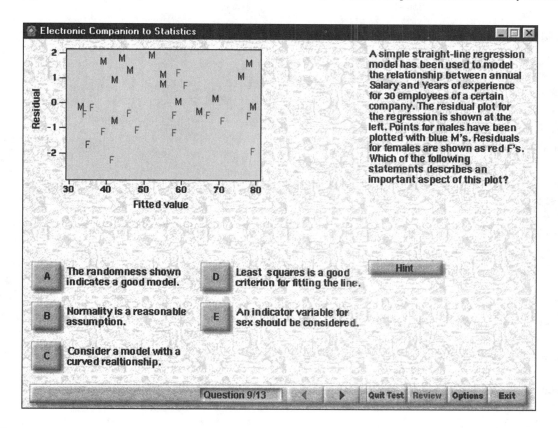

FIGURE 3

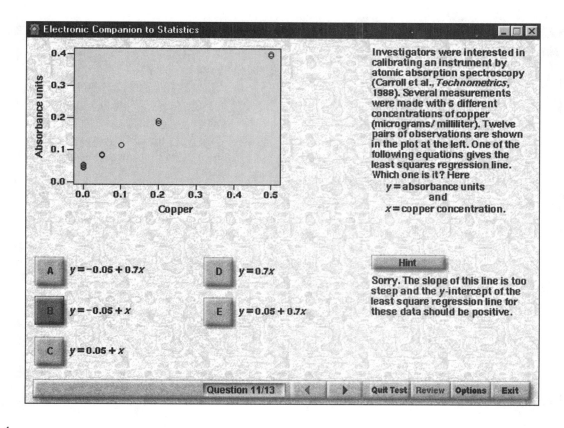

FIGURE 4

Incorporating *Visual Statistics* into Classes

It is probably easiest to see the many nice features of the *Visual Statistics* tools by considering a few examples. One of my favorite modules, and one I use very early in the course, is "Visualizing Univariate Data." After selecting one of a large number of data sets included with *Visual Statistics*, this module displays a histogram of the data in one window and either a dotplot or boxplot of the data in a second window. The user can easily change the number of class intervals for the histogram and see immediately the effect on the graph. I also like to have students look at a variety of different histogram shapes and see how properties of the histograms (skewness, outliers, etc.) are reflected in the corresponding boxplots. A sample screen from this module is shown in Figure 5.

The collection of data sets is rich enough that you can quickly look at a number of histograms with different properties using data sets that students can understand, such as divorce rates or median ages for the 50 U.S. states. Students like to guess which states are the outliers (although they are usually wrong—California doesn't have an unusually high divorce rate, and it is Utah, not Alaska that has an unusually low median age). I usually only spend about 10–15 minutes of class time on this, but it is very produc-

tive and much more interesting to the students than having me give the textbook definitions of terms like positively skewed.

Another module that I have found very useful is "Visualizing the Central Limit Theorem" (see Figure 6). The idea of a sampling distribution is one of the most difficult concepts for introductory statistics students. The simulation approach to illustrating sampling distributions in this module teaches the concept very effectively. The user chooses a population (the user can choose from normal or non-normal populations) and then selects a random sample from the population. The sample is highlighted, and the mean of the sample is added to an empirical distribution that is being formed in a second window. As the sampling process is repeated, the empirical sampling distribution is built up and features such as shape, center, and spread become apparent.

Since users can vary the sample size, population mean, population standard deviation, and population shape, they can use this tool to learn about factors that have an effect on properties of the sampling distribution.

I also like the "Visualizing Bivariate Data Analysis" module (see Figure 7), and use it to illustrate the concept of influential points in simple linear regression. Users can generate a scatterplot (using variables from the resident data

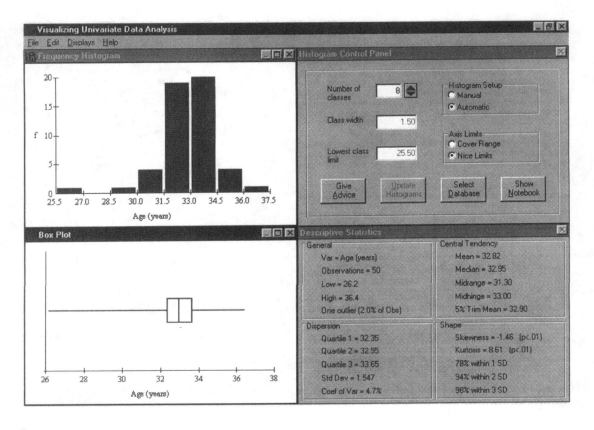

FIGURE 5

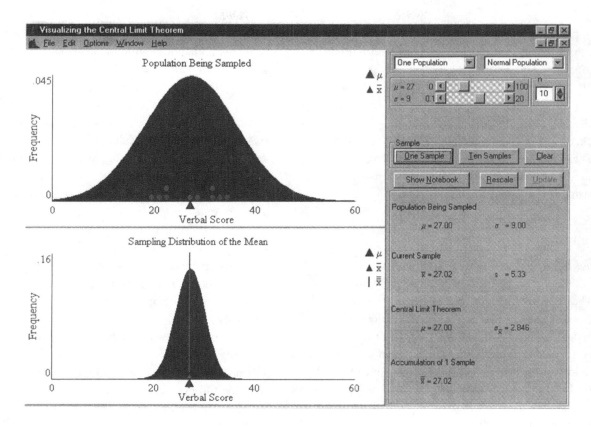

FIGURE 6

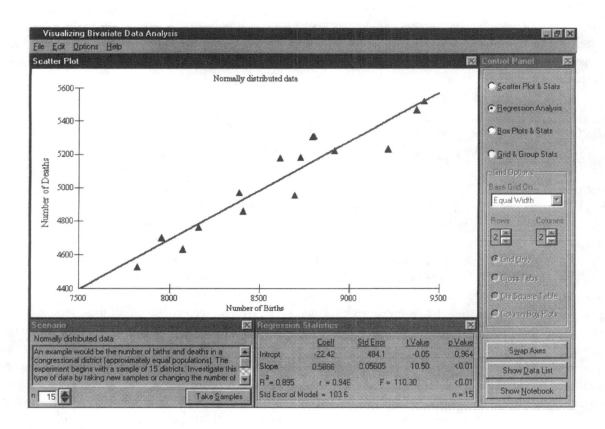

FIGURE 7

sets), plot the least squares line, and then drag points in the plot to different locations and see the effect on the line as it moves. I tell students they can move any point in the plot by 10 in either the x direction or the y direction, and ask them to figure out which point and what direction would result in the biggest change in the slope of the line. They quickly discover which points are influential and why.

These are just three of the well-designed tools that can be used to enhance instruction in the introductory course in many different ways.

Strengths of *Visual Statistics*

Visual Statistics has a number of strengths, which make it attractive as a supplement to a traditional textbook.

1. The software modules are excellent tools for illustrating statistical concepts. The graphical design is visually appealing and the modules are easy to use.
2. A large collection of data sets is included, so all exploration can be done in context, which is important. There is also a data editor that allows the instructor or student to add new data sets that are of current interest or are from the course textbook.
3. Students seem to prefer the "show me" approach to the "tell me" approach. (They can get the "tell me" approach from the textbook.) Students understand the underlying concepts better, using less class time! (This is REALLY true. It's hard, but worth trying, to give up some of your lecturing.)

StatConcepts, A Visual Tour of Statistical Ideas

StatConcepts, A Visual Tour of Statistical Ideas by H. Joseph Newton and Jane L. Harvil is a collection of computer-based labs designed to complement introductory statistics texts by providing a visual illustration of statistical concepts. The complete package consists of 28 labs, StataQuest, and a 308-page paperback companion book. StataQuest is a special student version of the statistics package Stata that is designed for the undergraduate introductory statistics market. It features a spreadsheet data editor and menu access to all of the methods typically covered in a first course in statistics. It is also possible to purchase a limited site license for the software, which consists of the labs and StataQuest. The table of contents parallels a typical introductory statistics course from probability through inference and least squares regression.

Many of the central ideas in introductory statistics (for example, probability, sampling distributions, and the interpretation of confidence level) rely on the idea of repetition. I often find myself in the classroom asking students to "imagine doing XXX over and over again and then try to picture ..." I then have to hope that what the students are imagining is what I think they are imagining, and that they can in turn relate it to a finished picture that I show them or that appears in the text. It is the desire to leave a bit less to imagination that, I think, motivated the authors to develop *StatConcepts*.

StatConcepts can enhance an introductory statistics course in a number of ways. Probably the two most common ways to incorporate the package are to use it for classroom demonstrations in a course that does not have a separate laboratory component or as the lab component of a lecture/lab course.

The course in which I have been using *StatConcepts* is a beginning course designed for students majoring in psychology, social science, and physical education and kinesiology. Typical class size is around forty. We have used different textbooks for this course over the years, most recently *Statistics: The Exploration and Analysis of Data* by Devore and Peck [1] and *The Basic Practice of Statistics* by Moore [2]. I have used *StatConcepts* primarily as a demonstration tool, so I will begin by indicating how I use it at Cal Poly and then will make some comments on how I think it could be used in a course that has a separate computer lab.

StatConcepts as a Demonstration Tool

The twenty-eight labs in StatConcepts include a mix of simulation-based demonstrations, static displays, or purely computational exercises. While all of the labs are well thought out and address important ideas in the introductory statistics course, for me the real strength of *StatConcepts* is in the simulation-based laboratories. I have found it particularly helpful in teaching the probability section of my course and in illustrating various concepts in sampling and sampling distributions.

When I incorporate one of these labs into my classroom presentation, I usually spend about 10 to 15 minutes of class time. I spend a few minutes introducing the demonstration, posing a question to be investigated (for example, "What do RANDOM samples look like?"). It is also important that I spend a couple of minutes at the end to bring closure to the activity and to ensure that students can relate what they have seen to statistical concepts. I usually try to focus this discussion by going back to the question posed at the beginning of the demonstration.

Early in the quarter, I use the "Random Sampling" lab (Chapter 2). This is a simple simulation lab that illustrates repeated sampling from a finite discrete population. The complete population is displayed, and each time a sample is selected, the selected points are highlighted in the population display and the corresponding sample mean is added to a display of sample means. I have found this lab to be particularly helpful in making two points: (1) random doesn't mean uniform or evenly spread, and (2) sample averages tend to differ less from sample to sample when the sample size is large than when it is small. Even though the idea of a sampling distribution is weeks away, students find this visual approach to be very intuitive.

After we talk about histograms, I incorporate some of the displays in the "How Are Populations Distributed" lab (Chapter 4). This lab allows the user to specify a population distribution (normal, t, chi-square, F, Beta, etc.) and then view a histogram based on a random sample of size 500 from this population. The population density curve is superimposed over the histogram on the display. The user can repeat the demonstration, with a different sample being selected on each repetition. Although my students have no idea what a chi-square or F density is at this point in the quarter, they can clearly see sample to sample variation in histogram shape and also the extent to which the sample histogram deviates from the population distribution. In the past, these are things that I have "told" my students, but it works much better if they can SEE it.

When I get to the point where I am ready to introduce the concept of the relative frequency interpretation of probability and how probabilities can be estimated via simulation, I use the "Relative Frequency and Probability" lab (Chapter 3) as an illustration. This lab uses a lotto game of selecting six balls from a population of balls numbered from 1 to 50. The goal is to estimate the probability of a pair (two consecutive numbers, such as 33, 34) being selected. The screen shows the 50 balls, and when six balls are selected at random, the selected balls are highlighted. Students can then see whether the draw includes a pair or not. This can be repeated several times, and then when students are comfortable with the process of simulation, they can speed up the selection process. With each repetition, *StatConcepts* updates the total number of draws, the number of draws containing a pair, and the relative frequency of occurrence of pairs. Since this is usually the first time I have used simulation to estimate a probability, I actually start with a physical process where we select six balls from a bucket of 50 numbered Ping-Pong balls before

moving to the computer simulation. I have found that doing this in three steps—physical process, computer process one trial at a time, and then automated computer process to carry out many trials—effectively teaches students the basic idea of simulation. This process also paves the way for a simulation-based development of the concept of sampling distributions.

Another lab that I have found to be very helpful is the "Least Squares" lab (Chapter 6). In this lab, the user specifies n, the true population slope, and population r^2. A sample is then selected from a population with the requested characteristics, and the lab shows the scatterplot of sampled points, the sample regression line, the population regression line, the sample r^2, and the population r^2. Sample residuals are also highlighted in the plot. Although it seems a bit unnatural to the students to specify a population r^2, it visually illustrates two important points. When using repeated samples from the same population settings: (1) the sample line varies from sample to sample, and (2) the sample line deviates from the true population line. It also gives students a sense of the potential magnitude of this deviation. I have found that using this demonstration leads to a much better understanding of what the standard error of the sample slope means and why it is important. This lab is also extremely helpful in explaining to students why prediction intervals are wider than the corresponding confidence intervals, because it clearly illustrates the two sources that contribute to prediction errors (versus the one source that contributes to estimation errors).

I use the "Central Limit Theorem" lab (Chapter 7) to illustrate the sampling distribution of the sample mean. This lab builds on ideas from the "Random Sampling" lab, so it is best to do Chapter 2 before Chapter 7 so that students understand the simulation behind Chapter 7. The concept of a sampling distribution is very abstract, and one that students often find difficult to understand. Again, this is a place where a simulation and visual approach works better than any string of words that I have been able to put together!

The final lab that I include is the "Minimum Variance Estimation" lab (Chapter 10). This lab illustrates the ideas of bias and precision by constructing Monte Carlo distributions of the mean and median for different population shapes. Some of the possible population shapes are uniform, normal, and t with small df. These choices make it possible to show cases where the distribution of the sample mean has a smaller variance than the distribution of the sample median, and vice-versa. After having worked through this lab, students have a much better understanding of what minimum variance means, and why it is an important consideration in estimation problems.

StatConcepts as the Lab Component of a Lecture/Lab Course

Although I use *StatConcepts* as a demonstration tool in my classes, it was really designed to be used as the basis for the laboratory component of a statistics course that is taught in a lecture/lab format. This format would require meeting at least one time per week in a computer lab. Since *StatConcepts* labs are built on top of StataQuest, which is also included in the package, it integrates particularly well into classes that intend to use StataQuest as the primary data analysis package. However, it could easily be used effectively in a course that relied on Minitab or some other package, since the StataQuest interface is only evident in a few of the more computationally-oriented labs. If you have access to a computer lab, but don't have the funds to purchase a stat package, the fact that *StatConcepts* comes with StataQuest may make it a very attractive package. The first lab in StatConcepts gives a detailed introduction to StataQuest, which you could omit if you use a different data analysis package.

To use *StatConcepts* as the basis for a lab, the 308-page companion book is invaluable. Each of the twenty-eight labs has both a guided tour of the lab and a set of exercises and questions that require the students to explore various aspects of the laboratory in further detail. The guided tour walks students through the essential features of the lab and points out the key concepts as they are illustrated. The lab instructor could use the guided tour as a demonstration, or the students could work their way through the guided tour individually. After completing the guided tour, students can work assigned exercises that require them to extend the use of the tools introduced in the guided tour, to think further about the key concepts, and to answer questions that require them to think carefully about these concepts. Handled in this way, and carefully coordinated with the lecture component of the class, these labs would truly enhance student understanding of concepts.

Why Incorporate *An Electronic Companion, Visual Statistics,* and *StatConcepts* into Your Introductory Statistics Course?

My experience over the years has been that many students complete their required introductory statistics course with the ability to apply cookbook recipes to carry out various inferential procedures. They can follow the standard seven-step procedure to get a conclusion in a hypothesis test, and can compute a confidence interval, a correlation coefficient, and a least squares regression line. However, many have very little understanding of why these things work the way we say they do. Why can they draw a particular conclusion after carrying out a test? What does confidence level mean? What is a sampling distribution, and why should I care what it looks like? This is very frustrating for both the student and the instructor. Much of the difficulty is the result of a heavy reliance on words and static pictures that we can put on a blackboard or reproduce in a textbook to explain very abstract concepts. While it is often true that a picture is worth a thousand words, it is my experience that a well-chosen *interactive* picture is worth at least 15,208 words! Even with interactive pictures, it is still critical to discuss the key features of the picture and why they are important, because students don't always see it immediately, but incorporating something visual and active is an invaluable starting point. The *Electronic Companion, Visual Statistics,* and *StatConcepts* allow this to happen. I believe that these tools, whether used as a presentation tool by the instructor, as the basis for a laboratory session, or by the student for study and review helps students to succeed in introductory statistics. These tools create interest and help students understand critical underlying concepts, which contributes to a successful educational experience for everyone—faculty and student alike.

References

1. Devore, Jay and Roxy Peck, *Statistics: The Exploration and Analysis of Data, Third Edition,* 1997, Duxbury Press, Belmont, CA.
2. Moore, David S., *The Basic Practice of Statistics, Second Edition,* 2000, W.H. Freeman, New York.

Introduction to ExplorStat

Dennis Wackerly
University of Florida

James Lang
Valencia Community College East

Overview

Quantitative reasoning skills are essential for the present and future generations of workers and citizens, if they are to be capable of filling the jobs necessary to keep America competitive in the world economy and making the decisions that are vital to societal advancement at home. A seemingly endless list of business leaders report on their inability to hire workers with appropriate quantitative skills for the jobs at hand, not to mention the jobs of the 21st century, and the mounting costs of retraining workers to handle the routine tasks of a technologically oriented world. The predominant issues related to quality of life, from global warming to acid rain, from the depletion of the ozone layer to the depletion of rain forests, from the unbridled growth of population to the unchecked decline in social security benefits, cannot be understood without a firm grasp on quantitative reasoning. The world runs on data and the interpretation of these data. If the data are not collected and interpreted properly, the consequences can be disastrous.

Today's college students grew up and live in a fast-paced world of rapid-fire TV commercials, action movies, and dynamic video games. Our culture does not prepare them to sit in a 50-minute lecture and absorb the material being presented on a topic, statistics, that seems remote and difficult. Even without the cultural bias, most experts on learning agree that the lecture-and-listen method of presenting information is quite inefficient. To move away from the traditional lecture format and to take advantage of the students' interest in the dynamic, this project has produced a series of computerized modules that will: (a) permit active demonstrations of statistical concepts during course lectures, and (b) allow the students to discover basic statistical concepts while engaged in hands-on activities at a computer work station.

Many statistics courses now emphasize the use of real data and make use of computers for data analysis. Modern software is excellent for this purpose since it allows for easy computation of statistical summaries and extensive use of graphics, all a step in the right direction. Modern statistics texts often support this trend by providing examples that are beyond the scope of hand computation.

This project, however, concentrates on exploring ways of using computer technology to maximize the interaction between the student and the subject matter for purposes of "discovering" basic concepts. For example, current computer software can quickly and accurately generate means and standard deviations for data sets, but our modules have been developed to help students understand what these measures mean and how they are interpreted. Existing computer software can be used to generate different graphical displays of data, but our modules enable students to learn how to understand and interpret these displays, learning which graphs best represent a particular data set, or which features of a data set are revealed in particular graphs. The fundamental concept of the sampling distribution of a statistic requires that students understand the results of calculating the value of a statistic in many repeated samples. Computing the mean of a set of numbers, or selecting a single random sample from a given population, can be done easily with standard statistical packages. However, it is much more difficult to generate and analyze the 100 or 1000 sample means needed to demonstrate the central limit theorem. It is even more difficult to accomplish this rapidly while allowing students to choose data from any one of the standard population distributions such as the normal or exponential, or even for distributions designed by the students. Students can run these modules repeatedly, obtaining different results on each individual run, and learning and gaining experience about the long-run performance of random phenomena. Other concepts, such as interpreting the mean as a balance point of the data arranged on a real number line, can be better introduced through computer programs specifically designed for illustrative purposes.

The innovative characteristics of the modules we have written are their ability to rapidly and easily generate data from specified statistical distributions and to graphically display distributions and other data characteristics, all under the control of the user. The user does not need to know a programming language or statistical analysis package to use these modules. The instructor who uses them can concentrate class time on explaining statistical concepts, not on teaching computer usage. While each module targets a specific statistical concept, the results are generic, that is, scenarios and units are not specified. The instructors can use these modules to demonstrate concepts, while at the same time using their own experience to motivate the problem and interpret the results. Part of our objective was to design these modules so that they can also be used in a laboratory by students to solve instructor-provided exercises. These exercises should be structured in a way such that the students will discover the concepts through experimentation with the modules, much in the way that students learn about other sciences.

ExplorStat is a set of HyperCard© stacks prepared for the purpose of *illustrating statistical concepts*. The stacks require either HyperCard or HyperCard Player version 2.2 or later. (Allocate 2,000K of memory to HyperCard to ensure efficient operation.) The HyperCard Player was included with older Macintosh computers when they were purchased. Download your own version of

ExplorStat (and the Hypercard Player) via the Web at: `http://www.stat.ufl.edu/users/dwack`.

The development of these materials was made possible by a grant from the National Science Foundation (DUE-9354419). We use these materials in two ways: in classroom demonstrations, where we use the modules in our presentations of the associated material, and in computer labs (typically after the classroom demonstrations), where students use the modules to explore and learn on their own. Our experience in using these materials has been very positive. Students seem to enjoy the demonstrations, but more importantly, grasp the material presented faster and with deeper understanding. We hope that you have similar experiences.

The Modules

Dot Diagram.   This module is designed to build intuition regarding the relationship between data sets, corresponding numerical characteristics (mean, median, standard deviation, quartiles), and graphical displays including histograms and box plots. You may opt to display the values of various statistics, a histogram, a box plot, or the numerical values in the data set. Whenever a data point is added, deleted or moved (using elementary mouse manipulations), all of the displayed information is immediately updated. The histogram and box plot (if selected) are redrawn, the values of the selected statistics are re-computed and re-plotted.

Sampling Path.   This module illustrates the behavior of the sample proportion of successes as a function of the size of the sample employed. One component of the module illustrates that the sample proportion of successes converges to the true population proportion of success as the sample size increases. The user can also examine the sampling distribution of the sample proportion of successes for two user-selected sample sizes. For larger sample sizes, it is seen that the sampling distribution is approximately mound shaped. Histograms for many sample sizes can be examined. Observations may be selected from a "bowl" that contains the user-specified proportion of successes. After each successive observation, the proportion of successes at that stage is plotted. What emerges is a sample path of the successive values of the proportion as the sample size builds. A single sample path can be plotted and extended illustrating that the sample proportion of successes gets close to (and stays close to) the true proportion of successes (user selected) in the population of interest.

Multiple sample paths can also be overlaid, making apparent the general trend of the sample paths to become closer to the true (user-selected) proportion of "successes" in the population. In addition, the set of sample paths can be "cut" at two user-selected sample sizes. Corresponding to each "cut" there are lists of numbers in the two boxes under the graph of the sample paths. These are the values associated with the entire set of sample paths if we "cut" through them at the values of the sample size that appear above each of the boxes. Under each box of data is the mean and standard deviation of the values of the observed sample proportions associated with the values of n that are indicated. Or, the user may opt to see the histograms that correspond to the sample values at each of these sample sizes. These initial histograms are given with identical horizontal axes to facilitate comparison of what is happening at the two values of n at which the "cuts" are made. The sample sizes at which the "cuts" occur are easily changed using the mouse to "drag" the cut point(s) to the desired location(s).

Random Sampling.   This module illustrates that, in the long run, random sampling (using a random number table) produces better results than subjective or "eyeball" sampling. This screen contains 100 rectangles of different areas. The objective is to select a sample of size 10, compute the area of each rectangle, and finally compute the average area of the 10 selected rectangles. The intention is to use this computed average based on the sample of size 10 to estimate the true average area of the entire set (population) of 100 rectangles. This activity can be implemented without a computer, but doing so makes the activity more tedious and time consuming. The user may select 10 "representative" rectangles by using the mouse to "click" on each of the 10 rectangles of his/her subjective choice. Upon clicking on a rectangle, the area of the rectangle appears on the screen and the rectangle and its identification number appear in inverse video (white on black). Once the selection of 10 is complete, the user may view the 10 areas selected and their average. A histogram summarizes the results of the last 50 times that users selected what they felt were representative samples of size 10 and computed the average area. The current user-selected value is indicated by a triangle. This display is intended to permit the user to see how his/her pick compared to those of other users. When this module is used repeatedly, the users' picks are updated to include the last 50 picks.

At a click of the mouse the computer uses a random number generator to *randomly select* 10 of the rectangles and computes their average area. A window pops up containing a histogram of the average areas of 10 rectangles for the last 50 computer picks (stored). Another mouse click results in a comparison of the histograms of the student picks and the computer picks. The true average area of the 100 rectangles is 7.42 and appears under a triangle on each histogram. This comparison permits the user to observe that the results obtained using random sampling tend to center on the true mean area (7.42) whereas the user picks tend to center at a larger value. This demonstrates the phenomenon of "size-biased sampling" wherein a disproportionately small number of "small" items tend to appear in what are perceived to be "representative" samples.

Sampling Distribution.   This module illustrates the sampling distribution of various statistics. The module can be used repeatedly to demonstrate the effect that the underlying population distribution and the sample size have on the sampling distribution of several different statistics. The idea of a sampling distribution is very difficult for most beginning students to grasp. This module makes it possible for users to see what a sampling distribution looks like—rather than trying to imagine what one might look like on the basis of a verbal description. Too often, beginning students are unaware that all statistics have sampling distributions. This module is designed to eliminate that misconception. If the module is used with large sample sizes and for appropriately chosen statistics, a very nice demonstration of the Central Limit Theorem is provided. Users may select samples from one of several populations. Or, the user may define his/her own population distribution by using the mouse to stretch or shrink the heights of boxes in a histogram. The module will reformat the shape that you specify to a relative frequency histogram, compute the resulting mean and standard deviation, and permit use of this distribution in any chosen simulation.

P-hat Sampling Distribution.   This module functions much like the Sampling Distribution module, but illustrates the sampling distribution of the sample proportion of successes. The user may select the value of the population proportion and the sample size to be taken. The fact that the sampling distribution of the sample proportion is approximately normal for large samples sizes—and not for small sample sizes—becomes apparent.

2″ × 2″ Table.   This module permits the user to explore relationships between probabilities of two events, their intersection, their union, and the impact that choices for these probabilities have on the conditional probabilities of one event given that the other has occurred. The probabilities of the events and the probability of their intersection are changed by moving sliders underneath the numerical values of the probabilities. When an attempt is made to move one of the probabilities to a value that is impossible (given the other values), the box in which the probability occurs will turn to inverse video (white on black) and a "beep" sounds (if the sound option has been toggled on). It is often instructive to pause and determine WHY the value selected is impossible. Once the probabilities of the two events and their intersections are determined, the conditional probabilities of each event given the other, the product of the marginal probabilities, the probability of the intersection and the probability of their union are calculated and displayed. If the probabilities selected in the table are inconsistent, all of the calculated probabilities are listed as undefined.

Medical Tests.   This module illustrates Bayes' Rule in the context of a medical diagnostic procedure. The sensitivity and specificity of the test and the incidence rate for a disease can be set by the user. The module computes the conditional probability that the person has the disease given that the test is positive and the conditional probability that the person is disease-free given that the test is negative. The results are usually surprising to a beginner learning Bayes' rule. Even individuals who have often used Bayes' Rule are sometimes surprised by the results obtained. It is instructive to discuss WHY these "surprising" results are valid—*after they have been discovered.*

Confidence Intervals.   This module illustrates the repeated sampling interpretation of the confidence coefficient associated with confidence intervals. It also illustrates the roles that the confidence coefficient, sample size, and parameter value(s) have on the lengths of confidence intervals. The parameter of interest can be either a population mean or a population proportion. If a proportion is selected, a slider will appear that permits the user to select the value of the population proportion from among the values $.1, .2, \ldots, .9$. Once the parameter and its value have been selected, that value is highlighted on the grid appearing on the right of the screen. Repeated samples can quickly be taken, with the resulting realized confidence intervals plotted on the grid. It is easily seen that different samples yield different intervals, some of which capture the true value of the parameter and some of which do not. For large samples, the proportion of intervals that capture the value of the parameter will approximate the (user-selected) confidence coefficient. The impact that the confidence coefficient and

sample size have on the length of the resulting intervals is graphically illustrated.

Hypothesis Testing.   This module illustrates how large sample hypothesis tests actually work. The user can explore the impact that the research hypothesis, the sample size, and the chosen probability of a type I error have on the proportion of the time, in repeated sampling, that the test procedure rejects the null hypothesis. This permits a very nice presentation of the interpretation of the size and power of a test without the need for mysterious formulas that beginning students fail to understand. The parameter of interest can be either a mean or a proportion. The research hypothesis can be upper, lower, or two-tailed. The size of the probability of a type I error is also at the discretion of the user.

All sorts of meaningful concepts associated with hypothesis testing can be illustrated with this module. If the actual value of the parameter and the value specified by the null hypothesis are the same, the proportion of times the null is rejected should be nearly equal to the user-selected value of α, if the sample size is large enough. Select p as the parameter of interest, set the "true" $p = 0.5$, and test $H_0 : p = 0.5$ versus $H_A : p \neq 0.5$ at the $\alpha = .10$ level. Is the proportion of time H_0 is rejected close to .10? Why?

If the true and hypothesized values of the parameter are not the same, an easily-understood demonstration of power is at hand. Explore what happens as the hypothesized value moves further away from the true value of the parameter and into the alternative hypothesis. Explore what happens as the value specified by the null hypothesis stays fixed at a "wrong" value, but the sample size increases. Demonstrate that if the null hypothesis is composite, the largest likelihood of rejecting the null occurs at the boundary value of the parameter. Abstractly, these ideas are typically beyond the understanding of beginning students, but can easily be illustrated using this module. The beginner can pick out patterns for him/her self with a little guidance from an instructor. Cumulative results are particularly useful for comparing results for different sample sizes for the same parameter value or different values of the parameter while holding the sample size fixed.

Least Squares.   This module illustrates what is meant by a least squares fit. The user can plot data, intuitively fit a straight line to the data using the "eyeball" method, compare the intuitively fit line to the least squares line, see how the sum of squares for error is computed, and immediately see the impact of high leverage points. Manipulate the slope and intercept of the line by using the mouse to grab the line and physically moving it! Note the change in SSE as the slope or intercept changes. Illustrate *how* SSE is calculated. Move, add, or delete data points using mouse drags and clicks.

Probability Simulator. This module illustrates what is meant by the *probability distribution* of a random variable. Use it to compare the simulated distributions with the theoretical model for distributions that are developed in an introductory course. The module uses a computerized version of a "bead box" to illustrate that there are lots of different random variables and that each has a distribution. Select the proportion of black beads in the bead box and the size of the sample by using sliders. If a sample size is selected, distributions that may be simulated are : the number of "successes," the number of runs, the number of runs of "successes," the length of the longest run, or the length of the longest run of "successes." Instead, the user may choose to explore the number of the trial on which the rth "success" occurs. Results are initially given in the form of frequency or relative frequency histograms. The user may choose to display the probabilities of each observed value or the cumulative probabilities of all values less than or equal to the numbers in the table. The theoretical "true" distributions for some of the variables are available and may be displayed at the discretion of the user.

ExplorStat Utilities. This module permits the instructor to edit or add data sets or exercises to be used in some of the modules (Dot Diagram, Least Squares, Random Sampling). Since this stack provides the only way to modify other stacks (except by an expert), our recommendation is that instructors remove this stack from the ExplorStat folder before students use the stacks.

A Companion Piece to ExplorStat

Maria I. Ripol
University of Florida

Introduction

The Department of Statistics at the University of Florida has traditionally been the source of all the core teaching on campus in the discipline of statistics. With an enrollment of over 42,000 students, the University of Florida is one of the nation's ten largest universities and one of the most academically diverse. Many of the undergraduate majors take their introductory statistics through two large service courses: STA 2122 for social science majors and STA 3023 for business, psychology, and other majors.

Since the early 1990's, the department has been operating a Teaching Computer Lab with 40 Macintosh computers, all of which run ExplorStat and Minitab. One of the computers in the lab is connected to an overhead projector to allow for demonstrations. The department created the lab with money from several NSF ILI (Instrumentation and Laboratory Improvement Programs for Undergraduate Education) grants and with matching funds provided by the College of Liberal Arts and Science. Undergraduate statistics majors staff the lab, which is used for regularly scheduled sections of STA 2122 on Tuesdays and Thursdays. On one or two other days of the week, the lab holds "open hours" for those STA 2122 students who need extra time to finish their work and for students taking other courses.

The department usually teaches eight sections per semester of STA 2122, Statistics for Social Sciences, and uses *The Basic Practice of Statistics*, by David S. Moore, a textbook that emphasizes statistical concepts and working with data, rather than mathematical theory. These sections enroll around 80 students each and meet with the instructor three times a week (on Mondays, Wednesdays, and Fridays). Once a week (either on Tuesday or Thursday) each of these sections splits into two groups of 40 students that meet in the lab with an undergraduate teaching assistant.

Students buy a Course Guide that includes the computer projects they will be working on during their weekly lab period. They complete eleven projects, each of which takes one or two weeks to complete. We encourage students to work with a partner (turning in only one project per pair) and to discuss their results with other students in the class. Project grades form a substantial part of the final grade in the course. Projects are synchronized with the lectures, so the computer activities reinforce the concepts and procedures learned in class. To this aim, we use two different applications for the projects: about half the projects are data analyses done in Minitab and the other half use ExplorStat modules to teach concepts.

The department teaches the other Introductory Statistics course, STA 3023 (which uses the book *Statistics* by Mc-

Clave, Dietrich, and Sincich), in four very large sections of over 300 students each. The lab cannot accommodate all those students on a regular basis, but the instructor can demonstrate ExplorStat in class by bringing a laptop computer and connecting it to an overhead projector. The Honors sections of STA 3023, however, are limited to under 25 students each, and, if the instructor so desires, he or she can bring the class to the lab several times during the semester during the regularly scheduled meeting time. In those instances, students typically work on exercises similar to those used in STA 2122, which are collected and graded. Many of these exercises are done in ExplorStat.

The lab instructor for STA 2122 begins each 50-minute session with a five- or ten-minute demonstration on the overhead projector. Because they must turn their swivel chairs away from their computer screens to observe the overhead projector, students are encouraged to pay attention to the demonstration. Before the students begin to work, the lab instructor goes through the main steps of the project using the appropriate ExplorStat module. Students follow along with their own copies of the projects in front of them. We describe below each of the ExplorStat modules that we use. We describe the Sampling Distribution project in more detail to provide a clearer picture of what it is like to teach with ExplorStat.

Project Descriptions

We use the Dot Diagrams module to introduce students to measures of center and spread and graphical displays of data. In this module, students move points on a number line to see the effect on the mean, median, and standard deviation, and optionally to see the effect on boxplots or histograms of the data. The instructor encourages students to play with the mouse and try slightly different placements of the points on the number line, since sometimes it can be tricky to get the dot exactly where the student wants it. The Dot Diagram module includes ten exercises on which the project questions are based. Some sample questions from the project on Dot Diagrams include:

- Arrange five numbers so that the mean is less than four out of five of them. (This illustrates the effect on the mean of an outlier or a skewed left distribution.)
- Arrange five numbers so that only two are within one standard deviation from the mean. (This illustrates that "flat" distributions have larger standard deviations than bell-shaped ones.)

We next use the Least Squares module to examine relationships between two quantitative variables. Again, students observe the effects of moving points, points on a

scatterplot. In "User Control" mode, students can try to find the best fitting line by moving the line up and down and tilting it in different directions. Students can see the effects of their actions by reading ExplorStat's display of the correlation coefficient, the sum of squares for error, and the equation of the line. When students switch to "Best Fit" mode, ExplorStat provides the least squares regression line. Again, the module includes some exercises, including some data sets with curvilinear relationships between x and y. This module illustrates beautifully the effect outliers can have on the least squares regression line and the difference between outliers "in the x-direction" and those "in the y-direction." Using "Best Fit" mode, students can grab the offending point with the mouse, move it up and down on the grid, and see how the least squares line moves along with it. This activity shows students that the distances they are trying to minimize are vertical distances, which is why points far away from the rest horizontally can have a large influence on the line.

Both of these modules are easy to use, the concepts they illustrate are uncomplicated, and the graphical displays usually reveal lessons clearly. Consequently, for these two projects, what the students turn in to the instructor is mostly a series of hand-written sketches of what the data points looked like on the screen, using the number line or grid provided by the Course Guide. ExplorStat does not have printing capabilities, and even though the Macintosh computers in our lab allow the user to take a "picture" of the screen and print it, it taxes the printers to have 640 students printing six or seven pages every week. Having the students draw a sketch is a simple and effective solution.

Next we introduce sampling distributions and statistical inference, which rely heavily on the idea of repeated sampling. These are hard concepts for most students to understand and ones that are very well suited to illustrating through simulations. Since most students have never seen simulations, we must explain carefully the process in lecture before students go to the lab to work on the Sampling Distribution project. It is also a good idea for the instructor to bring a computer to class before lab day to do a lengthier demonstration of the ExplorStat modules and to talk about the patterns students should see emerging. Students then go to the lab and do the project on their own, after the lab instructor first gives a brief review of how to run the module. During the next lecture, the instructor reviews the theoretical concepts and asks students if the results of their simulations are consistent with these concepts.

The Sampling Distribution, Confidence Intervals, and Hypothesis Testing modules all provide options that allow students to work at different speeds of sampling, so they can really appreciate what the simulation is doing. At the slowest speed, a sample is drawn, observation by observation, until all n values are obtained. Then the sample results are computed and plotted. Then another sample of size n is drawn, and its results—which will most likely differ from those of the first sample—are also plotted. Once the students comprehend this process, they can ask, what if I did this process many times? They can then increase the speed and have the computer take several samples (e.g., 50 or 100) and plot all the results; they can then repeat the sampling step several times until they have the results of several hundred samples. At this point they should see a pattern emerge. The students take as many samples as necessary, and even compare their results with those of their neighbors, until they are convinced of the pattern.

For these three modules, ExplorStat provides instructions on how to change parameter values, sample sizes, and the number of iterations of the sampling process. A Cumulative option on the menu saves the results of all the simulations. We ask students to write down the information on the worksheets provided and also to answer some questions about the patterns they see in the simulations.

An extended description

To give the reader a better idea of how the lab sessions work, we give here a more detailed description of how we implement the sampling distributions project. In the appendix to this article is a copy of the question sheet given to students and the answer sheet that they turn in.

Before the students arrive for the lab, they should have seen in class an explanation of the Central Limit Theorem and a demonstration of the Sampling Distribution module. In the lab, each student sits in front of a computer, with a partner sitting next to them at another computer.

The lab instructor opens the ExplorStat package first and then the Sampling Distribution module. To start, we sample from a discrete uniform population with mean 4.500 and standard deviation 2.872. The speed is on slow, and the sample size is set to $n = 4$ (see Figure 1). The instructor then clicks on the "Draw a Sample" button, and four random observations from the Uniform distribution are selected, say 9, 8, 8, and 2. ExplorStat gives the sample mean, 6.75, for these four observations and displays this sample mean on the graph (see Figure 2). By clicking on the "Draw a Sample" button again, a new random

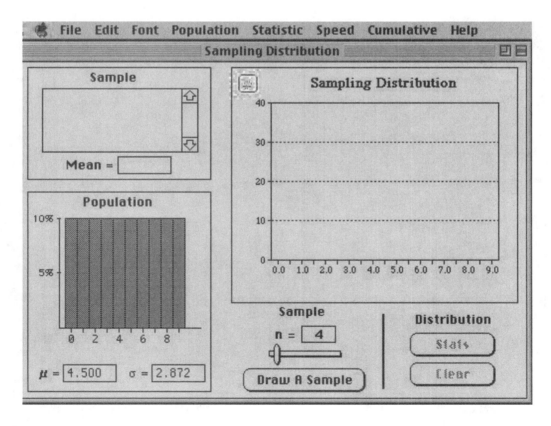

FIGURE 1

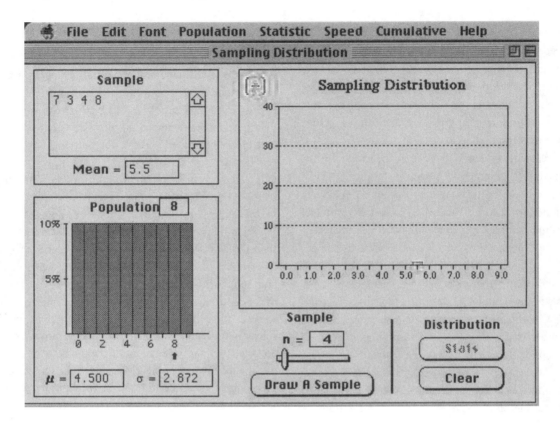

FIGURE 2

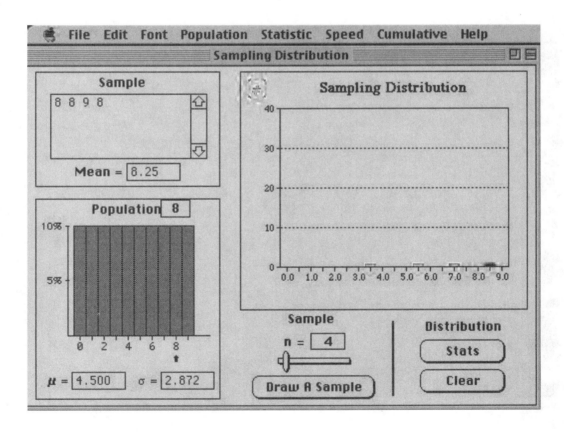

FIGURE 3

sample is selected and its mean is computed and displayed. These sample means will differ from each other; this process illustrates sampling variability. Figure 3 displays the results after four random samples.

Once the students understand the process, we want to know what happens if we take many samples. So the instructor changes the speed to fast so that ExplorStat will take 100 samples of size 4 and show their means on the graph. After a few hundred samples, the graph (which at this point displays counts on the y-axis) "goes off the scale" as shown in Figure 4. When we click on the # icon on the top left corner of the graph, the scale changes to percents and displays the full graph (see Figure 5). At this point, after a few hundred samples, a pattern emerges. The graph shows the shape of the distribution, and, when the instructor clicks on Stats, the module displays the mean and standard deviation of the sampling distribution of the sample mean (see Figure 6). These can be compared to the theoretical mean and standard deviation, $\mu = 4.5$ and $\sigma/\sqrt{n} = 2.782/\sqrt{4} = 1.391$.

The proportion of the observations within one, two, or three standard deviations of the mean are also displayed, to be compared with the 68%, 95%, and 99.7% expected of a normal distribution. Here we emphasize that $n = 4$ is not

a large sample size, and even if 500 samples or more were taken, the 68-95-99.7 rule would not be precisely met. Students tend to have a hard time differentiating between the sample size and the number of iterations of the simulation; the ExplorStat modules help solve this problem.

The sample size can be increased to, say, 50, and several hundred samples taken again (see Figure 7). When the instructor clicks on Stats again, the results are displayed (see Figure 8). Comparing these results to those obtained using $n = 4$, the instructor points out that the mean of the sampling distribution has not changed, but the standard deviation has decreased dramatically.

Before the students begin to work on their own, the instructor demonstrates how to select the population from the menu bar on top of the screen, which offers the following continuous distributions: uniform (which was used for the demonstration), mounded (bell-shaped), skewed, and M-shaped (bimodal).

As students work on the project, the instructor walks around the room answering questions. The project gives specific settings of the population and sample size, and asks students to record the results of their simulations at these settings on the worksheet provided. Students see, by comparing their results to those of their neighbors, that every-

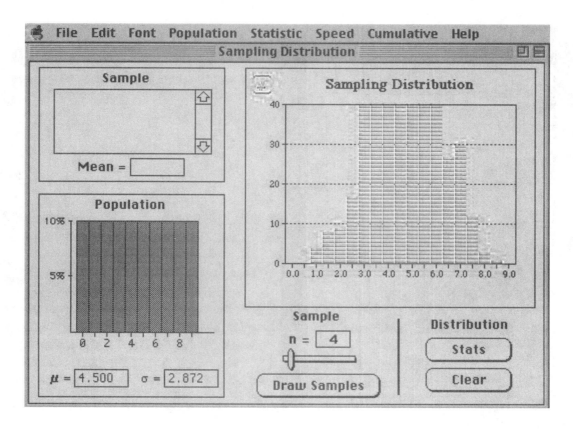

FIGURE 4

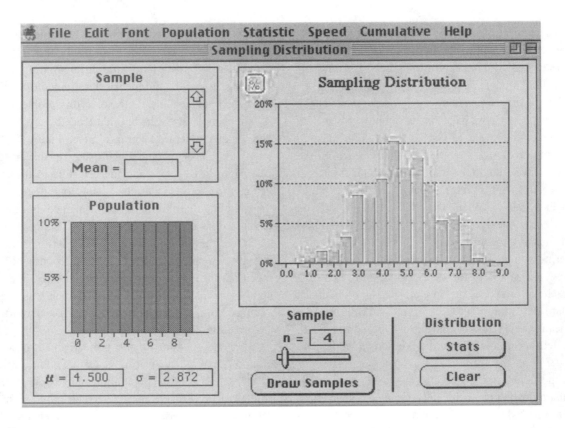

FIGURE 5

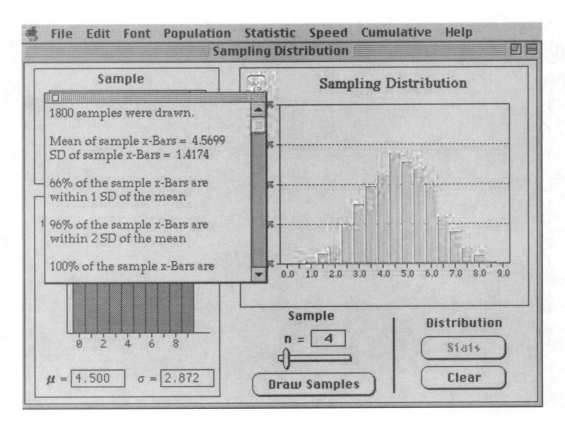

FIGURE 6

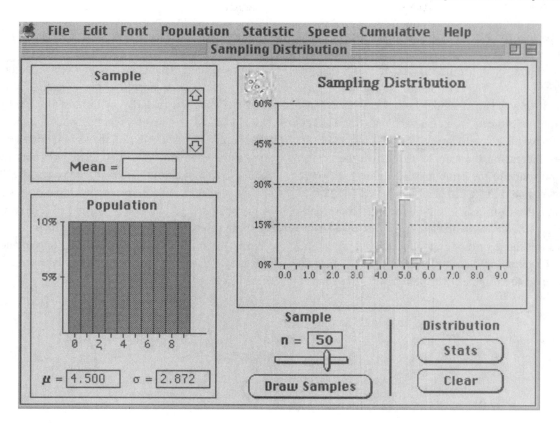

FIGURE 7

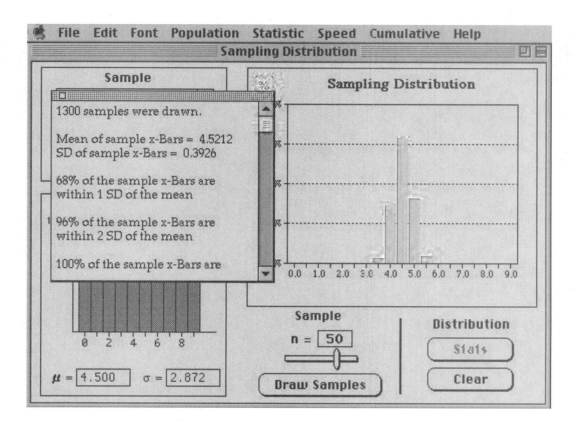

FIGURE 8

one is getting slightly different results, since they all have different random samples. However, overall the results are consistent with the theory. Students can then answer the questions asked on the project (in lab, if they have the time, or at home, if they wish to think about the issues more) before turning the projects in, in class, the next week. The students are asked:

- How does increasing the sample size affect the center, spread, and shape of the sampling distribution of x-bar? (The center shouldn't be affected, the spread should decrease, and the distribution should become more bell-shaped.)
- How does the shape of the original population affect the shape of the sampling distribution of x-bar? (The closer to bell-shaped the original distribution was, the smaller the sample size necessary for the distribution of x-bar to look bell-shaped.)

We have found ExplorStat to be a very effective tool for teaching statistical concepts to mathematically unsophisticated students. Particularly for the last three projects, the lesson is most effective when the students answer questions based on the results of the simulation. These questions should integrate the theoretical concepts learned in class (the Central Limit Theorem, the phrases "95% confidence" and "reject at alpha=.01") with the results produced by the computer simulations. Informal student surveys have found that most students consider the projects done in ExplorStat to be fun. Because ExplorStat is free and *easy to use*, it is attractive to administrators, instructors, and students alike.

Appendix
Sampling Distribution Project: Question and Answer Sheets

Project 3
DUE DATE: Friday, October 24

STA 3023 H
Fall 97

You may work in pairs or individually. If you work in pairs, turn in only one copy of the project with both names listed on it.

Purpose: To study the Sampling Distribution of x-bar, a sample mean, by simulating the process of repeated sampling.

Instructions:

1. Open the **ExplorStat** package to the **Sampling Distribution** module.

2. First, get comfortable with the program:
   Start with the slowest speed, and gradually increase it.
   When plot seems to go off the scale, change the # on upper left corner of the graph to %.
   Notice how the plots get more regular when you take a lot of samples.
   Experiment with different values of n (sample size), and different shapes for the distribution (under population). Note that these are all <u>discrete</u> distributions.

3. Set the speed to **Zap**, and the icon on the upper left corner of the graph to %.
   Using the worksheet provided in the back, for each **population** shape and sample size, **n**, fill out the table:
   a) compute theoretical mean and standard deviation with formulas given in class.
   b) sample <u>at least 500 points,</u> and describe the shape of the distribution.
   c) look under Stats to find observed mean, stdev, and proportions within 1, 2, 3 stdev of mean.

4. Briefly answer the following questions:

a) How does the sample size n affect the distribution of x-bar in terms of:

center?

spread?

shape?

b) How does the shape of the population affect the shape of the distribution of x-bar?

Settings		Theoretical		Observed		Proportion of observations in:			Shape
Population	n	mean	stdev	mean	stdev	$\bar{x} \pm s$	$\bar{x} \pm 2s$	$\bar{x} \pm 3s$	
Uniform	1	4.5	2.872						
Uniform	3								
Uniform	30								
Uniform	50								
Mounded	1	4.5	1.879						
Mounded	3								
Mounded	30								
Skewed	1	2.5	2.402						
Skewed	3								
Skewed	30								
Skewed	50								
M-shaped	1	3.5							
M-shaped	3								
M-shaped	30								
M-shaped	50								

Introduction to *ActivStats*®

Paul F. Velleman
*Cornell University and
Data Description, Inc.*

ActivStats is a multimedia presentation of the material typically covered in a first statistics course. It is intended to be used along with any or all of: a textbook, lectures, internet-based course supports, and classroom-based learning activities. *ActivStats* consists of approximately 250 individual Activities, each motivating, explaining, or reinforcing a single statistics concept. The Activities are organized so that students encounter them in a consistent order, but at a pace determined by the student. Students can learn a concept, apply it, and test their own understanding before proceeding to the next concept.

ActivStats is designed to complement statistics teaching in a variety of ways. Our goal has been to identify the "big ideas" of the introductory statistics course and to present them with innovative use of computer technology. Wherever possible, students discover important concepts for themselves. Every new method is immediately reinforced with applications to real data working with a statistics package. Interactive visualization tools give students an image to grasp to support the equations and definitions. *ActivStats* presents a Lesson Book environment organized into 24 *Lessons*. Lessons are between two and six pages long. Each page introduces the subject of the lesson and offers text to introduce each of several (typically three–five) Activities along with a goal statement (in red) and a clock to indicate the anticipated duration of the activity. When the student clicks the Activity's icon, a window opens to present the Activity.

Activities are of several kinds:

- **Videos** show statistics in use in a wide range of applications, helping to explain to students *why* they should study statistics. The problems discussed in the videos are discussed further in the associated activities. Some videos are from *Against All Odds* and *Decisions Through Data,* and some are original to *ActivStats*.

- **Expositions** present a brief narration, synchronized with text and pictures on the screen to explain a new concept or method. Most expositions pause every minute or so to ask questions and solicit student responses. Expositions focus on a single concept or method.

- **Interactive visualization tools** help students to understand concepts by working with them directly. Each tool is introduced with a narrated exposition that shows the tool at work, and is then followed by an invitation to the student to work with the tool herself. Students discover the sensitivity of some statistics (and the resistance of others) to outliers, what a correlation of 0.80 looks like, how a regression line can be fit by least squares, and many other fundamental concepts.

- **Simulations** help students discover and understand basic principles of randomness, probability, and inference. Students discover the law of large numbers, the Central Limit Theorem, the reasoning of hypothesis testing, and more by performing experiments for themselves.

- **Exercises** in *Data Desk,* a full-function graphical interface statistics package, allow students to apply newly learned skills immediately. Often the data analyzed is from the motivating video. *Data Desk* is included on the CD as part of *ActivStats*.

- **Case studies** illustrate more complete data analyses to put concepts in context.

- **Self-test quizzes** allow students to check their understanding of new terms and concepts.

Teaching activities end with a bullet-list summary of the major points of that activity. On returning to the *Lesson Book,* students find the activity "checked off" on the page (and in the Table of Contents), and see the original introductory paragraph on the page replaced by the bullet list summary. Thus, as a student completes activities, the lesson book becomes a review of the major points of the course.

Although the book metaphor gives students a comfortable environment, it is easier to become disoriented on a computer than with a physical book. For this reason, the *ActivStats* environment offers additional amenities to help students navigate and learn:

- A dynamic **Table of Contents** shows the outline of the course at the Lesson level, opens the current lesson to show each of its pages, opens the current page to show each of its activities, and indicates with check marks which activities have been completed. Students can navigate to any page by clicking on its title in the Table of Contents.

- **Asterisks** in the text of the Lesson book open supplementary examples and stories. Some of these are lighter illustrations (a discussion of Fisher's testimony that cancer may cause cigarette smoking, for example, in the Correlation lesson), many are worked examples drawn (with permission) from other textbooks, and some present background technical information.

- A complete **Glossary** of terms can be opened by itself or entered by clicking on any highlighted term in the lesson book or in an asterisk file. When the Glossary is entered via a hypertext link from the Lesson Book or an Asterisk file, the definitions often begin with a specific example taken directly from the context of the originating page or asterisk. Definitions are illustrated when appropriate, and have hypertext links to other related glossary terms.

- A complete hypertext **Index** shows for each term a list of places in *ActivStats* that reference that term. Clicking on elements of this list opens the Lesson book or asterisk page to the corresponding place.

- Students or teachers can drag the icon of any activity into a **Bookmarks** window and annotate the mark for later reference. Teachers can use this feature to note activities to use in class. Students can use it for study and review.

- Each lesson has extensive **homework exercises.** Many of these have datasets available at the click of a button for analysis in *Data Desk.* Some homework exercises are quoted (with permission) from David Moore's *Active Practice of Statistics,* from Alan Rossman's *Workshop Statistics,* from Mario Triola's *Elementary Statistics,* from *Statistics,* by McClave, Deitrich, and Sincich, and from *Elementary Statistics,* by Weiss. Others are original, using data generated by the students in experiments they perform on themselves, using the interactive visualization tools, or pursuing datasets used in the expositions for deeper understanding.

- Each lesson has one or more **projects**. Projects describe activities in which students or groups of students collect, generate, or discover on the internet original data for analysis.

- Each lesson has a built-in **web page**. If a web browser and internet connection are available, students can open these pages with a click and be directed from there to sites on the internet related to the material in that particular Lesson. Each of these pages holds a link to a site maintained by the author so that new links can be suggested as they arise.

- Students may choose the option of reading the **script** of any narration, either before listening to it or while listening to it. This capability is provided for students for whom English is not a primary language.

- *ActivStats* maintains for each student a Student Progress File in which students record their current progress in the course. When a student opens her progress file, her individual preferences are restored, and the Lesson book is opened to the last page she worked on.

- *ActivStats* includes **Data Desk documentation**, which is integrated into the Lessons at appropriate places, and is also available as a longer reference from the Appendix.

- *ActivStats* offers interactive tools that provide standard **statistics tables** both at the appropriate places in the course and direction from the Appendix. These tables look like those found in standard texts, but provide greater flexibility and graphical feedback than possible with printed tables.

Experience at a number of schools and with large and small classes has shown that a student who works through all of *ActivStats* and does a typical selection of homework exercises will spend between 50 and 70 hours working with *ActivStats* and will cover the usual syllabus of an introductory Statistics course or high school Advanced Placement Statistics course.

Teacher Support

ActivStats provides several tools to facilitate teaching.

- Each Lesson in *ActivStats* begins with an Asterisk file with **links to** corresponding sections of leading statistics texts. In addition, the Preferences include the option of selecting one of several texts to match with *ActivStats*. When a text is selected, *ActivStats's* lessons are placed in the same order as the topic sequence of the selected text and homework from that text is placed at the top of the homework lists in each lesson. (Homework numbering uses the abbreviation of the originating text, so regardless of the order, teachers can specify the exercises they want.)

- *ActivStats* provides an annotated **Dataset Browser** for all of the datasets available on the disk. Datasets are indexed by their titles and by the subject they are used to teach. A button takes you directly to the use in the Lesson Book. The Dataset browser makes it easy to find additional datasets for classroom examples, additional assignments, and examinations.

- **Teacher Extensions** allow teachers to add their own activities to the end of any (or every!) page of the Lesson Book.

- An active **Teachers' Discussion List** is maintained by the author, and can be subscribed to at www.datadesk.com/ActivStats/.

- Additional resources including a Teachers' Guide and web-based materials are available from Addison Wesley Longman, the publisher.

Background

ActivStats requires no more mathematics background than High School algebra. We have deliberately kept formal mathematics to a minimum to make the material in *ActivStats* widely approachable. It is widely used in universities, community colleges, high schools, and in a number of distance learning courses. *ActivStats* seems to be most successful with students who are themselves comfortable with computers—a growing fraction of today's students. Students who must first acclimate to computer-based learning may need some extra time to get up to speed. The *ActivStats* CD-ROM is transparently cross-platform, running on both Macintosh and Windows (95/98/NT) systems, which minimizes technical complications.

Summary

ActivStats has great depth and flexibility. By its nature as a teaching resource that emphasizes learning by participation and presents students with interactive animations and narrated expositions, it is difficult to describe verbally. I urge interested readers to visit the web site (www.datadesk.com/ActivStats) and to request an examination copy to work with for themselves. I also ask for feedback from both those who teach with *ActivStats* and those who decide not to so that we can improve *ActivStats*.

Companion Piece for
ActivStats

Amy Fisher
Miami University Middletown

Introduction

I first learned of *ActivStats* while attending the Chance Workshop at Dartmouth College in 1997. The Chance project [1], funded in part by the NSF, promotes the use of newspaper articles in addition to the content of the course to motivate student learning. The people involved with Chance had successfully used Data Desk, the statistical package that comes with *ActivStats,* in their own classes and were happy to distribute copies of *ActivStats* to all the participants.

The exposure to *ActivStats* at the Chance Workshop had convinced me to adopt *ActivStats,* but I was unsure how to implement it in my course. Some Chance instructors adopt texts that students are required to read on their own without benefit of formal lectures to re-explain content. I had never taught a Chance course in that way, because I did not think that my students would be motivated to do such work on their own. I teach at an open-admissions, regional campus of Miami University. The student population is diverse in age, academic experience, ability, and motivation, but the students do have one thing in common: nearly all are employed. The one overriding factor in student success is time management. Furthermore, with so many students lacking strong critical and mathematical skills, I hesitated assuming that students would be able to handle the rigors of reading a text on their own.

Then in November 1997, I attended the "International Conference on Teaching College Mathematics" in Chicago where Paul Velleman offered a workshop on *ActivStats*. I had already decided to try *ActivStats* in my spring 1998 introductory course, and I looked to the workshop to teach me how to incorporate *ActivStats* into my class. Paul Velleman reported that he has students work through *ActivStats* outside of class on their own. He convinced me to give it a try. The results were a resounding success.

ActivStats in My Class

Statistics 261 is an introductory, non-calculus-based, one-semester course for liberal education majors. Miami University requires all potential graduates to complete a course in "formal reasoning." The Miami Plan for Liberal Education emphasizes four goals for students: to think critically, to understand contexts, to engage with other learners, and to reflect and act. In attempting to meet these goals in my statistics course, I introduce many different learning scenarios. Although some lecturing is essential, students need opportunities to work with others in class, analyze arguments, understand concepts, and draw conclusions. To that end, I structure many classes with activities for small group work or class discussion. I expect students to come to class prepared to take an active part in these activities. I leave many of the content details to the students to work on outside of class.

How students are introduced to out-of-class assignments is crucial. After carefully explaining why I have adopted *ActivStats* in the course syllabus, I gently warn students about the amount of work I expect them to do. Besides working through the *ActivStats* lessons, I also require them to read another standard text, read and discuss articles, write reports, and analyze data. Of course, students must also practice statistics through traditional homework problems. Students are anxious about the course at first, but most persevere with good spirits, and their projects at the end of the term show that they develop good beginning analytical skills.

Our standard text in the spring of 1998 was *Seeing Through Statistics*, by Jessica Utts [3]. This text is a great companion to *ActivStats*. The Utts text teaches students how to analyze articles and displays; *ActivStats* teaches the content and concepts. I assigned chapters in the Utts text in an order compatible with *ActivStats*. I have also used David Moore's *Statistics: Concepts and Controversies* [2]. The order of topics in the Moore text matches that of the default ordering in *ActivStats*. The optional order of topics in *ActivStats* will match the more traditional texts that have probability earlier in the semester.

I have three essential prescriptions for the instructor considering using *ActivStats*; the first is to plan carefully. In order to use *ActivStats* efficiently, I worked through many of the lessons before the term began; I needed to understand what the students would experience when they started to use *ActivStats*. After working through the introductory lesson, I knew students would find this first lesson invaluable for learning the *ActivStats* system. *ActivStats* has so many opportunities for learning that I am sure we would have missed some if I hadn't worked through the examples, looked over the projects and homework, become familiar with Data Desk, and explored the Web sites before making assignments. Because each lesson has so many options for study, I am careful to structure assignments. Students will not work every problem or project just out of curiosity. An assignment of "work through lessons one through three" will get the same results as "read chapter one" from a standard text.

The second prescription is to keep students current on their *ActivStats* work. Because I prefer to spend class time on activities and discussions that enhance students' understanding and appreciation of statistical methods, students must do the work assigned outside of class. This outside

work includes both reading from Utts and lessons from *ActivStats,* and it is *ActivStats* that introduces students to the fundamental concepts and content of statistics. I use two strategies for motivating students to do the outside work. In his workshop, Paul Velleman suggested the strategy of giving simple *ActivStats* quizzes. *ActivStats* builds many drag-and-drop exercises into each lesson. These exercises are easy for students who have done the *ActivStats* seriously but are difficult to impossible for those who have not. These exercises make good, short, in-class quizzes. These quizzes keep students up on the material if based on the extrinsic reward of a grade, but once students see the benefit of staying current, they no longer need quizzes. The other strategy relates to class time spent on *ActivStats*: I answer content questions only at the beginning of class on activity days, which forces students to have the discipline to do the outside work.

My third prescription is to use Data Desk frequently. Data Desk, the statistical package of *ActivStats*, can be an integral part of classroom discussions. Often, I bring a computer to class in order to help analyze some data. Many *ActivStats* activities launch Data Desk for real data analysis. Using Data Desk in class emphasizes the importance of the *ActivStats* lessons and does so with a statistical package familiar to them. Live demonstrations help with *ActivStats* homework assignments and projects. Importing data into Data Desk is very easy, so I use Data Desk to analyze every example where data are available. Students see how to analyze real data and they realize that many techniques are available to them for their final projects.

Extended Example:
Using *ActivStats* to help teach bivariate descriptive statistics

ActivStats gives a multimedia presentation of statistics. The Lesson Book [4] is the "home base" of this presentation and combines features of a physical book—table of contents, index, glossary, book marking ability—with links to the various types of *ActivStats* activities that do the educational work for the course. Activities include expositions, interactive and data-gathering activities, data analysis using Data Desk, video clips, drag-and-drop exercises to allow students to check their understanding, and projects that ask students to collect and analyze data as a class.

Lesson 7, Scatterplots, comprises three main sections, each a separate Lesson Book page: (1) Scatterplots, which describes the basic concepts; (2) What to Look for in a Scatterplot, which teaches the direction-form-strength paradigm for interpreting a scatterplot; and (3) Reexpressing Data, which teaches fundamental concepts of re-expression. This third page is an optional, more advanced topic. Students access activities through icon links within the Lesson Book narrative. The narrative updates after each activity is completed. Within these three pages, *ActivStats* provides the following activities:

- A video clip about the Beanstalk Club, a social club in Boston, restricted to tall people, that motivates the question: Do people generally marry people of a similar height?
- An interactive exposition that introduces scatterplots.
- A tutorial on scatterplots with Data Desk.
- An interactive exposition on interpreting scatterplots by considering the direction, the form, and the strength of the relationship as well as paying attention to any outliers in the plot.
- A set of five drag-and-drop exercises that students use to test their newly acquired knowledge about scatterplots.
- A "case study," using a data set on 1991-model cars taken from *Consumer Reports,* that builds a predictive model for fuel economy. Students use Data Desk to create coded-scatterplots and to link between graphical objects.
- An animated exposition that motivates reasons to consider reexpressing data.
- An exposition that introduces power transformations.
- An interactive tutorial using Data Desk sliders that uses power transformations in a variety of simple cases to illustrate the effects of re-expression.
- An interactive Data Desk tutorial using sliders to re-express X and Y to attain linearity.

ActivStats also provides the following toolbar options for Lesson 7:

- A collection of 12 homework exercises about subjects like fast food sandwiches, Broadway shows, or educational spending.
- Two student projects that use class-generated data, one on heights and arm spans and the other on family sizes of students and their parents.
- Web sites related specifically to Lesson 7, such as links to web-based statistics textbooks and their coverage of scatterplots.

In its introductory Lesson 1, *ActivStats* encourages students to work "sequentially" because ". . . statistics is a sequential subject [4]." *ActivStats* also encourages students to take advantage of the multimedia and hypertext features but cautions, ". . . you'll find the material makes much more sense when you learn basic ideas first and then build on them [4]." I urge students to take this recommendation to heart. To reinforce this recommendation, I give students a

well-structured set of assignments and classroom activities that integrate *ActivStats* with other class resources.

Here is the syllabus from my course for the topic of scatterplots. I give students an abbreviated version of this schedule at the beginning of the year. They know when the *ActivStats* Lessons are scheduled, and they can work ahead. My students appreciate being able to work ahead with *ActivStats* since most students work more than 20 hours per week and they may not have enough time to work on a lesson on a particular night. At the beginning of each major unit, I hand out a more detailed schedule with homework assignments and due dates. Explanations of the activities follow.

Unit:
Scatterplots, Correlation, and Least Squares

Day 0: Motivation, last 20 minutes of class
Class Activity: Small group discussion (a)
Assignment: ActivStats Lesson 7
    Problems 4,5,6,9,14
    Due Date: (One week from class 0 or end of unit, whichever is greater)

Day 1:
Class Activity: Scatterplot activity (b)
    Student questions (c)
    Data Desk example (d)
Assignment: Utts: Chapter 10
    Problems 4,5,8 for class discussion
    Mini-project 2
    Due Date: (same as ActivStats problems)

Day 2:
Class Activity: Lecture/review (e)
    Class discussion of Utts assignment (f)
    Video (g)
Assignment: Response paper on video
    Due Date: (same)

Day 3:
Class Activity: Assessment article (h)
    (Intro to correlation)
Assignment: (ActivStats Lesson 8)

In Lesson 6, students learned how to compare two independent groups by using side-by-side boxplots and summary statistics. I schedule the first activity for Lesson 7 after a class assessment activity on Lesson 6.

(a) I hand out articles that describe situations where paired data is natural, such as pre- and post-test scores. Students read about the situation and form small groups. Discussion questions lead students to realize that more information can be gleaned from the data than in situations where side-by-side boxplots are helpful. If time permits, which would be unusual, we can reconvene as a class to review plotting points of paired data.

(b) Students have learned about scatterplots in their *ActivStats* homework. In this activity, I distribute several scatterplots for the student groups to analyze. They write paragraphs describing the story the plots are trying to tell and describe the scatterplots using the direction-form-strength paradigm.

(c) I try to allocate plenty of time for student questions. At this point, one student asked a question which led to a preliminary mini-lecture on correlation. Since a student brought up the topic naturally, I think all the students were more motivated for the next lesson in *ActivStats*.

(d) I anticipate that many students do not allocate enough time to completely understand all the information given in *ActivStats*. This activity is more a lecture/review time where I bring a computer to class and work an example problem much like the homework assignments using Data Desk. By this time, even the slackers understand enough to follow the discussion.

(e) I usually schedule some time to talk about whatever I feel needs to be talked about, which can lead to my giving a mini-lecture that fills in some details or stresses important points.

(f) The assignment in the Utts text has students reading material that encompasses Lessons 7, 8, and 9 in *ActivStats*. Students will be prepared to discuss questions concerning Lesson 7, and their questions about the rest of the material help motivate them for further *ActivStats* work. I will intersperse more problems from this chapter as well as Chapter 11 throughout the schedule for the entire unit.

(g) Students watch a video describing the history of the smoking-lung cancer debate. Although this video does not deal with scatterplots, now is the time to emphasize the problems involved with causation. Students have already learned about experimental design and analysis through earlier chapters in the Utts text. The Chapter 10 reading assignment has also prepared students for the association/causation problem. The response paper assignment asks students to write about the video, outlining how scientists decided without a controlled experiment that smoking indeed causes lung cancer.

(h) There are several possibilities for this activity. In one, I distribute a description of a data set with a scatterplot. Students individually write a response describing the scatterplot and the story behind the scatterplot. They also decide if causation is indicated by the study. Another activity would be to ask students to envision a scatterplot after reading a description of the data and the researcher's conclusions.

The last part of this third class becomes the introductory class for Lesson 8.

Student Reaction and Future Plans

Student evaluations highly favored both *ActivStats* and the use of Data Desk. There were the predictable complaints about how much time was spent outside of class, but students admitted to learning statistics. Students enjoyed the class activities and reported that the activities enhanced their learning.

One recommendation that many students made was to incorporate a lab day into each week where students could work on the *ActivStats* lessons with a teacher available. Since students really can work on *ActivStats* by themselves, I do not want to schedule labs simply for students to work on homework assignments. I plan on scheduling several labs for well-structured, in-class projects using Data Desk for analysis.

Having used two different companion texts with *ActivStats*, I plan to return to using the Utts text next year. *Seeing Through Statistics* gives the students different information than *ActivStats*. The Moore text is great, but I don't see the need for students to have two texts that give much the same information. *ActivStats* stands alone very well.

References

[1] Chance Home Page, `www.dartmouth.edu/~chance/`

[2] Moore, David S., *Statistics, Concepts and Controversies*, 4th ed., 1996, W.H. Freeman and Co., NY.

[3] Utts, Jessica M., *Seeing Through Statistics*, 1996, Duxbury Press, Belmont, CA.

[4] Velleman, Paul, *ActivStats*, 1998, Addison Wesley Interactive, Reading, MA.

A Time-Subject Index for *Against All Odds: Inside Statistics*[†]

Edward R. Mansfield
University of Alabama

Against All Odds: Inside Statistics is a collection of twenty-six, half-hour, video presentations that depict how statistics is used in society. This outstanding series was produced under the guidance of Dr. David Moore of Purdue University. The tapes are available from The Annenberg/CPB Collection, and are also offered free to schools that adopt certain textbooks. Using short excepts from the thirteen hours of video in the classroom can be an excellent way to introduce students of statistics to real problems. Contained in this paper is a listing *of the real-world setting, the specific statistical items discussed, and a time index* designed so that instructors can go directly to a desired story on a tape. As an example of how to use a tape in class, show the video of the space shuttle Challenger exploding! The impact on the class can be quite dramatic. Then discuss the data analysis problems as to why the tragedy happened.

Segments of the series that I think can be used effectively in a classroom setting are highlighted. A one- to four-star rating is used. These are my ratings; yours will vary. The portions of the tapes in which Teresa Amabile, series hostess from Brandeis University, teaches are generally not rated, since she is playing the role of the instructor, the task you will be performing in the classroom. Statistical terms are shown in **bold** type.

A VCR and a TV monitor are all that is needed. Knowing where specific segments start and end is greatly enhanced if your VCR has a "real time" counter as opposed to one that counts revolutions of the videocassette reel. Each tape in the series contains two 30-minute programs. All times in this paper are measured from the front of a tape, beginning at *the first video signal on the tape*. This signal is always "1-800-LEARNER," the phone number for information on the tape series. When this first appears, reset your VCR counter to "0:00." The time corresponding to "END OF PROGRAM" indicates the point at which the program credits start. Times on the left indicate the time index at which a segment begins. *Note, because of differences in the production runs made for duplicating this series, the "gap time" between the two programs on each tape may vary. Your tapes may have different gap times than mine; if so, note the difference and adjust all times on the even numbered programs accordingly.*

This listing for the *Proceedings* is an abreviated version. To get the full, detailed version, send an e-mail to emansfie@cba.ua.edu

Ask for file "asa95vid.doc".

Enjoy the series

[†] This article originally appeared in the *Proceedings of the Section on Statistical Education*, 1995, American Statistical Association, 341–345.

Overview of Stories

PROGRAM 1: What is Statistics?

4:48   Domino's Pizza.   ★★★

Note: Each of the following stories in Program 1 is presented in more detail in later programs.

Describing Data
13:53   Lighting strikes in Colorado. **Histogram.**
14:33   Growth hormones; heights of children.
15:26   Manatee deaths in Florida waters.
             Scatterplot.
16:05   Baseball players' salaries. **Correlation.**

Producing Data
16:50   Chesapeake Bay pollution.
17:54   Aspirin and heart attacks.
18:44   Frito-Lay Potato Chips. **Sampling.**
19:18   Political Polls.
20:35   The Space Shuttle Challenger.
             Joint probability.
21:24   Casino gambling.

Conclusion from Data
21:59   Discrimination within the FBI.
23:13   Duracell Batteries.
24:05   Shakespearean poetry.
             Salem Witch trials.
25:06   Welfare in Baltimore.
27:06   END OF PROGRAM.
             Tape continues

PROGRAM 2: Picturing Distributions

31:58   Charles Menard's 200 year old map/graph
33:55   Lighting strikes in Colorado.
             Histograms   ★★★
44:02   Scheduling TV Programs.   ★★★
52:17   Lowering health care costs.
             histograms, stem and leaf plots ★/2
             End of Tape

PROGRAM 3: Describing Distributions

3:30   National salary & wage data.
5:55   Wage inequities in Colorado   ★
16:07   Hot dogs' composition.   ★★
21:00   Musical analysis of urine data.   ★★
             Tape continues

PROGRAM 4: Normal Distributions

33:50   Baby "bust" problem.   ★
37:40   Aging of our population.   ★★★
46:07   Boston Bean Stalk Social Club.   ★
50:38   Baseball statistics.
             ".400" hitters?   ★★★
55:48   Ty Cobb, Ted Williams, and
             George Brett batting averages.   ★★
             End of Tape

PROGRAM 5: Normal Calculations

3:21   **Standardizing the normal distribution**
             with heights of American women.
7:07   GM Proving grounds.   ★
11:15   Does a new model car meet
             emission standards?
             using only n=5 prototypes?
14:10   Cholesterol values.   ★★
19:50   Sizes of military uniforms.   ★★
22:46   New army helmets
24:21   **Normal Quantile Plot.**
             Tape continues

PROGRAM 6: Time Series

32:17   Driving times to work in a **control chart.**

34:50   The body's internal clock.
             Time series.   ★/2
38:58   National economic statistics.
             Seasonal variation.
40:03   Ozone levels in the atmosphere.
             Seasonal var. and negative trend. ★★
41:03   Boston Marathon. **running median**
43:38   Brain's reaction time.   ★
47:27   Wall Street: Diversification reduces risk.
             Do stock market exist?   ★★★
             End of Tape

PROGRAM 7: Models for Growth

3:00   Children growth rates. Sara height.
       Alice in wonderland grows BIG.
       ★★★

9:20   **Linear growth, residual** patterns,
       Extrapolation problems.

14:00   Gypsy moths and **exponential growth.**
       ★★

20:17   Cartoon: The price of a chess board?
       ★★

23:30   Crude oil production. Use of **logarithm.**

Tape continues

PROGRAM 8: Describing Relationships

32:25   Manatees vs. motor boats in Florida.
       ★★★

37:55   Cavities vs. fluoride levels.
39:31   1970 Draft lottery.
       Median trace   ★★★
44:04   Obesity: metabolic rate vs.
       lean body mass   ★

End of Tape

PROGRAM 9: Correlation

1:36   Taste of chocolate cake and price?
3:45   **Correlation** illustrated with animated
       graphics.   ★★
5:42   Identical twins raised apart.   ★★★
16:22   Baseball players' salaries.   ★★
20:53   Education in the 60's. Coleman Report
       and Fred Mosteller.   ★

Tape continues

PROGRAM 10: Multi-dimensional Data Analysis

32:28   Chesapeake Bay pollution.   ★★
45:07   **Chernof faces, "Trees" and "stars."**
47:42   Bell Core graphics.
       Speech synthesis, 3-D plots and
       higher, and **brushing**.   ★★

End of Tape

PROGRAM 11: The Question of Causation

3:01   Cartoon: **Causation, Common response,**
       and coincidence.   ★★★★
5:42   **Simpson's Paradox.**
       "City University"   ★★★★
11:50   "Good" bad experiment with
       new borns.   ★★
12:47   The Wynder-Graham study.
       smoking <u>causes</u> cancer.   ★★★

Tape continues

PROGRAM 12: Experimental Design

32:46   **Observational** study of lobsters.   ★
36:14   The Physicians Health Study.
       Aspirin and heart attacks?   ★★★★
43:39   Is Ribavirin too good to be true?   ★★★
47:22   Disposition of domestic violence.
       Milwaukee, Wis. police dept.   ★
53:22   A fictional experiment to illustrate
       bad experimental practices.   ★★★★

End of Tape

PROGRAM 13: Blocking and Sampling

1:39   Dirty laundry, blocked and treated.
4:45   The perfect strawberry.   ★
13:28   Undercounting in the national
       census.   ★★★
19:45   Shere Hite's *Women and Love*.
20:48   Frito Lay potato chips.
       Sampling   ★★★★

Tape continues

PROGRAM 14: Samples and Surveys

32:03   A **stratified** national **sample.**
       Nice graphics.
34:41   A fish story.   ★
39:36   Bad interviewer techniques.   ★★★
41:21   National Opinion Research Center
       (NORC)
       (A must see segment.)   ★★★★
50:30   **Sampling distributions:**
       beads in a bowl illustrate
       precision in estimation.   ★★★

End of Tape

PROGRAM 15: What is Probability

4:32   Assessing probabilities of injury or
        death in everyday life.   ★
10:50   A magician shows randomness.   ★
17:49   Traffic control in New York City.
        Simulation model.   ★★

Tape continues

PROGRAM 16: Random Variables

33:36   Cheating on an AP Calculus exam.   ★
34:33   Space Shuttle Challenger.   ★★★★
43:02   Points in a profession basketball game.
49:10   Earthquakes in California.   ★
54:45   Distribution of ice cubes used per drink.

End of Tape

PROGRAM 17: Binomial Distributions

3:46   Boston Celtics Basketball.
        Free throws are **independent**
        in game situations.   ★★★
6:38   Stocks and T-bills.
        Expected rate of returns.
9:45   A finance class experiment.   ★★
16:23   **Binomial distribution.**
17:22   Sickle cell anemia.   ★
24:25   Quincunx: Falling balls.   ★★

Tape continues

PROGRAM 18: The Sample Mean and Control Charts

33:55   Roulette.
35:04   Interviews with gamblers.   ★★
40:44   The casino always wins.   ★★★★
47:03   Frito Lays Potato Chips.
        Statistical Process Control   ★★★
53:41   Dr. W. Edwards Deming.   ★★★★

End of Tape

PROGRAM 19: Confidence Intervals

3:11   Political Polls. **Margin of error**   ★★
6:37   Systolic blood pressure.
        Confidence interval.
11:35   Duracell batteries.   ★★
18:25   Rhesus monkeys in medical studies.   ★
21:21   The feeding behavior of marmosets.

Tape continues

PROGRAM 20: Significance Tests

34:18   Shakespearean Poetry.   ★★
49:06   Discrimination within the FBI.   ★★★

End of Tape

PROGRAM 21: Inference for One Mean

3:03   The t-distributions: 1908, the Guinness
        Brewery and William Gossett.
5:55   The National Institute of Standards and
        Technology.   ★★
10:33   CI for the mean of PCB concentrations.
13:30   NutraSweet,
        shelf life of a new cola.   ★★★
18:19   **Paired comparison test** of sweetness
        of cola.
21:08   Autism.   ★

Tape continues

PROGRAM 22: Comparing Two Means

33:32   Welfare in Baltimore.   ★★
45:05   Union Carbide product testing.   ★★★
51:00   SAT Exams. Can "coaching" help?
55:40   CI for the difference between the
        means.   ★★★

End of Tape

PROGRAM 23: Inference For Proportions

3:03   Measuring Unemployment Nationwide.
        The Bureau of Labor Statistics.   ★
11:58   Safety of City Water.   ★★★
20:15   The Salem Witch Trials.

Tape continues

PROGRAM 24: Inference for Two-Way Tables

34:11   Ancient Man.   Are Africanus and
          Robustus different?   ★★
43:30   Breast Cancer.   ★★
52:02   Mendel's Peas.   ★★

End of Tape

PROGRAM 25: Inference for Relationships

3:32   Are galaxies speeding away
          from earth?
          Edwin Hubble's work.   ★★★★
8:05   **Regression** using Hubble's
          original data on 24 galaxies.
14:08   Complications in the Hubble Constant.
          Rotating 3-D plot illustrates
          the "Swiss cheese concept"
          of universe.   ★★

Tape continues

PROGRAM 26: Case Study

35:49   How the drug, AZT, was tested and got to
          market.
36:57   **Phase 1: Observational Study.**
39:22   **Phase 2: A double blind experiment.**
          The Data Safety Monitoring Board
          Confirming the data analysis.
51:30   Getting AZT to patients.   **Statistical
          process control** in manufacturing.
53:07   A patient's perspective.   ★★★
          Safety and efficiency of a new drug.

End of Tape
End of series.

The following is an example of the more detailed index.   This includes starting and stopping times, as well as the elapsed time for each segment.   This detailed listing for all tapes would not fit in the limited space of the *Proceedings*.

If you would like a copy of the full index, send an e-mail to

emansfie@cba.ua.edu

Ask for file   "asa95vid.doc".

Example of the full detail index:

PROGRAM 13: Blocking and Sampling

0:00   1-800-Learner.
1:07   *Against All Odds* logo.
1:39   Teresa: Dirty laundry is blocked
          (cotton, synthetics) and treated
          (warm or cold water).
          Lesson Objectives:
          1. Blocking
          2. Sampling
          3. Census
4:45   STORY: The perfect strawberry.
          Horticulturists use a randomized
          complete block design to determine the
          best berry for market.
          Olivia Mageau, Horticulturist, & Gene
          Galletta, Ph.D., Geneticist.
8:43   Teresa: Reasons for blocking.
9:57   STORY continued: The evaluation
          of the berry data.   [6:53]   ★
11:38   Teresa: Reasons for multi-factor
          experiments.   [1:50]
13:28   STORY: Undercounting in the national
          census. This illustrates the difficulties
          of getting an exact count.
          Barbara Bailer, Statistician, &
          Peter Bounpane, US Census Bureau.
                            [5:08]   ★★★
18:36   Teresa: Why a sample instead of
          a census?
19:45   Shere Hite's *Women and Love*. 1987.
          An example of extremely biased
          sampling due to voluntary response.
                            [2:12]
20:48   STORY: Frito Lay potato chips.
          Sampling is used at many steps
          in the production of potato chips
          to insure a high quality product.
                            [5:49]   ★★★★
26:37   Teresa: Closing Comments.
27:08   END OF PROGRAM.

Tape continues

Abstract. Many excellent resources for supporting statistics instruction are freely and globally available on the World Wide Web. However, finding useful information among the ever-widening sprawl of on-line sites can be a daunting task. The purpose of this paper is to help sift through the range of possibilities and highlight some of the sites, which we have found to be the most helpful. We consider on-line access to electronic journals, discussion groups, applets, statistical software, teaching aids, and course materials. Special attention is paid to using the Web as a resource for both students and teachers to find or produce interesting datasets.

WWW Resources for Teaching Statistics

Robin H. Lock
St. Lawrence University

Introduction

The purpose of this paper is to direct readers to Web sites that typify the various sorts of resources that are currently available on the WWW to help support statistics instruction. Most of the links mentioned in this paper (denoted with italics type) can be accessed through the addresses given in the references or through an on-line outline of this paper which is located at `it.stlawu.edu/~rlock/maa51/www.html`. Due to the rapidly evolving nature of the Web, by the time this is in print (or read) some links may no longer be available or will have radically modified content. Fortunately, changes are often improvements and new resources are being added at a steady rate. The on-line outline will be updated periodically to provide a more current snapshot of the status of WWW resources for teaching statistics.

On-line Course Materials

An increasing number of instructors are using the Web to make course materials available to their students. For example, *Hal Stern's Statistics 101* page at Iowa State University contains links to the course syllabus, project assignment, past and current exams (with solutions), and homework exercises (again, with solutions). While this provides a convenient method for distributing information to a class, it also contributes a resource that allows statistics instructors at other institutions to peruse those course materials for hints and ideas to improve their own courses. A more elaborate example can be found at *Robert Hale's EdPsy 101* Web site at Penn State, which includes links to overheads used in class, a text-like summary of course material with embedded Java applets, an on-line stat package *(Statlets)*, a class discussion site, a glossary of statistical terms, tables, biographies of statisticians, and links to other statistics resources on the Web.

In addition to standard materials, a course Web page allows instructors to easily direct their students to Web resources at other sites. A good example is *Wlodzimierz Bryc's Elementary Probability and Statistics Course* at the University of Cincinnati that organizes links to a variety of other Web sites within a course materials Web page. AP Statistics instructors should check *Al Coon's AP Statistics* site at the Buckingham, Browne & Nichols School. Some nice examples of lab exercises (with samples of students' write-ups) can be found at *Beth Chance's Math 37—Probability and Statistics Course* at the University of the Pacific. For a variety of different courses, the Department of Statistics at the University of Illinois at Urbana/Champaign provides links to a wide range of *UIUC Statistics Course Web pages*.

On-line Texts

Going beyond materials for a local course, several individuals and groups have undertaken ambitious projects to develop full-featured textbooks for introductory statistics courses that can be accessed over the Web. While the coverage often follows familiar topics from traditional textbooks, the on-line texts offer new avenues for flexibility, multimedia capability, and the ability to link to other sites on the Web. Interesting examples include *SurfStat* being developed by Keith Dear at the University of Newcastle, *Hyperstat Online* by David Lane at Rice University, and *Statistics: The Study of Stability in Variation,* edited by Jan de Leeuw at UCLA. Hyperstat Online also provides links to several other Webtext projects. Commercial ventures in this area include Gary McClelland's *Seeing Statistics* (Duxbury) and CyberGnostics Inc's *CyberStats*.

JAVA Applets

The emergence of JAVA as a platform-independent Web programming language has allowed individuals to develop interactive demonstration software that can be accessed via any JAVA-capable browser. While most of what currently is done with statistical JAVA applets could be duplicated through traditional disk-based programs, the availability of these applications over the Web allows instructors to pick and choose among a variety of applications and (often) make them available to students without additional expense.

The *Globally Accessible Statistical Procedures* (GASP) initiative, centered at the University of South Carolina, showcases a number of interesting examples of what is possible through this medium. Click on a scatterplot to see how the addition of a new point affects the least squares line, or play a few rounds of the famous Monty Hall "Let's Make a Deal" problem to see if the switching strategy really is optimal. Links to similar *Interesting JAVA Applets* are also being collected at a Duke University Web site. Kyle Siegrist at the University of Alabama, Huntsville has produced a good collection of simulation applets with emphasis on applications in probability at his *Virtual Laboratories in Probability and Statistics*. The *CUWU Statistics Program* developed by John Marden at UIUC has a number of applets, including one of our favorites, a *Correlation Guessing Game* that allows students to match correlations with scatterplots and compete for a place on the worldwide "Top 20" list. For additional applet examples, the on-line texts described in the previous section all contain good collections of linkable applets. Two of the best efforts at developing full JAVA-based Web statistics packages can be found at NWP Associates' *Statlets* and Webster West's *WebStat*.

Electronic Journals

The *Journal of Statistics Education* (JSE) has been available electronically since its founding in 1993. The journal, now sponsored by the American Statistical Association (ASA), publishes fully refereed articles devoted to all aspects of teaching statistics at the post-secondary level. Most of the processing of these articles, including submission and review, takes place electronically. When an issue of JSE is "published," subscribers receive an e-mail message containing a table of contents and abstracts of articles in that issue. Since articles are available in HTML format through the Web, they may contain links to other sections of the article, other JSE articles, related Web pages, downloadable data files, graphics, executable program files, or video clips.

In addition to JSE, online newsletters related to teaching statistics are currently available through the ASA's *Section on Statistical Education*, the *Chance News* project, the *CTI Centre for Teaching Statistics*, and the *Statistics Teacher Network* published by the ASA-NCTM Joint Committee in Statistics and Probability.

Discussion Lists and Newsgroups

Electronic discussion lists allow instructors to share questions, ideas, and announcements and to debate issues related to teaching statistics, practicing statistics, and statistical computing. One of the earliest electronic discussion lists devoted to teaching issues was the *Edstat-l* list founded at North Carolina State University. One of the best lists for instructors teaching an introductory course is *APStat-l*, officially designed for the Advanced Placement Statistics course. A search through the archives of either of these lists can often yield valuable information (or help identify good contact people). The range of available discussion lists on topics related to statistics is quite remarkable, from those which focus on particular software packages (Minitab, SAS, Data Desk, . . .), to statistical topic areas (experimental design, time series, Bayesian analysis, . . .), or subject matter disciplines (econometrics, educational research, psychology, . . .), and geographical regions. The valuable *List of Statistical Lists* maintained by Mike Fuller gives a wealth of information on available discussion lists and newsgroups with hints for getting signed on.

Data, Data, and More Data

Need an example of a regression fit that is drastically altered by an influential point? Want to find some data to illustrate descriptive statistics that will appeal to students interested in environmental issues? Looking for a multivariate dataset to serve as the basis for next week's midterm examination? Have a student who loves horse racing and wants to use data from the Kentucky Derby for her project? The Web is the place to go to find loads of data sources, often in readily downloadable formats.

Our discussion of Web data is organized around different types of resources, starting with dataset archives, which contain collections of pre-packaged datasets designed specifically for instructional use. We also consider Web pages with links to data-rich Web sites, look at ways to use search engines to find data, and discuss how some students might study the Web itself as a source for project data.

A number of excellent Web sites contain collections of datasets that are primarily intended for educational purposes. For example, the *Journal of Statistics Education Dataset Archive* contains dozens of instructional datasets. For each dataset, one can find a documentation file that describes the variables in the dataset (and suggests some ways to use the data in class) and a separate ASCII file containing just the raw data. One can print the documentation file and use a "save as" feature, found on most Web browsers, to store a copy of the raw data file for later importation into a statistics package, or try a simple "cut & paste" operation to import the data. About half of the JSE datasets are linked to longer articles from the "Datasets and Stories" section of past JSE issues which give more detailed information on pedagogical uses for the data.

The *Data and Story Library* (DASL) has features similar to the JSE archive, giving raw data together with a context (story). DASL adds some interesting search capabilities that allow users to find datasets that illustrate certain statistical methods (regression, paired t-test, contingency table, . . .) or search for data dealing with a particular subject area (agriculture, environment, weather, . . .). One of the earliest public access dataset archives can be found at the *Statlib* server maintained at Carnegie Mellon University. This site contains a huge number of datasets (including all data from a number of popular texts). While *Statlib* doesn't have a convenient search engine (like DASL which is also housed at CMU) and pedagogical uses of some datasets are not so specifically detailed (as at JSE), the range of data available is impressive. *Statlib* also serves as a repository for a good deal of public domain statistical software and information about various statistical organizations.

Of course, all the datasets on the Web are not so neatly packaged for instructional use as in the dataset archives. Finding much of the data available on the Web often requires a good deal of patient digging through many sites to sift out usable nuggets of data. To assist in this process, a number of instructors have compiled lists of Web sites that are unusually productive sources of good data.

One of the best examples of such a site is *Dr. B's Wide World of Web Data* maintained by John Behrens at Arizona State University. Organized in an outline format according to subject areas (criminal justice, environment, food, history, . . .), this Web page provides loads of links to electronic data sources along with a sentence or two of commentary about each site. In many cases, the links are to "top-level" pages (e.g., *Social Security Administration*, *Census Bureau*, *U.S. Department of Education*, . . .) which still leave a good deal of work to find desired data, although direct links to one or two of those nuggets of data (e.g., counts of Social Security recipients by state and program) are often provided. An alternate source for connections to government data is *Fedstats*—billed as the "One-Stop Shopping" source for government data, with links to more than 70 federal agencies. Be sure to check out Fedstats A-Z quick links. For a more international flavor, the *CIA's World Factbook* gives loads of demographic information on countries. The University of Michigan's *Statistical Resources on the Web* has lots of links to data sources, including a page with links to *Foreign Government Data Sources* from an alphabetized list of countries.

Students are increasingly Web-savvy and eager to find their own data on the Web. Many are very comfortable using one of the many search engines to research areas of interest, but may have trouble getting to good raw data. To assist this process, we have developed a *DataSurfing on the World Wide Web* page as a starting point for students looking for project data. We have tracked their choices over several semesters and summarized the results at a page called *Student Choices for Web Data*. One quickly notes a propensity for students to choose data with sports-related themes. Thus, as an offshoot of the *DataSurfing* page, we created a more specialized *Sports Data Page* to provide links to current and archived data. Many of the sports links were originally found at the *Sports Statistics on the Web* page sponsored by the ASA's Section on Statistics in Sports.

While not specifically a page of links to existing data, a group at the University of Colorado at Boulder has produced an interesting site, the *Expersim Project*, which serves as a front end for simulation software originally developed at the University of Michigan. Several realistic scenarios are described and users may generate their own data by specifying an experimental design, controlling settings for several factors, and determining sample sizes. For some experience with sampling from a simulated population, visit Carl Schwarz' *StatVillage* to generate a sample from a hypothetical village based on real data from the census of Canada.

In addition to its more obvious data sources, the Web itself provides an interesting environment for generating questions to study. What percentage of Web pages are dead-ends (no links to other pages)? What proportion of links are to "dead" pages? How long does it take to download a typical Web page? How many "hits" will various search engines provide for common words? What proportion of pages include graphics? Web-veteran students can easily come up with project ideas that could be researched directly on the Web. Many such Web-based projects present an intriguing sampling problem. How can one obtain a random sample from a population of Web pages? One option is to sample within a category of Web pages from a search engine of lists such as Mike Conlon's links to *American Universities*. For a more general sample, one might try one of the "random link" pages (e.g., *URouLette* or *Yahoo's*

Random Link) that take users to randomly generated URL's from a given database.

Miscellaneous Sites

The *Statistical Education Section* of the ASA, the *Journal of Statistics Education Information Service,* and the *CTI Centre for Teaching Statistics* each maintain general Web sites with links to many locations of interest to statistics instructors. A collection of *Links to Statistical Software Providers* is maintained by Stata Corporation. Ann Cannon has produced a *List of Undergraduate Statistics Textbooks* that includes references to recent reviews. Other good sites to visit include Rex Bogg's *Exploring Data*, John Behren's *Statistical Instruction Internet Palette (SIIP)*, and Clay Helberg's *Statistics on the Web*.

Conclusion

The development of a World Wide Web has produced unprecedented means for instructors to easily share their ideas on ways to improve the teaching of statistics. The links presented here represent some of the types of resources that are currently available, but are by no means an exhaustive list of the many excellent Web sites that help support statistics instruction. Although the volume of on-line material may seem daunting, and the process of searching for worthwhile information can be frustrating, the rewards, both for instructors and students, can be quite substantial. If current trends continue, universal access to the Web should become easier, faster, and more common, on-line applications should become even more sophisticated, and useful resources should continue to appear at a steady rate.

Reference Links

Web addresses for all sites referenced (in italics) in this paper are given below, along with Web page authors where possible. All URL's should be entered through a browser as a single line with no spaces. An outline for the paper, including links to each of these sites (and more) can be found at: `it.stlawu.edu/~rlock/maa51/www.html`.

American Universities
    www.clas.ufl.edu/CLAS/american-universities.html

APStat-l Discussion List Archives
    forum.swarthmore.edu/epigone/apstat-l

Dr. B's Wide World of Web Data (Behrens)
    research.ed.asu.edu/siip/Webdata/

Bryc's Elementary Probability and Statistics Course
    math.uc.edu/~brycw/classes/147/

Census Bureau
    www.census.gov/

Chance Course Database (Snell)
    www.dartmouth.edu/~chance/index.html

Chance News
    www.dartmouth.edu/~chance/chance_news/news.html

Chance's Math 37 Probability & Statistics Course
    www.cs.uop.edu/cop/math/math37.html

CIA World Factbook
    www.odci.gov/cia/publications/factbook/index.html

Coon's AP Statistics
    www.bbns.org/us/math/ap_stats/

Correlation Guessing Game
    www.stat.uiuc.edu/~stat100/java/GCApplet/GCAppletFrame.html

CUWU Statistics Program
    neyman.stat.uiuc.edu:80/~stat100/cuwu/

CyberStats (CyberGnostics Inc.)
    www.cyberk.com

CTI Centre for Teaching Statistics
    www.stats.gla.ac.uk/cti/

DataSurfing on the World Wide Web (Lock)
    it.stlawu.edu/~rlock/datasurf.html

DASL — Data and Story Library
    lib.stat.cmu.edu/DASL/

Department of Education
    www.ed.gov

Edstat-l Discussion List Archives
    gopher://jse.stat.ncsu.edu/11/edstat

Expersim Project
    samiam.colorado.edu/~mcclella/expersim/expersim.html

Exploring Data (Boggs)
    curriculum.qed.qld.gov.au/kla/eda/

Fedstats
    www.fedstats.gov/

Foreign Government Data Sources (U. of Michigan)
    www.lib.umich.edu/libhome/Documents.center/stforeig.html

Globally Accessible Statistical Procedures (GASP)
www.stat.scarolina.edu/rsrch/gasp/

Hale's EdPsy101
espse.ed.psu.edu/espse/hale/edpsy101/

Hyperstat Online
www.ruf.rice.edu/~lane/hyperstat/index.html

Interesting JAVA Applets
www.stat.duke.edu/sites/java.html

Journal of Statistics Education
www.amstat.org/publications/jse/

Journal of Statistics Education Dataset Archive
www.amstat.org/publications/jse/archive.htm

Journal of Statistics Education Information Service
www.amstat.org/publications/jse/information.html

Links to Statistical Software Providers (Stata Corporation)
www.stata.com/support/links/stat_software.html

List of Statistical Lists (Fuller)
hardwick.ukc.ac.uk/cgi-bin/hpda.exe/mff/netres/statlist.html

List of Undergraduate Textbooks (Cannon)
wwwcsc.cornell-iowa.edu/~acannon/stated/booklist.html

Seeing Statistics (McClelland)
www.seeingstatistics.com

Social Security Administration
www.ssa.gov

Sports Data Page (Lock)
it.stlawu.edu/~rlock/sports.html

Sports Statistics on the Web (Box)
www.stat.duke.edu/~box/sis/sports.html

Stern's Statistics 101
www.public.iastate.edu/~hstern/stat101/stat101.html

StatVillage (Schwarz)
www.math.sfu.ca/stats/Innovation/StatVillage/index.html

Statistical Education Section of ASA
www2.ncsu.edu/ncsu/pams/stat/stated/homepage.html

Statistical Education Section Newsletter
renoir.vill.edu/cgi-bin/short/StatEd.cgi

Statistical Instruction Internet Palette (Behrens)
research.ed.asu.edu/siip/

Statistical Resources on the Web (U. of Michigan)
www.lib.umich.edu/libhome/Documents.center/stats.html

Statistics on the Web (Helberg)
www.execpc.com/~helberg/statistics.html

Statistics: The Study of Stability in Variation (de Leeuw)
www.stat.ucla.edu/textbook/

Statistics Teacher Network (newsletter)

`www.bio.ri.ccf.org/docs/ASA/stn.html`

Statlets (NWP Associates)

`www.statlets.com/`

Student Choices for Web Data (Lock)

`it.stlawu.edu/~rlock/pastdata.html`

SurfStat

`frey.newcastle.edu.au/Stats/surfstat/surfstat.html`

UIUC Statistics Course Web pages

`www.stat.uiuc.edu/courses.html`

URouLette

`www.uroulette.com`

Virtual Laboratories in Probability and Statistics (Siegrist)

`www.math.uah.edu/stat/`

WebStat (West)

`www.stat.sc.edu/~west/Webstat/`

Yahoo's Random Link

`random.yahoo.com/bin/ryl`

Section 6
Assessment

Changing emphases in content and pedagogy for introductory statististics courses have accompanied the evo-
lution of strategies for classroom assessment. The following pair of articles provides both general principles
and concrete recommendations for assessing students' learning. Joan Garfield's article, "Beyond Testing and
Grading: New Ways to Use Assessment To Improve Student Learning," offers a framework for how assessment practices in statistics courses need to evolve, based on considerations of the purposes of assessment that
extend much further than the assignment of grades. The article by Beth Chance, "Experiences with Authentic
Assessment Techniques in an Introductory Statistics Course," suggests a model for implementing various assessment strategies and describes lessons learned from her experiences with them. One of the common features
of these articles is their goal of developing assessment techniques that provide students with opportunities to
demonstrate their level of understanding, their ability to think critically about statistical issues, and their skill
in applying their knowledge to solve new problems.

A mathematician new to the teaching of statistics may well feel overwhelmed by the quantity of ideas
suggested here and by the daunting time commitment that would be required to implement them all. As both
Garfield and Chance suggest, teachers should not try to "do it all at once." Rather, instructors should gradually
integrate new assessment techniques to allow them to monitor the practice and improve on the implementation.
They should plan and evaluate what they are doing with colleagues, teaching assistants, and students. Instructors
(and administrators) should also be patient: techniques may not work perfectly the first time, but may still be
worth trying again.

Some considerations to guide an instructor's "first steps" toward implementing new methods of assessment
include the following:

- Students need to understand the value of assessment. Grading needs to be consistent and fair in the students'
  minds and it should be directly related to the goals of the course. The instructor should engage in open
  discussion with students about the assessment's goals and policies. Prior to the assessment, students should
  be provided with very clear guidelines of what is expected in their work.
- Feedback must be timely, constructive, and regenerative. Students need to be shown how they can improve
  their work and be given the opportunity to re-attempt similar tasks after incorporating the instructor's

feedback. This feedback is especially valuable for assessment that requires students to demonstrate mastery or assessment approaches that are novel to the students.

We provide an annotated bibliography of selected works on assessment.

Beyond Testing and Grading: New Ways to Use Assessment to Improve Student Learning[†]

Joan B. Garfield
University of Minnesota

Abstract. Changes in educational assessment are currently being implemented at all educational levels. In the area of statistics, traditional forms of student assessment have been criticized because they primarily provide a method for assigning numerical scores to determine letter grades, but rarely reveal information about how students actually understand and can reason with statistical ideas or apply their knowledge to solve statistical problems. However, as statistics instruction at the college level has been changing in response to calls for reform (e.g., [4]), there have been efforts to develop appropriate assessment methods and materials to measure students' understanding of probability and statistics and their ability to achieve more relevant goals, such as being able to explore data and to think critically using statistical reasoning.

This paper summarizes current trends in educational assessment and relates them to the assessment of student outcomes in a statistics course. A framework is presented for categorizing and developing appropriate assessment instruments and procedures. Suggestions are offered for teachers of statistics who wish to re-examine their classroom, and examples are offered of some innovative assessment approaches that have been used in introductory statistics courses.

An Evolving View of Assessment

The term "assessment" is often used in different contexts and means different things to different people. Most statistics faculty think of assessment in terms of testing and grading: scoring quizzes and exams and assigning course grades to students. We typically use assessment as a way to inform students about how well they are doing, or how well they did, in the courses we teach. A more current vision of assessment is that of a dynamic process that continuously yields information about student progress toward the achievement of learning goals [20]. This vision of assessment acknowledges that when the information gathered is consistent with learning goals and is used appropriately to inform instruction, it can enhance student learning as well as document it [20]. Rather than being an activity separate from instruction, assessment is now being viewed as an integral part of teaching and learning, and not just the culmination of instruction [19].

Because learning statistics has often been viewed as mastering a set of skills, procedures, and vocabulary, student assessment has focused on whether these have been mastered, by testing students' computational skills or their ability to retrieve information from memory [10]. Statistics items that appear on traditional tests typically test skills in

[†] This article is based upon [8] and [9], previous works by the author.

isolation of a problem context and do not test whether or not students understand statistical concepts, are able to integrate statistical knowledge to solve a problem, or are able to communicate effectively using the language of statistics. Research has shown that some students who produce a correct "solution" on a test item may not even understand the solution or the underlying question behind it [12].

As goals for statistics education continue to change to broader and more ambitious objectives, such as developing statistical thinkers who can apply their knowledge to solving real problems, a mismatch is revealed between traditional assessment and the desired student outcomes. It is no longer appropriate to assess student knowledge by having students compute answers and apply formulas, because these methods do not reveal the current goals of solving real problems and using statistical reasoning.

The reform movement in educational assessment encourages teachers to think about assessment more broadly than "testing" and using test results to assign grades and rank students (e.g., [22] and [17]). In the report on mathematics assessment, *Measuring What Counts* [19], some basic principles of mathematics assessment are described. Two of these principles, rephrased to focus on statistics instead of mathematics, are:

- The Content Principle: Assessment should reflect the statistical content that is most important for students to learn.
- The Learning Principle: Assessment should enhance the learning of statistics and support good instructional practice.

These principles lead directly to the use of alternative forms of assessment to provide more complete information about what students have learned and are able to do with their knowledge, and to provide more detailed and timely feedback to students about the quality of their learning. Assessment approaches now being used in many statistics courses better capture how students think, reason, and apply their learning, rather than merely having students "tell" the teacher what they have remembered or show that they can perform calculations or carry out procedures correctly (e.g., [6]). Some of these alternative methods include individual or group projects, portfolios of students' work, concept maps, critiques of articles in the news, and objective-format questions to assess higher order thinking.

The use of the new, alternative forms of assessment appears to have many advantages. For example, alternative methods tend to focus more on processes than exclusively on products. Use of multiple methods rather than a single test also provides a richer and more complete representation of student learning.

Before selecting alternatives to traditional testing, it is important to consider criteria for their appropriate use. In reviewing the National Council of Teachers of Mathematics [20] standards for assessment of mathematics learning, Webb and Romberg [27] provide criteria for assessment instruments and procedures that are relevant to the development or selection of statistical assessment materials as well. These criteria specify that good assessment should:
- Provide information that will contribute to decisions regarding the improvement of instruction.
- Be aligned with instructional goals.
- Provide information on what students know.
- Supplement other assessment results to provide a global description of what students know.

In considering these criteria, a broader view of assessment emerges, beyond that of testing and grading. In this view, assessment becomes an integral part of instruction, consists of multiple methods yielding complementary sources of information about student learning, and provides both the student and instructor with a more complete analysis of what has happened in a particular course.

Purposes of Assessment

Why should a statistics instructor consider implementing assessment methods other than traditional tests and quizzes in a college statistics course? The most compelling reason is because traditional forms of assessment rarely lead to improved teaching and learning and offer us limited understanding of our students: what attitudes and beliefs they bring to class, how they think about and understand statistics, and how well they are able to apply their knowledge. Without this knowledge, it is difficult to determine how to make changes or design instruction to improve student learning.

The primary purpose of any student assessment should be to improve student learning [20]. Some secondary purposes for gathering assessment information include:
- To provide individual information to students about how well they have learned a particular topic and where they are having difficulty.
- To provide information to the instructor about how well the class seems to understand a particular topic and what additional activities might need to be introduced, or whether it is time to move on to another topic.
- To provide diagnostic information to instructors about individual student's understanding or difficulties in understanding new material.

- To provide information to teachers about students' perceptions and reactions to the class, the material, the subject matter, or particular activities.
- To provide an overall indicator of students' success in achieving course goals.
- To help students determine their overall strengths and weaknesses in learning the course material.

Selection of appropriate assessment methods and instruments depends on the purpose of assessment: why the information is being gathered and how it will be used. If the purpose of a particular assessment activity is to determine how well students in the class have learned some important concepts or skills, this may result in a different instrument or approach than if the purpose is to provide quick feedback to students so that they may review material on a particular topic.

Regardless of the specific purpose of an assessment procedure, incorporating an assessment program in our classes offers us a way to reflect about what we are doing and to find out what is really happening in our classes. It provides us with a systematic way to gather and evaluate information to use to improve our knowledge, not only of students in a particular course, but our general knowledge of teaching statistics. By using assessment to identify what is not working, as well as what is working, we can help our students become more aware of their own success in learning statistics, as well as become better at assessing their own skills and knowledge.

What Should Be Assessed?

Because assessment is often viewed as driving the curriculum, and students learn to value what they know they will be tested on, we should assess what we value. First we need to determine what students should know and be able to do as a result of taking a statistics course. This information should be translated into clearly articulated goals and objectives (both broad and narrow) in order to determine what types of assessment are appropriate for evaluating attainment of these goals. One way to begin thinking about the main goals for a course is to consider what students will need to know and do to succeed in future courses or jobs.

Wiggins [29] suggests that we think of students as apprentices who are required to produce quality work, and are therefore assessed on their real performance and use of knowledge. Another way to determine important course goals is to decide what ideas you really want students to retain six months after completing your statistics class.

I believe that the main goals of an introductory statistics course are to develop an understanding of important concepts such as mean, variability, and correlation. We also want students to understand ideas such as the variability of sample statistics, the usefulness of the normal distribution as a model for data, and the importance of considering how a sample was selected in evaluating inferences based on that sample. We would like our students to be able to intelligently collect, analyze, and interpret data; to use statistical thinking and reasoning; and to communicate effectively using the language of statistics.

In addition to concepts, skills, and types of thinking, most instructors have general attitude goals for how we would like students to view statistics as a result of our courses. Such attitude goals include understanding how the discipline of statistics differs from mathematics, realizing that you do not have to be a mathematician to learn and understand statistics, believing that there are often different ways to solve a statistical problem, and recognizing that people may come to different conclusions based on the same data if they have different assumptions and use different methods of analysis.

Once we have articulated goals for students in our statistics classes, we are better able to specify what to focus on to determine what is really happening to students as they experience our courses. Are they learning to use statistical thinking and reasoning, to collect and analyze data, to write up and communicate the results of solving real statistical problems? Some goals may not be easy to assess individually, and may be more appropriately evaluated in the context of clusters of concepts and skills. For example, in order to evaluate whether students use statistical reasoning in drawing conclusions about a data set, students may need to be given the context of a report of a research study that requires them to evaluate several related pieces of information (e.g., distributions of variables, summary statistics, and inferences based on that data set). Determining if students have achieved the goal of understanding how to best represent a data set with a single number may require that students examine and evaluate several distributions of data.

How To Assess Student Learning

There are several ways to gather assessment data and each method offers different information regarding what students have learned. What all types of assessment have in common is that they consist of a situation, task, or questions; a student response; an interpretation (by the teacher or one who reviews the assessment information); an assignment of meaning to the interpretation; and reporting and recording of results [28].

Different assessment methods to use in a statistics class (both traditional and alternative methods) include:

- quizzes (including calculations and/or essay questions)
- minute papers (e.g., on what students have learned in a particular session, or what they found to be most confusing)
- essay questions/journal entries (explaining their understanding of concepts and principles)
- projects/reports (individual or group)
- portfolios (including a selection of different materials)
- exams (covering a broad range of material)
- attitude surveys (administered at different times, about the course, content, or view of statistics)
- written reports (of in-class activities or computer labs)
- open-ended questions or problems to solve
- enhanced multiple-choice questions where responses are designed to characterize students' reasoning.

Some examples of alternative forms of assessment listed above include the following:

1) *Individual or group projects:* Projects completed by individual students or groups of students typically involve posing a problem, designing an experiment or taking a sample, collecting and analyzing data, and interpreting the results. The project may be written up as a report, presented orally in class, or displayed on a poster. Projects may be assessed using a scoring rubric to assign points (such as 0, 1, 2) to different components of the project, such as:

   - Demonstrates understanding of the problem being addressed.
   - Uses appropriate methods to collect the data.
   - Uses appropriate methods to analyze the data.
   - Provides an adequate interpretation of the data analysis.
   - Discusses limitations of the project.
   - Communicates effectively in the written report.

   In this example, a maximum score of 12 would indicate the highest level of achievement. For further information on projects, see [18] or [24].

2) *Portfolios of student work:* A portfolio is a collection of a student's work, often gathered over an entire course. The selection is often done by both the student and teacher and may include a variety of components, such as computer output for data analyses, written interpretations of statistical analyses, and reflections on what has been learned. Keeler [14] describes the use of portfolios in a statistics class for graduate students. In this example, portfolios include:

- A mini-research paper, where students investigate a problem or question that can be answered by collecting binomial data.
- Six SAS and SPSSX programs the students have used and the output for these programs.
- A group project involving data collection and analysis, that has been presented to the class.
- Two midterm exams accompanied by students' analysis of their own performance and their corrections of wrong answers.
- A reflective journal.

As each assessment task is entered into the appropriate section of the portfolio, students are asked to respond to the following questions:

- What did you have trouble with in producing this product?
- How did you change the product after the initial feedback?
- How could the product still be improved?
- What was the most important thing you learned in producing this product?

3) *Concept maps:* Schau and Mattern [23] describe different uses of concept maps to assess students' understanding of conceptual connections. Concept maps include the concepts (referred to as nodes and often represented visually by ovals or rectangles) and the connections (referred to as links and often represented with arrows) that relate them. Students may be asked to construct their own maps for a particular statistical topic (e.g., hypothesis testing) or to fill in missing components from a partially constructed concept map. The general process for this second approach involves first constructing a master map. Keeping that map structure intact, some or all of the concept and/or relationship words are omitted. Students fill in these blanks either by generating the words or by selecting them from a list which may or may not include distracters. For examples of this type of assessment, see [23].

4) *Critiques of statistical ideas or issues in the news:* Students may be asked to read and critique a newspaper article responding to particular questions, such as:

- What do you think is the purpose of the research study described in this article?
- What method or methods were used to answer the research question?
- What questions would you like to ask the investigators in order to better understand the study?
- Are there any aspects of the study that might make you question the conclusions presented in the article?

Points may be awarded based on the completeness of each answer. For examples of assessment items that involve brief articles or graphs presented in the media, see [26].

5) *Objective format questions to assess higher level thinking:* Enhanced multiple-choice items or items that require students to match concepts or questions with appropriate explanations may be used to capture students' reasoning and measure conceptual understanding. Cobb [5] offers five principles for designing objective format questions that assess statistical thinking. One principle is to ask for comparative judgments, not just category matching. For example, a set of two-way tables is presented to students with data representing factors related to the death sentence. Each table displays frequencies for the breakdown of different independent variables (e.g., race of defendant, race of victim, prior record) by the same dependent variable (whether or not a convicted murderer is sentenced to death). Students are asked which factors in the tables are most strongly associated with whether a convicted murderer is sentenced to death. They need to compare the strength of the interaction between variables in each table to make this judgment. A second principle is to involve two or more modes of statistical thinking (e.g., both visual and verbal/intuitive thinking). An example is given where students are asked to match verbal descriptions to four different plots of data. For further information on objective-format tests, see [11], [13], or [30].

6) *Minute papers:* Minute papers are brief, anonymous written remarks provided by students, sometimes on an index card or half-sheet of paper, during the last few minutes of class. These remarks can cover a variety of topics, such as a summary of what students understand or do not understand on a topic, or students' reactions to various aspects of a course (e.g., the use of cooperative groups, the textbook, or the teacher's explanations in class). Some statistics teachers use minute papers to have students describe their understanding of a particular concept or procedure discussed in class that day, or to have them respond to the question: "What was the most confusing idea in today's class?" Another form of a minute paper is an open-ended student evaluation of the course, while the class is in progress.

Students' comments on these surveys may be tallied and sorted, and a list of things that can be responded to and that are possible (and reasonable) to change may emerge. The feedback from students sometimes lifts a teacher's spirits and often maintains a teacher's humility. The ultimate goal of obtaining this information on students' learning, attitudes, and understanding is to build a better understanding of the students' perceptions and experiences in the course and to suggest ways to improve teaching, making it a worthwhile endeavor despite the possible discomfort. For further information on minute papers, see [1].

7) *Performance assessment of statistical problem solving:* Although not typically used by teachers in their individual classes, the detailed scoring of open-ended statistical problems is now being used in the Advanced Placement Statistics Examination in the United States. A scoring rubric is used by test scorers to evaluate students' statistical knowledge and communication skills, using a scale of 0 to 4 for each scale [21]. A score of 4 on statistical knowledge means that the student completely understands a problem's statistical components, synthesizes a correct relationship among these components, uses appropriate and correctly executed statistical techniques, and provides reasonably correct answers. A score of 4 on the communication scale means that the student's explanation of what was done was clear, complete, organized, and correct; that appropriate assumptions and caveats are stated; that diagrams or plots used are appropriate; and that an appropriate and complete conclusion is stated.

The different assessment methods described above may be used in combination with each other as well as in combination with traditional quizzes and exams. Chance [2] provides an excellent model for combining different assessment components.

An Assessment Framework

An assessment framework emerges from the different aspects of assessment: what do we want to have happen to students in a statistics course, what are different methods and purposes for assessment, and what are some additional dimensions.

The first dimension of this framework is WHAT to assess, which may be broken down into: concepts, skills, applications, attitudes, and beliefs.

The second dimension of the framework is the PURPOSE of assessment: why the information is being gathered and how the information will be used (e.g., to inform students about strengths and weaknesses of learning or to inform the teacher about how to modify instruction).

The third dimension is WHO will do the assessment: the student, peers (such as members of the student's work group), or the teacher. It is important to point out that engaging the student in self-assessment is a critical and early part of the assessment process, and that no major piece of work should be turned in without self-criticism [29]. Students need to learn how to take a critical look at their own knowledge, skills, and applications of their knowledge and skills. They need to be given opportunities to step back from their work and think about what they did and what they learned [15]. This does not imply that a grade from a self-rating given by a student is to be recorded and used by the teacher in computing a course grade, but rather that students should have opportunities to apply scoring criteria to their own work and to other students' work so that they may learn how their ratings compare to those of their teacher.

The fourth dimension of the framework is the METHOD to be used (e.g., quiz, report, group project, individual project, writing, or portfolio).

The fifth dimension is the ACTION that is taken and the nature of the FEEDBACK given to students. This is a crucial component of the assessment process that provides the link between assessment and improved student learning.

This framework is not intended to imply that an intersection of categories for each of the four dimensions will yield a meaningful assessment technique. For example, measuring students' understanding of the concept of variability (WHAT to assess) for the PURPOSE of finding out if students understand this concept, using students in the group as assessors (WHO), with the METHOD being a quiz, and the ACTION/FEEDBACK being a numerical score, may not yield particularly meaningful and useful results. It also doesn't make sense to assess student attitudes towards computer labs (WHAT) by having peers (WHO) read and evaluate student essays (METHOD). Obviously, some categories of dimensions are more appropriately linked than others.

Another important point in applying this framework is that it is often difficult to assess a single concept in isolation of other concepts and skills. It may not be possible to assess understanding of standard deviation without understanding the concepts of mean, variability, and distribution. When given the task last fall, a group of statistics educators were unable to design an appropriate assessment for understanding the concept of "average" without bringing in several other concepts and skills.

Here are three examples of assessment activities illustrating the dimensions of the framework.

Example 1.

WHAT: Students' understanding of the Central Limit Theorem.

PURPOSE: To find out if students need to review text material or if the teacher needs to introduce additional activities designed to illustrate the concept (e.g., computer simulations of sampling distribution).

METHOD: An essay question written in class as a quiz, asking students to explain the theorem and illustrate it using an original example.

WHO: The instructor will evaluate the written responses.

ACTIONS/FEEDBACK: The instructor reads the essay responses and assigns a score of 0 (shows no understanding) to 3 (shows very clear understanding). Students with scores of 0 and 1 are assigned additional materials to read or activities to complete. Students with scores of 2 are given feedback on where their responses could be strengthened.

Example 2.

WHAT: Students' ability to apply basic exploratory data analysis skills.

PURPOSE: To determine if students are able to apply their skills to the collection, analysis, and interpretation of data.

METHOD: A student project, where instructions are given as to the sample size, format of report, etc. (e.g., [7]).

WHO: First the student completes a self-assessment using a copy of the rating sheet the instructor will use, which has been distributed prior to completing the project. Then, the instructor evaluates the project using an analytic scoring method (adapted from the holistic scoring method for evaluating student solutions to mathematical problems offered by Charles, Lester, and O'Daffer [3]). A score of 0 to 2 points for each of six categories is assigned, where 2 points indicates correct use, 1 point indicates partially correct use, and 0 points indicates incorrect use.

ACTIONS/FEEDBACK: Scores are assigned to each category and given back to students along with written comments, early enough in the course so that they may learn from this feedback in working on their next project.

Example 3.

WHAT: Students' perceptions of the use of cooperative group activities in learning statistics.

PURPOSE: To find out how well groups are working and to determine if groups or group procedures need to change.

METHOD: A "minute paper" is assigned during the last five minutes of class, where students are asked to write anonymously about their perceptions of what they like best and like least about their experience with group activities.

WHO: The teacher reads the minute papers.

ACTIONS/FEEDBACK: The teacher summarizes the responses, shares them with the class, and makes changes in groups or group methods as necessary.

Implications for Statistics Instructors

Given the calls for reform of statistical education and the new goals envisioned for students, it is crucial that we look carefully at what is happening to students in our classes. Without scrutinizing what is really happening to our students and using that information to make changes, it is unlikely that instruction will improve and unlikely that we will be able to achieve our new vision of statistical education. I would like to offer some suggestions for instructors contemplating alternative assessment procedures for their classes:

- Try to look at every assessment activity as a way to provide students with feedback on how to improve their learning and not just as an activity used to assign a grade.
- Don't try to do it all at once. Pick one method, try it for a while, and then gradually introduce and experiment with other techniques.
- Don't try to do it alone. Plan, review, and discuss with other colleagues or teaching assistants what you are doing and what you are learning from assessment information.
- Be open with the students about why and how they are being assessed [25].
- Make sure that you have opportunities to reflect on the assessment information you obtain, and monitor the impact of these results on your perceptions of the class and your teaching.
- Consult resources for ideas of different approaches to use and ways to evaluate assessment information (e.g., [1] and [16]).

The use of alternative assessment methods, particularly those involving papers and reports, often results in overwhelming amounts of paperwork to read and evaluate. Even with carefully constructed scoring rubrics, it takes time to evaluate and provide detailed feedback to students. Each time a new task is assigned, the instructor needs to be cognizant that the paper must be carefully read and good and timely feedback provided to students. It is much easier to have a teaching assistant score a multiple-choice test. However, students learn more from the challenging tasks of practicing their communication skills and integrating and applying their statistical knowledge, which they do when completing a project or written report.

A second caution deals with the courage sometimes required to administer an assessment to students and then carefully examine the responses. The results may reveal that instructors' perceptions of how well they have taught something, or how well students have learned something, may be incorrect. For example, when using minute papers in class, students might be asked to explain (in writing) their understanding of a particular concept (e.g., the standard error of the mean, a standard deviation, or what a sampling distribution represents). Asking the students to describe their understanding in these anonymous minute papers is easy. Reading their statements takes courage and patience. The often awkwardly-worded responses sometimes reveal a serious lack of understanding, despite the brilliance of an instructor's explanation or the most carefully designed in-class activity.

Finally, it is important to remember that assessment drives instruction, so be careful to assess what you believe is really important for students to learn. Use assessment to confirm, reinforce, and support your ideas of what students should be learning. Never lose track of the main purpose of assessment: to improve learning.

References

1. Angelo, T., and K. P. Cross, *Classroom Assessment Techniques,* 1993, Jossey-Bass, San Francisco.
2. Chance, B., "Experiences with Authentic Assessment Techniques in an Introductory Statistics Course." Originally appeared in the *Journal of Statistics Education,* reprinted in this volume on pp. 193–203.
3. Charles, R., F. Lester, and P. O'Daffer, *How to Evaluate Progress in Problem Solving,* 1987, National Council of Teachers of Mathematics, Reston, VA.
4. Cobb, G. W., "Teaching Statistics," in *Heeding the Call for Change: Suggestions for Curricular Action,* MAA Notes No. 22, edited by L. Steen, 1992, Mathematical Association of America, 3–43.
5. Cobb, G. W., "The Objective-Format Question in Statistics: Dead Horse, Old Bath Water, or Overlooked Baby?" Paper presented at the annual meeting of the American Educational Research Association, 1998, San Diego, CA.
6. EQUALS Staff, *Assessment Alternatives in Mathematics,* 1989, Lawrence Hall of Science, University of California, Berkeley, CA.
7. Garfield, J., "An Authentic Assessment of Students' Statistical Knowledge," in *National Council of Teachers of Mathematics 1993 Yearbook: Assessment in the Mathematics Classroom,* edited by N. Webb, 1993, Na-

tional Council of Teachers of Mathematics, Reston, VA, 187–196.

8. Garfield, J., "Beyond Testing and Grading: Using Assessment to Improve Students' Learning," *Journal of Statistics Education,* `www.amstat.org/publi-cations/jse/v2n1/garfield.html` (on line), **2**(1), 1994.

9. Garfield, J. and I. Gal, "Assessment and Statistics Education: Current Challenges and Directions," in the *International Statistical Review,* **67** (1999), 1–12.

10. Hawkins, A., F. Jolliffe, and L. Glickman, *Teaching Statistical Concepts,* 1992, Longman Group UK Limited, Harlow, Essex, England.

11. Hubbard, R., "Assessment and the Process of Learning Statistics," *Journal of Statistics Education,* `www.amstat.org/publications/jse/v5n1/hubbard.html` (on line), **5** (1), 1997.

12. Jolliffe, F., "Assessment of the Understanding of Statistical Concepts," in *Proceedings of the Third International Conference on Teaching Statistics, Vol. 1,* edited by D. Vere-Jones, 1991, Otago University Press, Otago, NZ, 461–466.

13. Jolliffe, F., "Issues in Constructing Assessment Instruments for the Classroom," in *The Assessment Challenge in Statistics Education,* edited by I. Gal and J. Garfield, 1997, IOS Press, Amsterdam.

14. Keeler, C., "Portfolio Assessment in Graduate Level Statistics Courses," in *The Assessment Challenge in Statistics Education,* edited by I. Gal and J. Garfield, 1997, IOS Press, Amsterdam, 165–178.

15. Kenney, P. and E. Silver, "Student Self-Assessment in Mathematics," in *National Council of Teachers of Mathematics 1993 Yearbook: Assessment in the Mathematics Classroom,* edited by N. Webb, 1993, NCTM, Reston, VA, 229–238.

16. Kulm, G. (ed.), *Assessing Higher Order Thinking in Mathematics,* 1990, AAAS, Washington, DC.

17. Lesh, R., and S. Lamon, *Assessment of Authentic Performance in School Mathematics,* 1992, AAAS, Washington, DC.

18. Mackisack, M., "What is the Use of Experiments Conducted by Statistics Students?," *Journal of Statistics Education,* `www.amstat.org/publications/jse/v2n1/mackisack.html` (on line), **2**(1), 1994.

19. Mathematical Sciences Education Board, *Measuring What Counts: A Conceptual Guide for Mathematical Assessment,* 1993, National Academy Press, Washington, DC.

20. National Council of Teachers of Mathematics, *Assessment Standards for School Mathematics,* 1995, Reston, VA.

21. Olsen, C., "What's a Rubric? Scoring the Open-ended Questions." Paper presented at the Joint Statistical Meetings, 1998, Dallas, TX.

22. Romberg, T. (ed.), *Mathematics Assessment and Evaluation: Imperatives for Mathematics Education,* 1992, State University of New York Press, Albany, NY.

23. Schau, C. and N. Mattern, "Assessing Students' Connected Understanding of Statistical Relationships," in *The Assessment Challenge in Statistics Education,* edited by I. Gal and J. Garfield, 1997, IOS Press, Amsterdam, 91–104.

24. Starkings, S., "Assessing Student Projects," in *The Assessment Challenge in Statistics Education,* edited by I. Gal and J. Garfield, 1997, IOS Press, Amsterdam, 139–151.

25. Stenmark, J., *Mathematics Assessment: Myths, Models, Good Questions, and Practical Suggestions,* 1991, National Council of Teachers of Mathematics, Reston, VA.

26. Watson, J., "Assessing Statistical Thinking Using the Media," in *The Assessment Challenge in Statistics Education,* edited by I. Gal and J. Garfield, 1997, IOS Press, Amsterdam, 107–121.

27. Webb, N. and T. Romberg, "Implications of the NCTM Standards for Mathematics Assessment," in *Mathematics Assessment and Evaluation: Imperatives for Mathematics Education,* edited by T. Romberg, 1992, State University of New York Press, Albany, NY.

28. Webb, N., "Assessment for the Mathematics Classroom," in *National Council of Teachers of Mathematics 1993 Yearbook: Assessment in the Mathematics Classroom,* edited by N. Webb, 1993, National Council of Teachers of Mathematics, Reston, VA, 1–6.

29. Wiggins, G., "The Truth May Make You Free, but the Test May Keep You Imprisoned," *AAHE Assessment Forum,* 1990, 17–31.

30. Wild, C., C. Triggs, and M. Pfannkuch, "Assessment on a Budget: Using Traditional Methods Imaginatively," in *The Assessment Challenge in Statistics Education,* edited by I. Gal and J. Garfield, 1997, IOS Press, Amsterdam, 205–220.

Experiences with Authentic Assessment Techniques in an Introductory Statistics Course[†]

Beth L. Chance
California Polytechnic State University, San Luis Obispo

Abstract. In an effort to align evaluation with new instructional goals, authentic assessment techniques [2, 5, 11] have recently been introduced in introductory statistics courses at the University of the Pacific. Such techniques include computer lab exercises, term projects with presentations and peer reviews, take-home final exam questions, and student journals. In this article, I discuss the University of the Pacific's goals and experiences with these techniques, along with strategies for more effective implementation.

Introduction

As instructional goals in statistics courses change, so must the assessment techniques used to evaluate progress towards these goals. Many statistics courses are shifting focus [4, 14], emphasizing skills such as the ability to interpret, evaluate, and apply statistical ideas over procedural calculations. Many of these outcomes are not adequately assessed using traditional tests, which too often emphasize the final numerical answer over the reasoning process [10, 15]. Thus, instructors need to accompany these new instructional aims with more authentic assessment techniques that address students' ability to evaluate and utilize statistical knowledge in new domains, communicate and justify statistical results, and produce and interpret computer output. Further, students need to receive feedback not only on their exam performance, but also constructive indications of their strengths and weaknesses, guidelines for improving their understanding, and challenges to extend their knowledge. The instructor needs to know not only how the students are mastering the material, but also how to improve instructional techniques and enhance statistical understanding. Since students' attitudes towards statistics can affect their learning [9], an assessment program should also include a way of judging how students are reacting to the material, including their impression of the relevance and fairness of the assessment process. Above all, assessment should mirror the skills students will need in order to be effective consumers and evaluators of statistical information.

Towards these goals, I have incorporated several techniques into my courses that seem well suited to statistics instruction. These techniques include a computer laboratory component, a term project with peer reviews and oral presentations, a take-home component to the final exam, minute papers, and student journals. In this paper, I first discuss my goals for these assessment procedures and how my implementation of these techniques has evolved. Based

---

[†] This article appeared originally in the *Journal of Statistics Education*, **5**, (3), 1997 when the author was teaching at the University of the Pacific.

on what I find works and doesn't work in my courses, I describe what I feel are the essential features of effective assessment techniques in the introductory statistics course.

Background

The University of the Pacific is a small (4,000 students), private, comprehensive university. One of the University's goals is to maintain small class sizes, allowing more personalized instruction. The main statistics course, Math 37, fulfills a General Education requirement and is taken by students in numerous disciplines, such as business, science (computer, natural, social, sports), physical therapy, humanities, and pharmacy. Business is the most common major (Fall 1995: 36%, Spring 1996: 61%), and students come from all years (Fall 1995: 62% juniors, Spring 1996: 77% freshman and sophomores). The prerequisite is intermediate algebra, and the course is worth four credits. A different course is generally taken by mathematics and engineering majors. Typically, Math 37 is the only statistics course these students will see, and there are various levels of mathematics and computer anxiety and competency among the students. From surveys distributed the first day of class, most students indicate they are taking the course to fulfill a requirement for their major or to fulfill the General Education requirement (Fall 1995: 80%, Spring 1996: 92%). When asked their initial interest level in statistics, on a scale of one to five with five being high, 79% in the Fall and 88% in the Spring indicated an interest level of three or below. I believe authentic assessment techniques should work well in this environment due to the focus on student-centered learning at my university and the flexibility I am given by my department in structuring the course.

Goals of Incorporating Nontraditional Techniques

When designing my course, I identified several ways I wanted to enhance students' statistical learning experience and my assessment of that experience. In particular, I wanted to better gauge the students' understanding of statistical ways of thinking, evaluate their communication and collaboration skills, measure their statistical and computer literacy, and monitor their interest in statistics. To see if these goals were met, I felt I needed to move beyond traditional assessment techniques and incorporate several nontraditional techniques in conjunction with traditional exams, homework exercises, and quizzes. Below I discuss how I combined several different assessment components together to address these goals. The Appendix

gives an overview of how these different techniques are implemented in my introductory course.

Understanding the Statistical Process. I want my students to think of statistics as not just plugging numbers into formulas, but as a process for gaining information. Thus, I feel it is important to evaluate student understanding of this process by requiring them to complete such a process from beginning (conception of the question of interest) to end (presentation of results). One way to accomplish this is through semester-long projects. Use of projects in statistics courses has received considerable discussion in the literature [8, 10, 11, 12, 17]. My goals include seeing how students apply their knowledge to real (and possibly messy) data that they collect, while integrating ideas from many parts of the course (data collection, description, and analysis) into one complete package. By using the same project throughout the semester, students are able to rework their plan as new ideas occur, illustrating the dynamic nature of the process. Students also have an application to constantly refer to as new topics are covered in lecture. While the students' final projects may not incorporate all of the statistical techniques covered during the course, they need to evaluate each idea to judge its suitability for incorporation. Thus, the students are determining the necessary components for their analysis. I feel this leads to more creativity in the projects, and better mastery of the statistical ideas, than when I tell them to apply one specific idea.

Students also see this cycle in their labs and final exam. Five of their fourteen labs require students to collect the data themselves and then complete a technical report detailing their data collection procedures (e.g., precautions, operational definitions), analysis, diagnostic checks, and final conclusions. Students must discuss pitfalls in the data collection and analysis, and suggest potential improvements. At the end of the course, to further assess their ability to apply what they have learned, I now incorporate a take-home component to the final exam. Students are given a series of questions pertaining to a new data set. Students identify an appropriate test procedure based on the question asked, perform the computer analysis (choosing informative graphs and relevant diagnostic procedures), and interpret the results. Students need to integrate different portions of the course and review several potential approaches to the problem. Students are graded on their ability to identify and justify appropriate techniques, perform the analysis, and interpret their results to formulate a conclusion.

These assessment techniques provide the instructor with an authentic performance assessment that cannot be obtained solely from traditional, timed, in-class exams. In particular, these approaches judge whether students can move beyond the textbook and apply the statistical concepts to new situations.

Statistical and Computer Literacy.   Another assessment goal in my course is to judge whether students possess sufficient knowledge to interpret statistical arguments and computer output. Many current newspaper articles are discussed in the course, and I often ask students to evaluate the merits of the numerical arguments and generalizations. For example, many of the homework assignments and test questions involve recent articles, following the model given in the CHANCE course [21]. Students are also asked to critique classmates' project reports. These reviews are completed in 10 to 20 minutes at the end of one class, reviewed by the instructor, and then returned to the groups the next class period. Each project group receives two to four reviews. It would also be possible to grade the peer reviewer on the quality of the review to see if he or she can evaluate the proposal critically. In both these cases, I can see whether the students understand the ideas well enough to distinguish between good and bad uses of statistics.

While many questions can ask students to evaluate computer output, it is also important for students to work with computers directly, producing statistical output and interpreting that output in their own words. This was my initial justification for incorporating weekly computer lab sessions into the course. In most of these labs, students work with Minitab to analyze existing or self-collected data. The rest of the labs are directly aimed at enhancing student understanding of statistical concepts. These labs work with programs developed by delMas [6] to develop visual understanding of concepts such as the standard normal curve, sampling distributions, and probability. Thus, students use the computer as a tool for analysis and for obtaining deeper conceptual understanding. In all of these labs, students' explanations of what they learned are emphasized.

Communication and Collaboration Skills.   Writing and being able to explain ideas to others have become important components of my course. In the lab write-ups, students either explain an important statistical concept at length, or identify, execute, and justify the relevant statistical procedure. I feel some of the students' most significant learning gains come from debating ideas with each other, so I encourage students to work in pairs on the lab write-ups to further increase this practice. Requiring students to explain ideas in their own words also greatly augments my ability to judge their level of understanding, while giving the students repetitive practice with the language of statistics

and further internalization of the concepts. (For research on how giving explanations helps, see, for example, Rosenshine and Meister [18].)

My method for allocating points on assignments reinforces the importance I give to the different components. When I grade the full lab write-ups, 50% of the points are given for discussion. Thus, students learn that interpretations and explanations are important and highly valued components of the analysis. Students find the writing component quite time consuming, often indicating that their least favorite lab is "any full lab write-up." They can have tremendous difficulty explaining their reasoning, reinforcing my belief in its necessity. The most common feedback I give is "Why?" or "How do you know this is true?" as I try to teach the students to build a logical argument based only on the statistical evidence. In grading the labs, it is important to reward thoughtfulness and creativity, and especially to allow multiple interpretations of the same idea as long as the interpretations have been justified.

Another way I sometimes address the need for writing is through the use of student journals. I use many in-class activities (primarily based on those found in Scheaffer, Gnanadesikan, Watkins, and Witmer, [19]), but I notice that while students find the in-class activities entertaining, they often miss the important statistical concept involved unless they are asked to further reflect on the ideas. Thus, when I use journals, I require students to include some explanation of the activity, such as a simple paragraph explaining what the activity was about or answers to a series of directed questions. I also require chapter summaries to encourage students to continually review the material, blending lectures with text explanations and tying topics together. Due dates of project reports roughly correspond with midterms to help students assimilate the ideas they are reviewing. Hearing presentations of other project groups enhances review for the final exam. These additional reflections greatly aid students' understanding of the underlying ideas.

Peer reviews and oral presentations require the students to express their understanding to each other. I find that if only I present examples in class, students often don't participate fully and then later cannot extend the knowledge. Now each week, three to four students are responsible for presenting homework solutions on the board, with no prior notice. Also, at the end of the semester, each project group is required to give a presentation of their results to the class. The rest of the class and I evaluate these presentations. From homework and project presentations, I learn much more about the student's or group's ability to communicate results, as well as their ability to summarize the important points and to effectively convey results visually.

In each of these tasks, students must learn to utilize the statistical terminology in a coherent manner and to explain the ideas to themselves, to other students, and to me. This requires them to develop a deeper understanding of statistical concepts.

Learning to function in groups should also be an important component of statistics education. Thus, the term projects are completed by teams of three to five students. In extreme situations (e.g., commuting from another city), students have been allowed to work individually. However, I encourage the group experience to foster debate and discussion among the group members, as well as to model their future working environment. The first semester I tried project groups, I learned that students at the University of the Pacific can have trouble working together in groups. To address these difficulties, I have given them more opportunities to work with other students (e.g., in-class activities) prior to selecting groups. Also, I now split the grades into an individual component and a group component. A student's final grade is based on a group grade (85%) and an individual grade (15%) that varies among the team members if there is a severe discrepancy in effort. This discrepancy is identified by confidential input from the group members at the end of the semester. The discrepancy has to be clear before points are adjusted. Knowing from the beginning that their teammates will provide this information has eliminated many of the potential problems. Contracts for projects can also be included, detailing which parts of the project each person will work on. Some instructors have also recommended including a quiz or test question requiring the individual students to demonstrate knowledge of the group project. Overall, I believe learning to work in groups should be a requirement, but the instructor needs to incorporate some flexibility and individual responsibility into the grading.

Establishing a Dynamic Assessment Process.   I also want to utilize assessment practices that allow students to reevaluate their work, in order to establish a dialogue with the instructor and improve students' own self-evaluation skills. Through reevaluation of their work, students can develop their knowledge over time. For example, I grade the lab reports "progressively," requiring slightly higher levels of explanation as they proceed through the labs and incorporate the earlier feedback. Pairing students also allows me to provide more immediate feedback. Another process for continual review is the use of periodic project reports. Four times during the semester each group is asked to submit a report on their current progress for the instructor to review. This allows me to give guidance, prompt the students with

questions, and answer their questions at several points during the semester while they are thinking about different stages of the project. I find this has greatly enhanced my ability to monitor and challenge the teams. Students see that statistics is an evolving process, and they also learn to justify their decisions.

Similarly, with the journals, the only grade that counts is their final grade, and I encourage students to resubmit earlier work to increase their credit. My goal is for students to continually reflect on a concept until they understand it fully. This approach has been most effective with the lab reports, as I do see a tremendous improvement in the quality of the reports over the semester. It is important for students to be able to revisit an idea, so they can clear up misconceptions and enhance their understanding.

It is also important for students to learn to assess their own work. In the journals, I require self-evaluations so students will think critically about their own participation in the course and knowledge of the material. I have found that many of my students do not ask questions in class or office hours, and so I hope that by having them submit questions through the journal, I can establish a dialogue with them and provide personally directed feedback in a nonthreatening environment.

Increasing Student Interest in Statistics.   Since my students do not enter the course with much interest in the material, I want my assessment program to monitor and enhance their interest levels. Thus, I choose techniques that are effective not only as instructional and assessment tools, but also as motivational tools. This is important because I believe increasing their interest will also increase their learning and retention of the material. Students often agree, as shown in the following comments.

> "Doing the project did help strengthen my knowledge of proportions. When I actually had to sit down and do the calculations I found that the results made much more sense than before."

> "When you apply what we've learned to the real world we see everyday it makes more sense and becomes more interesting."

> "Putting the ideas to use further implants them into the brain cells."

To maximize interest, I allow students to pick their own project topics. I want to be sure the topic is of interest to the students, and I encourage them to expand on activities from other courses. This fosters student creativity and ownership in the topic. Students appreciate seeing a "real-world application."

"It certainly made it more interesting to see that we could actually use what we learned in class."

"It was good to analyze something we were interested in."

"It was good to be able to use what we learned in a study we conducted ourselves."

"The project helped me to see the practical use of statistics. This type of project was more interesting than just computing data for homework."

By allowing some flexibility in what topics the students examine, they will better see the relevance of statistics and want to learn the ideas. When asked if they enjoyed the project, 79% of Spring 1996 students ($n = 63$) said yes; 86% said the project helped them understand the material; 62% said the project increased their interest in the material.

Similarly, I find increasing the number of labs where students collect data about themselves and their classmates increases their interest in the answers. I also incorporate an "Other" category in the journal assignment. Students must contribute experiences they have with statistics outside the course, for example, an interesting article or news reference. My aim is to give students the opportunity to expand their knowledge and find interesting uses of statistics in the world around them.

To track student interest levels, I ask the class to complete minute papers at various points during the semester. These papers, which are completed at the end of a class period and can be turned in anonymously, are designed to inform me how I can improve the course or identify concepts that need further explanation. Students are also asked again at the end of the semester to rate their interest level in statistics, revealing how their views have changed. For example, typically I've found 10% to 20% of the students have an initial interest level of four or higher, but over 50% do at the end of the semester. I can also compare these numbers across semesters. Thus, I have very quick and efficient ways of tracking student opinions during the course, allowing immediate adjustments.

Essential Features of Effective Assessment Techiques

After implementing the above strategies in various stages, I have found the following guidelines to be essential to the success of the evaluation process.

Provide Students with Timely, Constructive, Regenerative Feedback.   Assessment techniques should provide a dialogue between the instructor and the student. The feedback needs to identify the problem to the student and provide guidance for how he or she may proceed. On homework, instead of simply telling students the correct answers, I try to show them how their solutions are insufficient and guide them towards an improved solution. When I use student graders, I also distribute homework solutions for further review. One student explained, "The solutions handed out were more helpful to determine how to fix what I'd done wrong."

Students also need to be given the opportunity to reevaluate their work and receive additional feedback. The journals are an excellent way to maintain ongoing discussions with the students. However, I find that many students may not naturally take the opportunity to resubmit earlier work. Conversely, the project reports have worked well to continually monitor students' efforts and provide hints at different stages of the process, and students have found them valuable. The lab reports also allow me to provide feedback on data collection issues before the group project has been completed. The "full" write-ups provide the students with lots of practice before they produce the final project report. These approaches reinforce to students that statistics is an evolving process, while allowing me to monitor their methods as they are being developed.

I find peer reviews of student projects quite helpful. These reviews show students what others in the course are doing, and provide additional feedback from their peers. This feedback is sometimes more valuable to the students than the instructor's input. Overall, the student feedback is quite constructive, providing input that is prompt and rich with several new perspectives. These techniques provide the students with information they can use in their next assignment, instead of giving them only a final interpretation of their work at the end of the term.

Promote Self-Reflection and Higher-Order Thinking. It is important to develop students' ability to evaluate their own work and challenge themselves. Decreasing the amount of specific instructions in the labs as the semester progresses allows me to measure students' level of self-guidance and independence. The labs have proven more and more successful as I incorporate students' suggestions on how to clarify the instructions. For example, at the students' request, the lab instructions now include an index, glossary, and frequently asked questions section. By minimizing the computer learning time, students are able to concentrate longer on the conceptual points of the lab. I also now hire a temporary student assistant each semester to provide feedback on the lab exercises and the clarity of the instructions while I am developing them. I find this has greatly enhanced my ability to present the material at the appropriate level for the students, so they can focus on the concepts being addressed.

The index, glossary, and frequently asked questions sections also help me to assess the students' ability to help themselves when they encounter a problem. Including these sections has certainly helped to provide students with guidance, but I am still trying to find the proper balance between leading and telling. I could also include more grading information in the lab instructions, but I think it is important for the students to learn to identify the components of an effective statistical analysis or explanation for themselves. I want students to do much of the discovery for themselves, because what students construct for themselves they will understand better and remember longer [16].

Often it is difficult to get students to become more independent learners. For example, with the journals, many students didn't appreciate the opportunity to outline the chapters and summarize the relevant points for later review. I thought students would like the opportunity to receive feedback and credit for review techniques they were already utilizing, but the study habits of my students are not at this level. Still, I think it is advantageous for students to generate their own summaries, and I continue to ask them to develop their own review sheets (which I look over) instead of relying on the instructor. (An overview of research on how students actively construct knowledge is presented in Anderson [1]).

Students also had mixed reactions about the "Other" category of the journals. A few students took the opportunity to expand their knowledge and find interesting examples in the world around them, but most did not. Thus, instead of increasing their opportunity to see the relevance of statistics, the requirement instead tended to add to their anxiety about the course load.

It is important to put students in situations that require the skills you are trying to assess. For example, I use the take-home component of the final exam to allow students to show me what they can produce independently. By putting them in the role of a statistician, I challenge them to develop a solution to a new problem on their own. I encourage them to ask questions about the computer commands, as this is not my main focus, and I want them to be able to move on with the problem. However, if they ask for statistical knowledge, they are "charged" by losing points if I tell them the answer. I indicate that this is similar to having to pay an external consultant when they need statistical expertise. Usually, if I tell them a question will cost them, students accept the challenge to think more about the problem. I hope by offering myself as a resource I

also reduce unpermitted collaboration. Students are given the freedom to demonstrate to me how they can use the knowledge they have gained in the course.

Provide Students with Guidelines of What is Expected. Almost every time I have implemented a new technique, I have erred in not providing the students with enough guidance as to what I expect. This is primarily because I have not fully developed the ideas ahead of time. Students have commented that they "did not always know what to write about the different activities" or "what the point was." To address these difficulties, I now give quizzes to preview exam questions, include project checklists in the syllabus, supply a detailed lab manual, and make model papers available for review.

For example, initially my in-class exams were slightly different from what students were expecting because the exams focused as much on the conceptual topics in the course as on the calculations. Now I give biweekly quizzes, partly for evaluation, but also to introduce students to the types of questions that may appear on an exam. The quiz questions are quite conceptual in nature, typically requiring more thought than the homework problems. I alleviate some test anxiety with this approach, and indicate to students the topics I find most important. I have found this to be sufficient exposure to the exams, and do not provide exams from previous semesters for study.

For the projects, I attempt to incorporate the suggestions made by Sevin: give clear, detailed instructions; provide feedback and guidance [20, p. 160]. For example, I give students a checklist in their syllabus explaining what needs to be discussed in the final project report. A clear timeline for the periodic project reports is also included. Students are also given access to a web page of previous project topics to review at their convenience. This gives the students more of a framework for the project, and encourages them to extend themselves beyond what was done previously.

The largest initial problem when developing lab exercises was the students' computer anxiety and lack of experience. I now produce a lab manual that is given to the students at the beginning of the semester (as part of a lab fee paid with the course). The manual, modeled after those by Egge, Foley, Haskins, and Johnson [7] and Spurrier, Edwards, and Thombs [22], includes instructions for the 14 lab assignments, sections on how to use the computers, Microsoft Word, and Minitab, as well as the index, glossary, and frequently asked questions sections. The manual provides detailed computer steps, including pictures of the menus they will see, for all of the labs throughout the semester. Guidelines for the full lab write-ups are also included (similar to [22]). Thus, the manual provides students with a constant reference and knowledge of what is expected of them.

Each week, a lab write-up that received one of the highest grades is posted in the lab and on the course web page. The goal is for students to review these papers, feel pride if their paper is selected, see the work of their peers (and thus what they are also capable of), and notice that there can be multiple interpretations and conclusions for the same data. I purposely post these materials after the lab is due, so that students can utilize the feedback for their next lab but cannot use the papers as templates for each lab. Unfortunately, fewer than 20% of students indicated that they reviewed these model papers. In fact, three students indicated that they were not aware of their existence. Perhaps this is one reason students still felt there wasn't enough guidance on what was expected in the lab write-ups. In the future, I need to increase student awareness of this resource.

Lack of guidance also appeared to be a problem with the journals. A definitive set of guidelines for the journals, similar to those for the projects and labs, given at the beginning of the semester, would probably help significantly. In the future, I will be more clear about which topics will be included in the journals and what I expect from students. For example, the journal questions are now distributed as handouts, with more focused questions to be addressed, rather than requiring merely a simple summary. These handouts also include graphs of data collected in class for students to reflect on and utilize to support their conclusions. I now also include an initial practice example and distribute a model explanation of the activity.

In short, students need to be given enough direction to start the problem, but not so much that their approach becomes rote. Evaluation techniques should give students the ability to continue to learn and develop, while being flexible enough to allow students to develop in their own ways.

Make Sure the Assessment is Consistent and Fair. Students always know if they are getting different grades for the same work and may discount feedback if they don't feel it is valid. This is especially a concern to me because grading the labs and projects can be time consuming (approximately 15 to 20 minutes for full lab write-ups, 30 minutes for projects). Development of point systems (how much is taken off for each type of mistake) and scoring rubrics has proven quite helpful for consistency, and can be reused in subsequent semesters. The point system can also be revealed to students if they desire additional information on the grading process.

For example, I use a breakdown sheet for the projects each semester: 20 points for oral presentation, 20 points for the quality of the write-up, 20 points for the data collection design, 20 points for choice and correctness of the analysis, and 20 points for interpretation of the results. During the project presentations, students rate the following features on a five point scale: introduction, organization, clarification, visual aids, and conclusions. Comments and suggestions from the class are summarized into a final feedback report for the group. Such sheets have helped my consistency from semester to semester and have clarified to the students what I am looking for.

For the journals, I grade the explanations of in-class activities on a three-point scale with 0 = incomplete, 1 = severe misunderstanding, 2 = partially correct, 3 = correct [10]. Half points are often assigned. This point system allows me to assign grades more quickly, but such totals often need to be adjusted to assign letter grades. Furthermore, a three was seldom given initially, as I hope to encourage further reflection. However, if students don't resubmit their work, the grading can seem harsh to them.

Most of the student complaints about lack of fairness came with the journals. While several students expressed appreciation in the course evaluations that their questions were answered personally and in detail, others felt their grade shouldn't be lowered because they did not have questions. Evaluating the self-evaluations also proved problematic. I tried to make it clear that these self-evaluations are different from the in-class minute papers, in that students should reflect on their efforts (instead of mine). I gave full credit if I felt the student was being constructive and insightful. However, students didn't see how I could grade their opinions. Again, more clarity is needed regarding my expectations.

Make Sure Students Understand the Goals of the Evaluation. For the assessment technique to be informative, students need to understand why it is being used and why it is important. Otherwise the evaluation will probably not be an accurate reflection of their abilities, and their anxiety about the course may increase.

Initially, students saw the lab activities and journals as time consuming and not adding to their knowledge. Of the students working with journals, 66% found them too time consuming, with 41% pinpointing the chapter summaries as the most time consuming component. One of the main problems with my implementation of the journal technique was not explaining to students the concept of the journal. Students didn't really understand what I meant by "journal," thinking of a diary that had to be completed daily.

Furthermore, students did not understand how the journals assessed a component of their learning that is separate from the traditional homework assignments. One approach I may adopt is to have the journals substitute for the homework assignments for one week, or at the end of a large block of material, but feasibility of this may depend on the pace of the course. I will also encourage students to keep their journal entries on the computer so that later revision will be less troublesome. Journal entries can also be submitted through e-mail.

Some students don't see the data collection and writing components of the course as "worth the effort." I need to further emphasize why these tasks are being asked of them and what I want them to get out of the experience. This will help the students concentrate on expressing what they have learned instead of dwelling on how long the task is taking. Some students have expressed appreciation, though perhaps reluctantly, for the gain in understanding of the material, despite the additional work:

"I hated doing them (journals), but I realize now that they really helped in learning the concepts."

"(I didn't like) writing about the chapter summaries, but it did help me get some of the concepts down."

Furthermore, students need to realize how each assessment tool is different. This was evident when journals were first introduced:

"You already provided most of the service the journal was meant to be for."

"If I have a problem, I would go straight and ask you and you can judge my understanding by looking at my homework and lab assignment."

Comments like this illustrate why students did not easily accept the journal component. Conversely, students can more easily see the purposes of the take-home component of the final exam and the lab activities.

I believe additional clarification of the distinct goals of the different assessment activities will increase student participation. Students will better appreciate what they are learning from the activities, and the assessment will more accurately reflect students' abilities.

Make Sure the Assessment is Well Integrated Into the Course.   For evaluation procedures to be successful, they need to be well organized and complementary to the lecture material. All assessment components should be described at the beginning of the course. Consideration also needs to be given to the amount of time required by the students and the instructor for each component. If too many tasks are assigned, neither the students nor the instructor will be able to devote sufficient energy to each task, and the speed and consistency of the assessment will decline.

Initially, labs and journals were not well received because of my lack of organization and the need for better integration of the journal and lab assignments with traditional homework assignments. I find I have more success when I make a point of briefly mentioning the labs and the projects during the lecture time. These reminders are helpful to illustrate to the students when and where the ideas fit in. I have also been able to better time the lab exercises to be concurrent with lecture topics, although this can lead to a rather rigid syllabus. It is important for students to see that all these ideas are related, and not just several disjoint tasks.

Students will also resent an assessment activity if they feel the time required is excessive.

"The labs didn't really help because I was too busy trying to get it done that I didn't learn anything."

Students claim that a lab requiring 15 minutes of observation outside of class is unreasonable. They prefer smaller tasks or data collected in class. The lab activities became more successful after I introduced the separate lab hour into the course and incorporated more of the data collection into the lecture time. During the lab, half of the class meets at a time. Students work in pairs on the lab assignment, with the instructor available for immediate assistance and clarification. Students appreciate having access to the instructor and seem able to approach the computer with higher efficiency and less anxiety. When designing lab assignments, I plan them so the computer work can be completed during this lab hour, with the students' explanations and interpretations being incorporated on their own during the week. I also reduced the number of full lab write-ups to five of the fourteen labs. These changes allow students time to absorb the ideas and to incorporate ideas from lecture into their lab reports. Reducing the number of full lab write-ups and encouraging students to work in pairs also reduces the grading load.

Furthermore, the assessment strategies need to complement each other. I think this is accomplished with the activities I am currently using, providing me with a more complete picture of student understanding and performance. Each technique gives me different sources of information, whereas, as Garfield [11] states, a single indicator would limit the amount of information I receive. Still, too many competing assignments can overwhelm the students or seem too repetitive. I must be careful not to use so many distinct indicators that they overload the students and are no longer effective. Currently, I do not require a separate journal assignment, but I do integrate some of the questions into the homework. While undergraduates grade most of the homework problems, I grade these more open-ended questions. This approach achieves many of the journal goals. I also include exam questions that directly relate to the main ideas I want the students to learn from the labs and in-class activities. (For example, Scheaffer et al., [19], include assessment questions after each activity.) This reminds students to reflect on the learning goals of these activities.

I concur with Garfield's [11] suggestion to attempt to incorporate only one new assessment technique at a time. These techniques can be quite time consuming and demanding on the instructor, and need to be well organized and thought out ahead of time. Both the instructor and the administration need to be cognizant of the additional demands required by these techniques. Successful implementation will not be instantaneous, but will require continual review and redevelopment. My current system of weekly homework, biweekly quizzes, weekly labs, and a semester-long project seems to be at the upper limit of what I can ask of my students and of myself.

Summary

I have found that traditional assessment techniques often do not sufficiently inform me as to whether my students possess the skills I desire. For example, at what level do they understand the material? Will they be able to read and critique articles in their field? Can they read and debate statistical evidence? Can they make reasoned arguments with data and explain their ideas to others? Can they read and interpret computer output? Can they use what they have learned? I have found the techniques discussed here to be quite effective in expanding my knowledge base about the students, including where they are struggling and what topics need to be reviewed. Still, such techniques should be implemented gradually and with careful planning. For example, I did not find the journals added significantly to the techniques I had already implemented, but instead created an excessive workload. However, I think journals could successfully be substituted for more traditional homework assignments or in situations where more individualized assessment is not otherwise possible. At the university level, we often have tremendous flexibility in the types of assessment we can incorporate into a course. Furthermore, as students become accustomed to such approaches, we will be able to more easily expand their use. I find the above techniques to be excellent tools for informing me about what students know and can do. At the same time, these techniques tell me whether students appreciate statistics and computers. They also allow me to provide prompt feedback that is meaningful to the students. Such information is crucial to both the instructor and the students, and is much richer than that provided by traditional techniques.

Appendix
Current Assessment Components

Math 37 is a four unit course with three 80-minute lectures per week and one 50-minute lab per week for 15 weeks. Sections are limited to 45 students. The text is Moore and McCabe [13]. The following assessment components are incorporated in Math 37:

* Two in-class midterms (15% each)

* Final exam (15%)
  85% from in-class exam, 15% from take-home exam distributed one week before traditional in-class final. Students work individually on distinct questions. Sources of data: ASA datasets, *Journal of Statistics Education*, casebooks [e.g., 3].

* Weekly homework assignments (15%)
  Due on Friday. Randomly selected students present "practice problem" solutions to the class on Wednesday.

* Weekly computer labs (15%)
  Students meet for one hour per week in computer lab with instructor and have one week to complete lab write-up. Sections are limited to 23 students. Lab manuals are handed out the first week. Students complete nine 25-point labs and five 50-point labs ("full labs"). The full lab write-ups are graded on presentation (10%), computer output (40%), and interpretation of results (50%).

* Quizzes (10%)
  Eight to ten quizzes given, lowest two grades dropped.

* Term Project (15%)
  Groups of three to five work together on one project over the semester. Projects are graded on data collection design (20%), analysis (20%), interpretation (20%), written report (20%), and final oral presentation to the class (20%). Grade given is 85% group grade and 15% individual grade. Previous project topics can be viewed at `www.uop.edu/cop/math/chance/projects.html`.

Groups submit four periodic project reports:

o Report 1 (Week 4): Topic, population, type of study, sampling frame.

o Report 2 (Week 6): Data collection with copy of design or survey. Submitted for peer review.

○ Report 3 (Week 11): Preliminary descriptive statistics, goals for analysis.
○ Report 4 (Week 12): Final selection of statistical tests.
○ Rough Draft (Week 14): Optional.
○ Final Report and Presentations (Week 15)

In the peer reviews, students are asked to review the proposed study, indicating where the study is lacking in clarity or has potential biases. The instructor looks over the reviews and returns them to the groups.

∗ If journals are used, they are worth one-half of the homework grade. A 3-point scoring rubric is used to assign points for write-ups on ten in-class activities, and a 2-point rubric is used for ten chapter summaries. There are 10 points total for self-evaluations, 10 points total for questions on the material, and 10 points total for finding "other" applications. Journals are collected every 2 to 3 weeks.

References

1. Anderson, J. R., *The Architecture of Cognition*, 1983, Harvard University Press, Cambridge, MA.
2. Archbald, D. and F. Newmann, *Beyond Standardized Testing: Assessing Authentic Academic Achievement in the Secondary School*, 1988, National Association of Secondary School Principals, Reston, VA.
3. Chatterjee, S., M. Handcock, and J. Simonoff, *A Casebook for a First Course in Statistics and Data Analysis*, 1996, John Wiley and Sons, New York.
4. Cobb, G., "Teaching Statistics," in *Heeding the Call for Change: Suggestions for Curricular Action*, MAA Notes No. 22, edited by L. Steen, 1992, Mathematical Association of America, 3–43.
5. Crowley, M. L., "Student Mathematics Portfolio: More Than a Display Case," *The Mathematics Teacher*, **87**, 1993, 544–547.
6. delMas, R., "A Framework for the Development of Software for Teaching Statistical Concepts," *Proceedings of the 1996 International Association of Statistics Education (IASE) Roundtable*, 1996, Granada, Spain, 85–99.
7. Egge, E., S. Foley, L. Haskins, and R. Johnson, *Statistics Lab Manual*, 3rd edition, 1995, Carleton College, Mathematics and Computer Science Department, Northfield, MN.
8. Fillebrown, S., "Using Projects in an Elementary Statistics Course for Non-Science Majors," *Journal of Statistics Education*, www.amstat.org/publications/jse/v2n2/fillebrown.html (on line), **2**(2), 1994.
9. Gal, I. and L. Ginsburg, "The Role of Beliefs and Attitudes in Learning Statistics: Towards an Assessment Framework," *Journal of Statistics Education*, www.amstat.org/publications/jse/v2n2/gal.html (on line), **2**(2), 1994.
10. Garfield, J., *An Authentic Assessment of Students' Statistical Knowledge*, 1993, in *National Council of Teachers of Mathematics 1993 Yearbook: Assessment in the Mathematics Classroom*, edited by N. Webb, Reston, VA: NCTM, 187–196.
11. ——, "Beyond Testing and Grading: Using Assessment to Improve Student Learning," *Journal of Statistics Education*, www.amstat.org/publications/jse/v2n1/garfield.html (on line), **2**(1), 1994.
12. Mackisack, M., "What is the Use of Experiments Conducted by Statistics Students?" *Journal of Statistics Education*, www.amstat.org/publications/jse/v2n1/mackisack.html (on line), **2**(1), 1994.
13. Moore, D. S. and G. P. McCabe, *Introduction to the Practice of Statistics, Second Edition*, 1993, W. H. Freeman, New York.
14. National Council of Teachers of Mathematics, *Curriculum and Evaluation Standards for School Mathematics*, 1989, Reston, VA.
15. ——, *Assessment Standards for School Mathematics*, 1993, Reston, VA.
16. Resnick, L., *Education and Learning to Think*, 1987, National Research Council, Washington, DC.
17. Roberts, H. V., "Student-Conducted Projects in Introductory Statistics Courses," in *Statistics for the Twenty-First Century*, MAA Notes No. 26, edited by F. Gordon and S. Gordon, 1992, Mathematical Association of America, 109–121.
18. Rosenshine, B. and C. Meister, "Reciprocal Teaching: A Review of the Research," *Review of Educational Research*, **64**(4), 1994, 479–530.
19. Scheaffer, R., M. Gnanadesikan, A. Watkins, and J. Witmer, *Activity-Based Statistics*, 1996, Springer-Verlag, New York.
20. Sevin, A., "Some Tips for Helping Students in Introductory Statistics Classes Carry Out Successful Data Analysis Projects," *Proceedings of the Section on Statistical Education of the American Statistical Association*, 1995, 159–164.
21. Snell, J. L., and J. Finn, "A Course Called 'Chance'," *Chance*, **5**(3-4), 1992, 12–16.
22. Spurrier, J. D., D. Edwards, and L. A. Thombs, *Elementary Statistics Lab Manual*, 1995, Wadsworth Publishing Co., Belmont, CA.

Bibliography on Assessment

Angelo, T. and K. Cross, *A Handbook of Classroom Assessment Techniques for College Teachers*, 1993, Jossey-Bass, San Francisco.

A wonderful collection of practical ways to assess how well students are learning what you are teaching and for giving the instructor student feedback on various course components: includes ideas like the minute paper and the punctuated lecture.

Gal, Iddo and Joan B. Garfield (eds.), *The Assessment Challenge in Statistics Education*, 1997, IOS Press, Amsterdam.

A collection of articles, both conceptual and practical, on issues of assessment in statistics education.

Wiggins, Grant, "Toward an Assessment Worthy of the Liberal Arts," in *Heeding the Call for Change*, MAA Notes No. 22, edited by Lynn Arthur Steen, 1992, The Mathematical Association of America, 50–162.

Wiggins provides us with one of the most provocative essays on the subject of assessment, starting with evidence from Plato's Meno and progressing toward "10 tentative principles" of assessment that might lead students to developing habits of real thought.

Author Contact Information

The following list includes authors who wrote original articles or companion pieces for the volume, but does not include authors of the commercially available products described in the volume.

Karla Ballman, Ph.D.
Section of Biostatistics
Harwick Building
Mayo Clinic
200 First Street SW
Rochester, MN 55905
Ballman.Karla@mayo.edu

Beth Chance
College of Science and Mathematics
Cal Poly
San Luis Obispo, CA 93407
bchance@calpoly.edu

George Cobb
Dept. of Mathematics, Statistics, and Computer Science
Mount Holyoke College
South Hadley, MA 01075
gcobb@mtholyoke.edu

Amy Fisher
Miami University Middletown
4200 E. University Blvd.
Middletown, OH 45042
fisherma@muohio.edu

Joan Garfield
University of Minnesota
332 Burton Hall
178 Pleasant St. SE
Minneapolis, MN 55410
jbg@vx.acs.umn.edu

Sneh Gulati
Department of Statistics
Florida International University
University Park
Miami, FL 33199
gulati@servms.fiu.edu

Katherine Taylor Halvorsen
Department of Mathematics
Smith College
Northampton, MA 01063
khalvors@science.smith.edu

Robert W. Hayden
Department of Mathematics
Plymouth State College MSC#29
Plymouth, New Hampshire 03264
hayden@oz.plymouth.edu

Patrick Hopfensperger
Homestead High School
5000 W. Mequon Rd
Mequon, WI 53092
phopfens@mtsd.k12.wi.us

Bruce King
31 Brookfield Lane
New Milford, CT 06776
wbln2357@ntplx.net

Robin Lock
Mathematics Department
St. Lawrence University
Canton, NY 13617
rlock@vm.stlawu.edu

Edd Mansfield
Management Science and Statistics
University of Alabama
Tuscaloosa, AL 35487-0226
emansfie@cba.ua.edu

Thomas Moore
Department of Mathematics and Computer Science
Grinnell College
Grinnell, IA 50112
mooret@grinnell.edu

Roxy Peck
College of Science and Mathematics
Cal Poly
San Luis Obispo, CA 93407
rpeck@calpoly.edu

Maria Ripol
Department of Statistics
222 Griffin-Floyd Hall
University of Florida
Gainesville, FL 32611-2049
mripol@stat.ufl.edu

Rosemary A. Roberts
Mathematics
8600 College Station
Bowdoin College
Brunswick, Maine 04011-8486
rroberts@bowdoin.edu

Michael Seyfried
Department of Mathematics and Computer Science
1871 Old Main Drive
Shippensburg University
Shippensburg, PA 17257
mdseyf@ark.ship.edu

Norean Radke Sharpe
Department of Mathematics and Science
Babson College
Forest Street
Babson Park, MA 02457
sharpen@babson.edu

Robert L. Wardrop, Professor
Department of Statistics
University of Wisconsin–Madison
1210 West Dayton, Madison, WI 53706
wardrop@stat.wisc.edu